A Journey Through Our **]**

The Story of the Jamaican People in Leeds
&
The Work of the Jamaica Society (Leeds)

Melody Walker

A Jamaica Society (Leeds) Publication

Published by the Jamaica Society (Leeds)
277 Chapeltown Road
Leeds, LS7 3HA

ISBN 0-9546279-0-3

© 2003 Copyright The Jamaica Society (Leeds)

All rights reserved. No part of this publication may be reproduced, stored within a retrieval system, or transmitted, in any form or by any means without the prior permission in writing of The Jamaica Society (Leeds)

Printed: Lear Stationers & Printers Ltd., Wolverhampton

Layout: Paul Aiken

Editor: Maureen Baker

This book is dedicated to
the members of the Jamaica Society (Leeds) past and present;
the Jamaican community in Leeds
and to future generations of Jamaicans born in Leeds.

In memory of one of our founding members, Errol James, MBE, JP

Sponsored By

with support from the
Yorkshire Bank Trust

Contents

Acknowledgements .... vi-vii
Foreword – Ambassador the Hon. David Muirhead, OJ, QC viii
Introduction 1
Granny Inna England by Khadijah Ibrahiim 4
Chapter 1 – The Arrival 9
Black Diamonds by Laurah Pitter 29
Chapter 2 – Leeds, Our Home? 31
Christmas Come by Marva Buchannan 68
Chapter 3 – The Formation of the Jamaica Society (Leeds) 71
Photo Spread 115
Ancestral Architects by Marva Buchannan 122
Reflections of a Jamaican Elder by Edley White 124
Chapter 4 – A Place of Our Own 125
Saturday Night, Sunday Morning by Laurah Pitter 150
Chapter 5 – The Next Generation 151
Riddims Talking by Khadijah Ibrahiim 181
Chapter 6 – The Journey Continues 183
Epilogue 187
Bibliographical Notes 189
Glossary 198
Bibliography 203
About the Writer 206

Acknowledgements

Trying to whittle down over fifty years of history into a few hundred pages is never an easy task. Fortunately, it is less daunting to thank the people and organisations which have provided the resources to complete an important aspect of the history of the Jamaican community in Leeds. The Jamaica Society (Leeds) would like to thank the following funding organisations: Local Heritage Initiative, Yorkshire Bank Trust, Nationwide Funding, Local Regeneration Funds, Lloyds TSB Trust, Resourcing the Community, CIT ChapelAllerton/University and Harehills/Burmantofts Wards and to Awards for All for sponsoring the art exhibition and its accompanying CD ROM.

Many thanks to the members of the History Committee for their many hours of volunteer time that they have put into supervising the project: Travis Johnson, Lynford Fletcher, Ratrica 'Nettie' White and Theresa Condor. Special thanks to Nettie White for providing the delicious Jamaican soup for the young participants at the workshops, and to Elizabeth and Travis Johnson for waiting around many late nights to ferry home the transcribers.

We express our deepest gratitude to Wesley Grant and Steadroy Lewis for giving a lot of time to the setting up of the computer network - the time they spent on this job exceeded their compensation.

The project would not have been completed without the expertise of a number of local artists and facilitators who worked with the young participants: thanks to Paul Aiken, Ansell Broderick, Marcia Brown, Garnet Dore, Khadijah Ibrahiim, Jenny Eugene, Musufing Njie and Linton Robinson.

Once again, the members of the Jamaica Society (Leeds) rose to the occasion and made themselves available for interviews, discussion sessions and participation in the workshops, thanks for showing continued dedication and commitment to the organisation. Special thanks to Finley Wray who now lives in the USA but made himself accessible by telephone, and to the following members who turned up repeatedly to speak to the young people: Glen English, Travis Johnson, Roy Mitchell and June Wood.

We cannot forget the participation of those from the wider Jamaican community: His Excellency The Most Hon. Sir Howard Cooke, Governor General of Jamaica, Ambassador the Hon. David Muirhead, Delores Cooper, Paulette Simpson, Clinton Cameron, Veryl Harriott, Celine North, Councillor Norma Hutchinson, Sandra Simpson, Marcia Hylton, Angelique Johnson and Windrush passenger, Alford Gardner; we appreciate your insight and perspectives.

The Society would also like to thank the more than forty young people who participated in the project, your interpretation on the lives of your predecessors has greatly enhanced the value of this project. We extend our appreciation to the parents for allowing their children to participate. We cannot forget the young participants from the Mandela Centre who also participated in the series of workshops: we are grateful to

Bridget Robinson and Owen Sinclair for making this happen.

Others have given their stamp of approval to this project and we appreciate the confidence you have demonstrated towards our organisation: Brian Walker, former Leader of the Council, Bernadette Allen and Derek Lawrence.

The Society would like to acknowledge the book's editor, Maureen Baker, whose knowledge of the development of the Caribbean community in Leeds has helped to shape this book. We recognise the contributions of our readers, Angela and Michael Senior and especially Marva Buchannan who brought to this process a wealth of knowledge on Jamaican history and culture, and whose input helped to preserve the authenticity of the voices in the book. The Society is indebted to Nicole Swaby, who came just in time to help with the transcribing of the taped interviews and workshop materials that were amassed over the course of this project. Special thanks to Annesse James-Taylor for providing the Society with information and photographs of the late Errol James.

This project was certainly a community effort and once again we would like to thank all those who have been involved. Over the years, many of our members and a number of organisations have given their unqualified support to the Society, we would like to take this opportunity to express our deepest gratitude to all of you. As we say in Jamaica, *one hand cyan clap*: we could not have done it without all of you.

Foreword

It is sometimes a daunting task to have to read a book with the intention of providing a foreword.

Reading this book however, was both pleasurable and profitable as it afforded me the opportunity to relive my own experiences which largely coincided with those attested to and documented herein as I arrived in England in 1954 and departed for Jamaica in December 1959.

During the intervening years, I read for the Bar and thereafter had the enviable opportunity of being appointed the Community and Industrial Relations Officer at the West Indies Welfare Service attached to the Colonial Office to assist our migrants, mostly Jamaicans, to find accommodation and employment in the many areas in the United Kingdom where we settled - hence my deep involvement.

The circle of arrival in 1954, departure in 1959 was completed by my arrival in July 1999 as the Jamaican High Commissioner in which position I remained until August 2002.

The story of Jamaicans and the Jamaica Society (Leeds) so powerfully and eloquently recorded in the book, *A Journey Through Our History*, brings to mind the adage "ad astra per aspera", "High achievement through overcoming difficulties"

The author has done a great deal of research and additionally has had the great advantage of interviews with living persons whose experiences and achievements are recorded and therefore provide an unchallengeable authenticity to the events recounted.

It assures inexhaustible material for research but more importantly, provides young persons not only with a source of pride in the achievements of their elders, but with aspiration and confidence for them to build superstructures on the firm human and material foundations laid by their forebears.

The Society's defined goals to this end are well directed, recognising as it does that "One of the Jamaica Society (Leeds) main objectives is the advancement of education." It coincides with the declaration of the Right Honourable Prime Minister that "'education, education, education" is the path to high attainment thereby allowing our people to play a fuller role not only in their own lives but also in the life of the wider community. The Society will undoubtedly find new and exciting ways to capture the interest of our young people and thereby continue to attain this objective.

A Journey Through Our History: The Story of the Jamaican People in Leeds and the Work of the Jamaica Society (Leeds) is worthy of our highest praise and is destined to enjoy a special place on the bookshelf- always near at hand.

Ambassador the Hon. David Muirhead, OJ, QC
July 2003

If yuh wan' good, yuh nose haffi run
Jamaican Proverb

Success comes through hard work
English translation

Introduction

In 1992 at the London School of Economics, the late Right Hon. Michael Manley, former Prime Minister of Jamaica delivered a lecture to commemorate the life and work of his father, The Right Excellent Norman Manley, National Hero of Jamaica. On completing the address, Michael Manley concluded, "if we fail to act to give to ourselves the advantages of a greater collective strength and planning, reality and voice, the generations to come will not forgive the leaders of today." While he was speaking of the wider challenges of regional unification, his words have also given clarity to the mission undertaken by the Jamaica Society (Leeds) - to bring together the Jamaican people scattered across the four corners of the West Yorkshire City of Leeds.

The need to create a community of Jamaicans who would work towards building and contributing to the City of Leeds presented itself in 1977 - almost 30 years after the first set of Jamaicans settled in and around the metropolis. The vision of the founding members of the Jamaica Society (Leeds) was predicated on 'unity of strength'. Strength, determination and persistence were hallmark qualities of the generation of Jamaicans who migrated to the UK during the post war years: they were essential to Caribbean people's very survival. In order to create such an organisation, it was necessary to harness these attributes. The strength of any organisation lies in the strength of its people; ergo, to fully appreciate the history of the Jamaica Society (Leeds), one has to know the history of the Jamaican people in Leeds. The two are intertwined. Their struggle to create a better life for themselves in the 'Mother Country' also became the struggle for racial equality, social justice and for recognition as a burgeoning community worthy of respect. Using various channels to lobby for change, members of the Jamaican community have contributed enormously to the development of community life in Leeds. A number of them have thrown the same zeal and energy into building the Jamaica Society (Leeds) that has been around for a quarter of a century.

The Jamaica Society (Leeds) emerged out of a recognised need for Jamaicans to have a collective impact on the City of Leeds and became the vehicle that had made it possible. The Society has cemented itself in the consciousness of generations of Caribbean people in Leeds, city officials, politicians and ordinary citizens. It has stood out as exemplar to Jamaican societies and associations around the UK and has functioned as an essential contact point for the Jamaican High Commission. The erection of its headquarters at 277 Chapeltown Road stands as a monument to their collective achievements as a people. Jamaicans got together and resurrected the building known as Jamaica House from the ruins of urban decay. In the process, they created a space that in their eyes symbolically represents 'a little piece of Jamaica on British soil.'

When Jamaicans migrated to Britain, they brought with them the force of their national character and a deep-rooted heritage. Their contribution to the British landscape can be found in the legacy of the health sector, the transport services, politics, the trade union movement, and industry. Its influence on British culture is reflected in music, television shows and urban street talk - handed down from one generation to the next. The Jamaica Society (Leeds) believes that in the same vein that these aspects of Jamaican cultural heritage can survive through the generations, in like manner the total history of the Jamaican people should endure - more relevantly, their historic journey across the Atlantic to the UK in the 1940s.

When the Society's oldest living member Edley White suggested to the membership that the Society should document its history, the decision was taken that the second and third generations of Jamaicans living in the city should also participate in the documentation process. For the past twenty-five years, the Society's work has been centred on fulfilling the needs of people born in Jamaica and whose domicile is in the UK. The profile of the population that the Society was established to serve has changed dramatically with a growing number of its members being of pension age. At this juncture in its history, the Society is aware that in order to survive it has to remain relevant to the next generation.

This book, *A Journey Through Our History* began as a cross-generational and multimedia oral history project. A yearlong programme, *Our Journey! Our History!* was designed and implemented. It brought together the generations of Jamaicans (elders and young people) to explore new and exciting ways to record the history of the Jamaican people in Leeds and the social impact of the Jamaica Society (Leeds). Building on their oral cultural traditions, the Jamaican elders shared with the younger generation through participatory storytelling sessions and video taped interviews, their stories and experiences of migration to the UK, and their efforts to build a united Jamaican community in Leeds. As the young participants began to explore their history, it revealed how little they knew. Many did not know how and why Caribbean people had come to Britain. After learning about their history, the young people documented their knowledge through paintings, creative writings and computer-generated timelines. Some of the young people's impressions and interpretations are featured in this book.

The project was also designed to address some of the needs of the younger generation which were identified as feelings of displacement, rejection, low self esteem and lack of visible role models. It took on the challenge to re-educate the younger generation on the achievements of their predecessors who have been an integral part of the British society - socially, economically and culturally. These people reside in their communities, as their neighbours, parents and grandparents. The young people were encouraged to use their ancestral and cultural heritage as a source of empowerment. According to Jamaica's first National Hero, The Right Excellent Marcus Garvey, the history of a people, the history of an organisation is the signpost for that people's destiny, that organisation's destiny. Therefore, the history of the Jamaican people in Leeds could inspire and guide the younger generation towards greater achievements. Equally, the project aimed to demonstrate to the younger generation the importance of community volunteerism and participation. It was one way of persuading young people of Jamaican descent that they too can make a valuable contribution to the communities they inhabit in the future.

The aims and objectives of this book are also similar, and bring together the different generations' perspectives with specific focus on the following:

- To document through oral accounts the experiences of Jamaicans who settled in the City of Leeds and surrounding districts - starting with the Jamaican ex-servicemen who settled in Leeds after World War Two, and ending with the Jamaicans who came in larger numbers from the 1950s to the early 1960s.

- To recount the stories and experiences of the Jamaican people's pioneering efforts to build a viable community in Leeds.

- To highlight the Jamaicans who played their part and contributed to improving the life of the inhabitants of Leeds.

- To demonstrate how Jamaicans have concentrated their energies to serve their community through the work of the Jamaica Society (Leeds).

- To examine the role of the next generation of Jamaicans born in the UK in carrying on the work of the Jamaica Society (Leeds).

- And, to explore the role that Jamaican people's historical and cultural heritage has played in their struggle to build a community in Leeds, and to ascertain the significance of the knowledge of one's cultural heritage on successive generations.

A Journey Through Our History preserves the orality of the process by maintaining the voices and texture of the stories in the words of the Jamaicans interviewed. The narrative also relies largely on the perspectives of the Jamaicans who are members of the Jamaica Society (Leeds). This is their story.

MI GRANNY INNA INGLAND

Lawd God mi granny cry
Mi nuh no how mi a go survive inna dis yah land

Windrush liner dock 1948
Wid hopes and dreams
Immigrants!
      Migrants!
           De people dem SCREAM…
But Ingland people send fe dem cum
To educate de people and build up dem economy

Granny cum
Smile face!
      Shine face!
           Complexion glean
Mi mumma cum too wid did same hopes and dreams

And each week cum,
Dem drop dem pardner hand
      And one by one dem send fe dem pickney, who nuh born yah
           To Ingland green pastures wid dem king and dem queen.

Leaving behind the things they loved
Mango, Coconut,
      Salt'fish and Ackee,
           Fry fish and Bammy,
                 Sweet hot pepper,
                      Jamaican Sun.

Lawd God mi granny cry
Mi nuh know how mi a go survive inna dis yah land
And me bawl

      Lawd God
Cos mi nuh no who me 'fraida more

De people, who make mi granny bawl so

Mi granny and her fiery tongue
      Mi mumma wid her switch
            She said cum yah rude pickney

          …If a lick yuh, yuh –

But granny tell mi say
      …a Ingland people send fe dem cum
And me no granny nuh tell no lie

Granny said dem tell her when she first cum a Ingland
This is the best we've got
You won't get better than this.

De one dutty bedroom dem waan gi har an' her pickney dem
But she never bodda lick pon nobody door too tuff
Cos dem PUSH dem sign UP inna dem window an' pon dem door

Saying…
      NO BLACKS! NO IRISH and NO DOGS!

    DAWG!
        DAWG!
A wah dem tek mi fah doh-ee?

But de water it a leak
And a cum down t'rough de crack inna de ceiling
One bar heater and de paraffin soon done
And you puppa deh yah yankee him a drink white rum.

...An' mumma say unno fi tek time
Cos Co-operation POP drink nice when de syrup it done
      Spice bun and cheese!
            Sunday! Rice and peas!
And Miss Maisy she push' in de door
And tun off de Blue Spot radio gram and sings the Lord's praise.

...And granny SAY! De rain it nah stop fall
And the cold a bite her inna har bone, down trodden snow
And little if any sun a shine.

...And granny bawl
and she bawl
Singing...
      Dem cudda little mi dis and little mi dat
           Dem give you little a dis and a little a dat
                Little a dis and little a dat
                Little - of - dis

Until she end up have to stay

...But granny drop her pardner hand
And she work night and day inna de hospital
And she buy her house inna Ingland
And she educate all of her pickney
So nobody could a tell dem no foolishness
So dem can stand strong

...And granny tell mi say
Windrush liner dock 1948
Wid hopes and dreams
Immigrants!
      Migrants!
           De people dem SCREAM

But a Ingland people send fe dem cum
To educate the people and build up dem economy

Granny cum
Smile face
      Shine face
           Complexion glean
Mi mumma cum too wid did same hopes and dreams

Returning granny back
Den de preacher tand-up in him pulpit
Reading, chanting verse and text from scripture:
St John: chapter 14 verse 1
"LET not your heart be troubled"
as tight throat voices from loved one shadowed chorus
and de choir sings in harmonious ceremony

"Then sing my soul, my saviour God to thee
How great thou art"

How great thou art!
…and how powerful are these tears dat roll down pon 4 generations of skin and beauty
Returning granny back to her Maker
Holding pan her dutch pot of knowledge
Calling pan her Being
Den de spirit bawl out

Ahhh…
You caan't bury DIS YA HISTORY
HER-stories come from far and beyond
Africa fertile lands
to Kingston's back yards
Climbing ackee trees walking through cane fields
Suckling on sweet saps

To Ingland's cold shore
Greeted with twisted faces burdened with ignorance and a bitterness
A legacy of a superficial ruling class of the seas and waves
Columbus's heresy buried in their bellies

...So now here I am
I stand today in dis yah land
Not a Failure
      But the Progression in succession of Granny's dutch pot of knowledge and wisdom
           Because granny was a
                Builder!
                AND a Survivor!
Of old England's green pastures wid dem KING and dem QUEEN.

Khadijah Ibrahiim
© 2001, 2003
(Dedicated to the memory of a loving grandmother Lucilda Wynters 1923 -1999)

1 THE ARRIVAL

It was 1944. Five young Jamaican men, Glen English, Errol James, Marcus 'Roy' Mitchell, Noel Edwards and Alford Gardner volunteered like scores of other Caribbean men and women to serve alongside the British in the Second World War. These men would be among the first set of Caribbean people to settle in the growing West Yorkshire City of Leeds after the war, setting the stage for a larger migration of their people into the region and other parts of the United Kingdom. Unwittingly, they were pioneers. It was the beginning of the Jamaican community in Leeds. Four of these men would go on to play crucial roles in either the establishment or development of the Jamaica Society (Leeds). The Caribbean community in Leeds like others across the country sprang from the courage of a handful of men like these into a vibrant and tenacious force that would irrevocably change the socio-political, economic and cultural landscape of Britain.

Jamaicans in World War Two

Thousands of Jamaican men and women volunteered for the war effort. They responded enthusiastically to Britain's call, 'Come and fight for the Mother Country'. Jamaican volunteers with others from the British Commonwealth joined the Navy, Air Force, Marines, Army, Air & Sea Rescue, Nursing Services and the Auxiliary Territorial Service (which recruited women in non-fighting roles). A number of them also joined the elite ranks of fighter pilots in the Royal Air Force, but the vast majority served as ground crew and support staff. The largest recruitment of Caribbean service personnel took place in 1944, (though others were serving in the war from 1940). It was the spirit of goodwill, co-operation and loyalty that led the Jamaican men and women to volunteer for the service. These principles would eventually become the cornerstone of the Jamaican community in Leeds, and would later influence the organic structure and function of the Jamaica Society (Leeds). The initial part they played in Britain was as contributors, and they would continue in that role as more and more Jamaicans arrived and settled in and around the city, some years later.

However, the demands of World War Two did not give the Jamaican servicemen and women a great deal of time to consider the possibility of settling in the UK. Their participation meant they could finally visit the once inaccessible lands of England and above all, it provided them with opportunities to acquire new skills and professional training in a number of areas. It whetted their ambitious palates.

> "I came to the UK in April 1944. I came because I had already joined the RAF in Jamaica and they just transported us to come across to continue our basic Air Force training. I was seventeen

when I joined. But I told them I was eighteen; I was really big so nobody questioned it. I set off hoping to be one of their aircrew, but before the course got on the way we were told that they didn't need anymore aircrew, so personnel like myself would have to do ground crew training. I took that up and became an Air Force air engine personnel and my career basically started from there." – *Glen English*

"I came to the UK the backend of November 1944. I had just left school at the time and there were loads of adverts going up around the place saying: 'The Mother Country Needs You'. So I decided to join the RAF and that's why I'm here. When I joined the RAF, we were at a training camp by the name of Wymeswold. Over a period of time, there were notices going up all around the camp saying: 'There is a Trades Desk. Anyone who would like to join should put their names to it'. I put my name to it and what I chose was Transport. I was sent away to a camp called Netheravon to train as a driver, and then further on I took another Trades Test which comes under HGV which means 'Heavy Goods Vehicle Driving'. I passed that, and then I became a driving instructor, so I was teaching other soldiers to drive. Over a number of years, I continued to work in Transport." – *Roy Mitchell*

Some Jamaican men volunteered because they were itching to follow in the footsteps of their grandfathers and fathers who had served in World War One. The stories that were recounted about the Great War left an indelible impression on them and increased their eagerness to sign up for the World War Two efforts. It was an irresistible call to adventure.

"I came to the UK to fight in the war on June 3, 1944. When I joined the RAF, I aimed to fly. It was the in thing you see. My dad, he came to the 1914-18 war. He was always on about the things that happened in that war and he more or less said that he had a good experience. So I thought to myself, I've left school and doing nothing, I just failed my third year, I didn't get a ticket to go to America on the Farm Workers' programme. They said that I was too small. The RAF turned up and I said, 'Yes, I would try.' They started recruiting for the RAF and they started going around the island and everyday I'd pick up the Gleaner and it'd say: 'They have tested so many boys - two hundred boys and they have selected seven'. All the time you'd hear so many boys were failing. When they had reached Montego Bay and I went and I took the test. I was among thirteen which they had picked and so it was that I joined the RAF.

"I had some right good friends who I knew had joined up - lads from Montego Bay. When we were leaving Mama shouted to one of them named Lloyd. She said, 'Lloyd, look after Ford!'

He said, 'Yes, Miss Lou, you can bet!' I had no fear of being alone, even though I was small. I had no problem because I was with three lads who were body builders. I wasn't afraid. It was an adventure!" – *Alford Gardener*

The journey over to the UK on British troopships was fraught with unforgettable and nail-biting events. Chief among them were the threats of real or imagined attacks by enemy vessels. These events brought home the horrifying reality of war; fear gnawed at the young service personnel's consciences, when they realised that their wartime adventure could cost them their lives.

"It was November 1944 when we set sail from Palisadoes to come to England. As a matter of fact, we had on board seventeen hundred men or should I say troopers on the *HMS Carthage* which included men from Trinidad, Barbados and most of the Caribbean islands. On the way coming over we were fired on by the enemy- the Germans- near to Bermuda and we had to take refuge in Bermuda for a couple of days before we set sail again. It was just a matter that we got the report from the captain that we were fired upon. All I heard was a rumble like thunder in the water. I thought it was submarines. But because we were inexperienced, we didn't know what it was until after everything was over. There was no damage done, so we were rescued into Bermuda for a few days. None of us were allowed to come off the ship in Bermuda, but they brought fresh supplies onto our ship. So we refuelled and set off again. We got as far as the River Clyde in Scotland, that's where we landed and we were aboard the ship overnight until next morning. We were taken off the ship and lined up to be sent off to different camps across England. To tell you the truth, when we landed in Scotland, it was like going into an icebox; it was bitter, bitter cold. It was the first time we experienced frost, we didn't know what it was. Everyone was rubbing their hands and rubbing their feet and crying about the cold. We got over that okay once we got to our camps. My first camp was North Weald. When we got to the camp we had to be lined up and numbered off and all the lot of it. The number I was given I still have that number today. Because once I got that number I have never forgotten it. My number is 724804." – *Roy Mitchell*

"I came over on the *SS Cuba*. An old ship and that was a right ole ship. The first night on the Cuba was the roughest sea I ever ran into - it was something! When the wave picked it up and tossed it one way, nearly everybody on the ship was sick. We were supposed to go into Guantanomo Bay I think in four days and it took us fourteen days. From Jamaica to Cuba! (*Cuba is 90 miles from Jamaica*). Apparently, one of the engines broke down. But rumours started going around that we were a decoy ship, because all black men were on our ship, so we were bait for German submarines. There was a lot of praying. Anyway, we finally reached Guantanomo Bay and from Guantanomo Bay we went to Newport Mews in America. When we got off the ship, everybody got sprayed from the captain right down. The ship had been out so long they thought anything could have been on it. They then sent us up to Camp Patrick Henry, I think it was in Virginia. We were supposed to be changing from one ship to the next. We stayed at Camp Patrick Henry for a week. That was a cracking week. Everything was lavish. We left to go to New York to get this ship, *HMS Esperance Bay* which took us to England. It took us another fourteen days to finally reach England and we got off the boat at Liverpool." – *Alford Gardner (He was 18 when he volunteered.)*

The Jamaicans' arrival into Britain was a culture shock that went both ways. The Jamaicans watched with bewilderment as stacks and stacks of chimneys belched out black smoke and soot. It was a chilling introduction to British industrialisation and urbanisation; a betrayal of the pastoral splendour they anticipated. Etched in its urban landscape was the foreknowledge of a more devastating betrayal that Caribbean people would experience in post war Britain. Meanwhile, the local people's reaction to their arrival was a mixture of gratitude, bemusement and low-keyed antagonism. The inhabitants of the colonies in the vast British Empire had suddenly become visible: live and in colour.

"When we arrived, we went across to Filey just down the bottom of Yorkshire. A lot of English people were dead scared of us. They had never seen so many black men. Then another thing that baffled them, it was over a thousand of us from the West Indies yet we had different skin colours. There were different shades of black. Then there were blue-eyed, blond-haired white men among us and they were all talking the same way as the black West Indians, the Chinese West Indians and the Indian West Indians who were all Jamaicans.

"When I had time off from camp, I would go to Manchester or Bolton or Burnley for a week. I had friends in those places. They were all Englishmen and women. Some of them you met at the dancehall. For instance, you would meet the daughter at the dancehall and she would take you home. Another time, I met this family at the Tower Ballroom and the dad took me home. So that's how I met people. They took me home and treated me like one of the family. Honest to goodness, I met some good people and I also met some right bad people. You just ignore the rogues and get on with life". – *Alford Gardner*

Within its colonies, Britain had instituted a rigid colour hierarchy which was understood by the indigenous people, though they were totally opposed to it. However, on British mainland there were no legal or political structures that relegated people of colour to specific facilities or areas. The Jamaican service personnel were aware of this and refused to accept the resistance they would meet because of their colour. The American servicemen who were used to a legal colour bar in their country posed the biggest racial threat.

"It was something of a mixed situation. In the Air Force, while we were at camp, most of the other guys there were pretty respectful towards us from the West Indies. Also, at that time the Air Force was short of manpower and they were pleased that somebody from the Commonwealth had come all this way to help in the war effort, so they were quite accommodating. People used to get invited to people's homes for teas and such things. It was different in the small rural areas outside of cities where they had never met black people before. Whether there was a group of West Indians or you were alone, you got the impression that for the local English people all sort of mixed emotions about your race or colour would run through their heads. Some people were trying to stereotype you and didn't quite know how to handle you and it created some problems. I found the constant scrutiny by these people particularly annoying. People looked at you and kept looking at you, which was very unnerving. It made you a little bit self-conscious and you began to think, 'what's wrong with me?' I felt like saying: 'For heaven's sake, stop looking at me and get on with your business.' But after a while I got used to that. When we went out for a drink in the evenings and we would go in the local pubs, especially if you were at a camp well away from the cities, you would have problems with the locals. Sometimes other servicemen from other parts of the world were there…" – *Glen English*

"When Americans were here, you would get to the pub and all of a sudden you would hear: 'You can't come in'. My argument was this: 'You are in England, you are not in America, so there is no way you can say we can't come in'. So what you would do was to go in anyway and they would say you should get out. So, tomorrow night more of us would go prepared for a skirmish. I tell you something, we very rarely lost! When we lost a fight, the odds were usually too great. When the odds were too great we took off. It was no use staying around and getting beaten up for being too brave.

"I tell you something else, I used to go London very regularly, and when you go to a dance-hall, the doormen would tell you that you could not come in without a partner. So, you would see a girl and you would ask her and she would say, 'Oh, no.' You would see another girl and she would say, 'Oh, yes, I'll come with you.' We would reach the door and the doormen would say, 'You can't come in!' Even though they had told you the first time that you could not come in without a partner, yet with a partner you still could not come in. You would find the odd dancehall that would make you come in. The best dancehalls were at Blackpool - the Tower Ballroom or the Winter Gardens. Also, at Bolton they had a nice little dancehall called the Aspen Hall. Lovely little place. Lovely little fights too at Aspen Hall. When the sailors would come home and find their wives and girlfriends going out with black men, they'd come and challenge you in the dancehall. But you can't have that, so it would lead to fisticuffs.

"I remember when we got to Camp Patrick (Virginia, USA) and the white men in America said, 'Do that!' We told them where to get off and they realised that they were dealing with a different lot of people altogether. The lads realised that we did not believe all that rubbish that if you were black you could not go here or there. We are Jamaicans we do what we like. No, that was not for us at all." – *Alford Gardner*

The Jamaican people's indignant response to the racial barriers they encountered was a striking memento to the national character and psyche. Jamaicans are lovers of equality and liberty. Throughout its colonial history, Jamaica earned the reputation of having more slave revolts than any other colony in the British Empire. Jamaicans refused to timidly accept a life of repression and struck a bid for freedom. This national cultural reaction would be accurately summed up many years later by former Jamaican Prime Minister, Michael Manley: "we [Jamaicans] intend to walk through the world on our feet and not on our knees."

Dealing with unfriendly local people or discriminating American servicemen was the least of the Jamaican's battles; such incidents were sporadic at that time. However, two decades later, Caribbean people would launch organised political activities to legislate against racial discrimination that was institutionally entrenched -threatening their civil rights and even their mortality. But during the war, they were focussed on defending King and the Mother Country. Jamaicans died alongside British men and those on the ground who remained in England performed their tasks efficiently and exceptionally.

"I remember one incident that happened when I was working at Dunkswell in Devon. There was an aircraft that we were working on and when the propeller was spun, it would vibrate at high speeds and nobody could find the reason. We took the whole thing apart; took the propeller off, examined it, looked at the markings, and put it back together and the same thing happened. Then later that night I was thinking about it. We had looked at it and the markings locked up, but we were 180 degrees out of line. The next day I came back and I told the chief this and he was very dismissive, but I insisted that it was worth trying and he agreed. I tried it and it worked. After that I was made an area man for a while." – *Glen English*

"Filey was where we did square bashing (drilling exercises). I think it was for twelve weeks. Once you did your square bashing you did different courses. I got transferred to Wheaton to do my motor mechanics course. After I finished the course and I got transferred to Moreton-in-Marsh and my flight was called Flight Five. I tell you something about Jamaicans. On the station where I was working as a motor mechanic, two Jamaicans came to the station and let me tell you something, they were very good mechanics. Every vehicle and every thing that could run we had them running. There were three armoured cars where we were which were stuck there for a long time, but we had them running in no time. When these two lads came there they had everything running beautifully. Everything was going well and we were right proud of what we were doing because everything was going nicely." – *Alford Gardner*

The Jamaican servicemen and women were prepared for a long, protracted war. The attitude at the time was that as soon as the war was over, they would return home. They looked forward to going home as heroes and heroines, and to share their experiences with friends and families. Having acquired new and valuable skills, they knew they could return to Jamaica and contribute meaningfully to its development. When the war ended in 1945, many of the camps remained open and it would be three years before there was a large exodus of Caribbean service personnel returning home.

"In 1948, when I finished my time in the RAF the Colonial Government wrote to me and several others saying: 'Since you've dropped your studies to join the Air Force, we are prepared to give you some training to update your education'. I said I wanted to be a Design Engineer and they arranged a course for me. I had to go up to the offices at Cambridge to take some tests. Which I did and I got through, so they offered me the course I wanted. Some of the lectures were actually taken at Cambridge University itself. But during the day I was at college in Letchworth doing practical work. At the end of it, I got a certificate to say I had done all these different subjects: Maths, Engineering, Science, Design and Craftsmanship. I finished up as a draughtsman. I was still in the Forces while I was doing this course, so I had to go back in to be demobilized. When I was demobilized, I got a job as a junior draughtsman at a firm in Leeds. And that was really where my career kicked off." – *Glen English*

Errol James, Glen English and Roy Mitchell were among a very small number of Jamaican men, who remained behind and settled in Leeds. After leaving the RAF, Roy Mitchell joined the Leeds Rifles (Territorial Army) and spent the next fifteen and a half years of his service life as a part time driving instructor. Mitchell contends that in the early days immediately following the war, he could 'count the number of black people who lived in Leeds on one hand.' Meanwhile, their fellow Jamaicans accepted their free passage home from the British government, and returned to their country of perennial sunshine, white sand beaches, sweet sugar cane and mento music, (a precursor to reggae music).

> "One weekend, I decided to go over to Manchester, because I wanted to see some people. When I got there, all the boys from my station were in Manchester. The camps were closing down all over the place. So, I did my course and went home in '47. It was the natural thing to do because good heavens, I missed my family that much. It wasn't just a sudden decision. It was a case that I was going to do so many years in England then I would go home. Now the name of the ship that I took to go back to Jamaica I can't remember but I know I took the ship at Portsmouth. When we reached the Caribbean, the lads mainly from Trinidad started playing calypso and knocking little bits. Then all of a sudden it got a little louder. Then the other lads started knocking things from all around; anything that could make a sound. Pling! Pling! Pling! Ting! Tiddy-ting! One rhythm started and all of a sudden the whole of the top deck lined up with English people. We didn't know we had English people on board. They were all in evening gowns because they were having a dance, yet they all stopped to admire the sound coming from below. That was like three nights out to Jamaica. Then the captain came and he said, 'We've got forty-eight hours to Jamaica and we're cruising.' The Caribbean sea was just like a carpet- calm and smooth, not a ripple. When we reached Kingston the night, everybody was happy. I mean you're home." – *Alford Gardner*

But this celebratory mood would be short lived. The sight that greeted them on arrival into the Kingston Harbour struck an ominous note; it was an augury of things to come.

> "When we sailed into San Juan, Puerto Rico, it was beautiful. All the guys said, 'Look at San Juan. When we get into Kingston, it will look beautiful too.' When we woke up the next morning and looked out at Kingston. Honest to goodness! All you could see was the hills of Rockfort. It was dead rough. All you could see were these ugly rocks." – *Alford Gardner*

The Windrush Generation

The Jamaican servicemen and women were returning home to a Jamaica that was known for its tropical splendour. Jamaica's physical beauty was legendary. When Christopher Columbus stumbled upon Jamaica in 1494, he described it as "the fairest island eyes have beheld…" Even the name Jamaica which originated from the Arawakan word Xaymaca and means 'a land of wood and water', evokes the picture-postcard image of the landscape. The returnees made their way home to the capital city, or to their towns and villages situated by the seaside or nestled at the foot of a hill, or in the valley of a mountain with its lush vegetation hydrated by one or more of the island's scores of rivers and waterfalls. Their hometowns held memories of the smell of breadfruits roasting on wood fires, the laughter of children fishing for crayfish in the streams, and the times when the sweet juices of mangoes, coconuts, sweetsops, star-apples and naseberries filled their bellies. Whether it was the euphoria of returning home as former players on the side of victory, or the memories of their island home, their expectations were high.

Sadly, years of British colonisation had failed to bring economic prosperity to the majority of working class Jamaicans. In 1948, Jamaica was still a plantation economy with a heavy reliance on a limited number of export crops such as sugar and bananas. The mining of bauxite had yet not commenced. The country was still recovering from the devastating economic effects of the 1944 hurricane. The Jamaican economy remained stagnant and the population was growing. Britain was too busy repairing its infrastructure and economy destroyed by the war to offer any concrete assistance. Poverty was widespread. The Jamaican workers and peasants were either unemployed or underemployed. On the whole, Jamaicans were searching and waiting for new economic prospects. This was the harsh economic and social reality that faced the returning ex-servicemen and women. But as quickly as the taste of victory turned sour, a glimmer of hope would appear on the horizon of Kingston Harbour.

It started out as gossip among a few in some quarters of Jamaica that an old German troopship, the *SS Empire Windrush* would be docking into Kingston Harbour to transport fare paying Jamaicans to England. It attracted the attention of the ex-servicemen and countless other Jamaicans who dreamed of escaping a country stuck in an economic quagmire. The news gripped the entire nation and many began making preparations for the appearance of this ship - real or imagined. The veracity of this rumour was finally confirmed by an advertisement which appeared in the national newspaper, the Gleaner. Passengers were being offered a special rate of 28 pounds and 10 shillings for a one-way trip to England.

> "I heard about the *Windrush* from one of my sisters who lived in Kingston. At the place where she was boarding, there was a chap who worked in the Colonial Secretary's Office and he got the word that the *Windrush* was coming to Jamaica and it was taking men back to England for twenty-eight quid. My sister rang the Post Office and left a message about the ship coming down and she told me to more or less prepare. I thought I haven't even got twenty-eight pence! A few weeks after, an advertisement appeared in the Gleaner. It said you should come and book your passage on this ship. My brother, Gladstone heard about it the night and the following day he went to Kingston to book. He had £50 saved and put away. I said, 'Papa, I'd like to go back to England but I don't even have a cent.' He said, 'It's alright, you can have the money when you

ready'. I went to Kingston when the *Windrush* came and there was a big queue. That day there was almost two hundred people in the queue." – *Alford Gardner*

Even those who could not afford the fare were determined to get on board. One Leeds-bound Windrush passenger knew four ex-RAF men who did not have the money for the passage. He and his brother helped them to stowaway. The passengers had devised ways of distracting the authorities to prevent the detection of the stowaways. The passengers' generosity extended to sharing their food and sleeping arrangements with the stowaways. It was their way of saying they understood each other's situation back in Jamaica. The *SS Empire Windrush* left Jamaica on May 24, 1948. Significantly, it was Empire Day. For hundreds of years, Britain has had a largely one-way impact on the colonies that made up its Empire. Britain exported its people to populate its colonies and to assume key roles in the administration of government, business and culture. Now it was a colony's turn to export its people to Britain.

As the *Windrush* sailed towards England, the news of its impending arrival with over 400 Jamaicans threw Government Ministers and Civil Servants into a frenzy. The arrival was neither government planned nor approved. After a flurry of communiqués between different government departments and the Colonial Secretary's Office in Jamaica, a letter to the Parliamentary backbenchers from then Prime Minister Clement Attlee cleared up the apparent fear and confusion among the government administrators by asserting that British citizens of Dominion and Colonial origins irrespective of race or colour, should be freely admitted to the United Kingdom. On June 22, 1948, the *SS Empire Windrush* docked at Tilbury harbour in Essex.

On disembarking, six of the Windrush passengers set their destinations as Leeds. Four of them have been identified as Noel Edwards and his "good friend", Winston Stewart, Alford Gardner and his brother Gladstone. Only one of the four named resides in Leeds today. Both Edwards and Stewart are deceased and Gladstone Gardner has returned to Jamaica. Noel Edwards and Alford Gardner were both ex-servicemen and acted as guides for their travelling companions. Two of the more than a dozen stowaways on the *Windrush* also accompanied one of the parties that left for the northern city.

They left behind the passengers hopeful about the future and fearful of the unexpected - and under the vigilant eyes of the British press. Many of the national newspapers along with the two leading newspapers in Leeds announced the arrival of the Jamaican men on the *Windrush*.

The coverage by these two West Yorkshire newspapers gave no indication that the wider public were concerned about the arrivals of the Jamaican men. What Noel Edwards and his fellow Windrushians had to face was a Britain that was not used to a large scale inflow of immigrants of a different colour. Britain already had a number of Irish and Eastern European migrants, many invited to rebuild the post war economy and infrastructure. Labour was still short because over 300,000 British people had died because of the war, and the indigenous population showed preference for working in the relative high tech industries, or migrated

Job hunters here from Jamaica

When the ex-troopship Empire Windrush berthed at Tilbury today, her deck was crowded with 492 Jamaicans who have come to Britain to seek work.

Because of the dock strike the Jamaicans organised unloading. Fifty-two of the men volunteered for the Services, 204 have prospects of work and 236 are without work.

- *Yorkshire Evening Post, June 22, 1948*

Help for Unexpected Jamaicans
Welfare men board ship

Colonial Office welfare officials boarded the former trooper, Empire Windrush tonight "to tell the 412 Jamaicans on board what arrangements had been made for them in England."

"We don't know what work they can do or how old they are," a Ministry of Labour official said tonight. "All we can do is direct them to the local employment exchange."

- *Yorkshire Post, June 22, 1948*

by the thousands to Canada, New Zealand and Australia. Britain had also expanded its nationalised transport and health sectors, and there were increased investments in other industries such as wool, textile and engineering. An accessible and willing pool of Caribbean workers was exactly what Britain needed. As the *Windrush* passengers found employment in the industries and areas that were experiencing labour shortage, an idea was born. The UK government institutions set about recruiting workers for the transport and health sectors from the Caribbean territories. The Windrushians' gamble had paid off. They would later inspire a much larger wave of Caribbean people to risk everything and make the journey across the Atlantic in search of a better life for themselves and their families.

The Search for a Better Life

1950s Jamaica was still gripped in a sea of social change. There was the continued struggle for self-government, the rights of the workers and the provision of jobs for the masses. The economic downturn in the Jamaican economy persisted even with the commencement of bauxite mining by North American Corporations. One of the failed predictions during this period was that bauxite mining would energise the Jamaican economy, and bring about prosperity through the creation of a large number of job opportunities.

Chapter 1

The major political parties promised industrial expansion programmes that would create over 150,000 new jobs resulting from overseas investments. Deep fissures began to show in the industrialisation plans. In fact, only 13,000 new jobs were created from the mid 1950s to the late 60s, while the Jamaican workforce was growing at a rate of approximately 20,000 each year. The persistent economic downturn forced many Jamaicans to search for jobs overseas. In the 1950s, they boarded ships destined for the UK, including banana boats that were laden with the export crop for the British market.

"I came to the UK in September 1954. Job prospects, I should imagine. Things were not looking too good in Jamaica for young people. On the whole, there wasn't too much to look forward to. My family owned a little shop and I was helping to run it. But then I was helping to run it down also. My intention was to come to work in England for a few years and to return home with a fortune, because we were told that the streets of London were paved with gold." – *Allen Ebanks*

"I came because Jamaica was so poor and you couldn't get work. My sister and brother came before me and sent for me. I was doing sewing when I was in Jamaica. I used to sew all sorts and sell them in Coronation Market in Kingston." – *Mavis Cole*

"I came here in 1956, about June to see what it was like and to better myself because things weren't all that right with me. I had friends who were over here and I was encouraged from the reply I got from them. So, I decided it was time to have a go. You see, we know one another's position from home and what they used to say was give it a go because it was better off than what you were doing in Jamaica. I was doing a bit of cultivation to keep me going and helping out other people. The bit of farming that I did was practically a dead end." – *Samuel Barrett*

"After I left school, I worked with a surveyor for three months. I didn't have anything to do after that, so I just helped the old man out in the fields until I came to England. My cousin was coming and he was lonely and needed company and he said, 'Why don't you come with me?' So, I came to the UK in 1958 on 28th of April. I got a cow from my father and my father had also bought for me a horse and colt some time ago and I sold them. I also had some sugar cane and I sold that so that's how I came to England. I came by boat, it was supposed to take twelve days but I think it took more." – *Lincoln Cole*

Over 160,000 Jamaicans migrated to the UK during that period. Many of them were small farmers who had struggled to remain sustainable and profitable. Even plantation owners were migrating: citing unfavourable returns on small and medium scale agricultural production as one of the reasons for resettlement.

"My family wanted to go to Canada. My dad had a big sugar cane plantation but he was still considered a small farmer because there were bigger estates. The bigger estates could pay out more money to the workers, so after awhile my dad could not get workers because he could not afford to pay that sort of money." – *Celine North*

"I came in 1954. I came because the grass is greener on the other side of the mountain. Jamaicans were coming here because things were bad in Jamaica at the time. I had just come home from America after spending three years there. When I was in Jamaica, I was a farmer. I had my own land which I got under a government scheme. I went to a school called Holmwood and after I finished there they turned us into student farmers. They gave us some land, some money to employ people, to build houses and that sort of thing. But it was not profitable. Or, we could not make it good enough, one of the two things. So I decided to travel because as the saying goes: *fowl scratchin' here, him nuh find it here, him find it over there.*" – *Edley White*

By the 1960s, the majority of Jamaicans who came, did so on the recommendation of another friend or family member.

"I came to the UK in April 1962. I came because my sister was here doing her training. The day before I left Jamaica, I got a letter from her saying she was going to Canada but I came even though she was not here. I came straight to Leeds to my cousin at Harehills Terrace, near Roundhay Road." – *Maizie Pinnock*

"My father came here and he spent five years and so I said that I would come and do the same." – *Lynford Fletcher*

"I was working in Montego Bay at the time and I also had some livestock. I worked in a dress shop, making cover buttons and buckles. The life in Montego Bay was great if you liked that kind of life but there was no future in it. I didn't really have to come to England but there were some ups and downs and I needed a change. At that time my brother had emigrated to England. He left Jamaica in 1956. I wrote to him and explained the conditions in my life and that I wanted to join him in the UK. He said, 'Yes. Sell up the livestock and I will help you with the rest.' So I talked it over with the children's father and he agreed to move too. It was on December 10, 1960 that we finally migrated to England." – *Phyllis Hines*

Another set came to study or to have the experience of travelling outside of the region and to see for themselves the glory of the Mother Country they heard so much about at school, and later from friends, or read about in story books.

"I came to the UK in April 1962. I came because I thought it was a good opportunity for me to have a better life. I came mainly to train as a nurse." – *Florence Williams*

"I came to the UK in 1962. At the time several of my friends had made the decision to do so. I suppose we saw it as an adventure and the prospect of better educational opportunities."
– *Travis Johnson*

"I came to the UK in April 1965. I left Jamaica to start my nursing career at Royal Bath Hospital in Harrogate. I came with my mother, my father was already here and my elder sister who came here in the 1960s to join her husband. I had not seen my dad for a long time and it was very emotional when we met, especially seeing my sister at the airport too. I had only four days to spend with them and then I was off to Harrogate from Brixton, London. I had to leave home and my parents." – *Yvonne English*

"I arrived in the UK in October 1961. My intention on leaving Jamaica was to come to the UK to study. I had already applied for my training as a State Registered Nurse (SRN). The whole idea was to study here for four years - three years at SRN training, one year studying to become a Health Visitor. Then, I would spend a year working, another year travelling around Europe and I'd return home in six years." – *Elizabeth Johnson*

"I came in September 1965. I was taught in school that England was the Mother Country. So a lot of us would always dream of visiting the Mother Country. One day, my dad asked me, 'What do you want to do when you have finished school?' I said that I would like to travel; I would like to go to England. Then he said, 'If that's what you want to do then OK'. I can remember him going to the bank to draw the money. I was excited. I came to Bradford to stay with my aunty. It was the very first time that I travelled that distance on an aeroplane. I had never travelled on a aeroplane before." – *Councillor Norma Hutchinson*

Critically, the Jamaicans who had migrated for five years or more could afford to pay for the passage of the children they had left behind in Jamaica. This was one of the immeasurable costs of migration. Migration had changed the structure and emotional psychology of many families, leaving them hanging precariously in the balance. Children as young as a few months old were left behind with grandparents, aunts and uncles. Their arrival to the UK would mark the first time some of them could remember seeing their parents. It was very difficult for some of the children to accept this arrangement, but their parents were making a medium term sacrifice that they believed would pay off in the long term. It was a painful trade off for a higher standard of living and access to better educational opportunities. Or, so it seemed.

"I arrived in England on the 21st of August 1971. My mother who was living in England at the time had sent for my brother and me. My mother had been planning to send for us for a long time, but when my grandmother took very poorly, she decided that it was now time. She only sent for my younger brother and me because she felt that my older brother and sister could fend for themselves. I was eleven at that time and my brother was ten. I wouldn't say I was excited, because I was leaving my older brother and sister; it was like leaving part of you behind. I didn't know what I was expecting, I didn't know where I was going. All I knew was that I was going to my mother in England. I didn't know anything about England. My grandparents, they didn't tell me much. When I came, I met my mother for the first time because she left me when I was three years old. My grandparents used to show us photographs of our mother, but I can't remember if I had a photo of her or not when I was travelling to England. I know that it would have been the first time I would meet my mother in person.

"When I got here I just cried. When it was going into the winter and it was going to snow, I cried some more. I'd never forget that. It felt like living with a stranger, it was like starting all over again. My brother and I wanted to go back to Jamaica because we missed our grandparents. They were kind to us. They were the only people I knew from I was a child. I tried absconding from home many times, but I got into trouble for running away. First, I went to stay with my grandma, my mom's husband's mother. The other time I went to stay with a friend. It was like three times that I ran away. My grandmother phoned my mom and she came and got me. The next time she got the police to find me. I didn't know how my mother felt at the time. Just looking at her I knew she was strict. My relationship with my mother is very good now and we have developed an understanding. We're not children anymore, so the relationship is better." – *June Wood*

Chapter 1

"My mother came here in the '50s. I was quite young. I think I was about eleven. I don't think I missed her too much because I didn't actually live with my mom. I lived with my grandparents who brought me up, so I was loved and cared for by them. When I came to England in 1961, she was like a stranger to me, so of course, living with her it was hard, I cried many times. I don't think our relationship as a mother/daughter relationship was close as I would have expected, but after a very long while we became friends. I think we built a lot of bridges there, so that was nice." – *Yvonne Hylton*

"I came to the UK in 1965. My parents sent for me. I was fourteen years of age when I arrived in England. I was very excited to see my mother. When I met my mother, at first I didn't know her, but she knew me. It felt a bit strange but we got use to each other." – *Theresa Condor*

Some Caribbean people took the risk of bringing their children at the onset brushing aside any fears or uncertainties that they might have had. Parents, who anticipated the fallout from leaving their children behind, followed a strict savings regime to ensure that the responsibility of raising their children would remain theirs.

"When my daughter came here to live with me, she was a bit standoffish. She never called me Mom, she called me Aunty, because she said her mom was back in Jamaica. It started when she was in Jamaica. Every week I'd write to my mom to find out how my daughter was getting on, and how she was progressing in school. In every letter I always would say, I am your mom. And you know, when she answered me back she would say my mom is here with me in Jamaica. I said, 'Oh, what have I done?' So, I said to myself, 'OK then we'll see'. When she came to live with me here, I used to give her a lot of loving. I used to hug her up and say to her, 'I am your Mummy'. Eventually she changed and started call me, Mommy." – *Francis Williams*

"I had a son at home in Jamaica. He was only ten months when I left him with my mother. When I sent for him he was nearly four. Oh, it was lovely seeing him again. It was the intention that I would come to England but not to stay long, but things didn't work out that way. So, I decided that I wanted to see him grow up with me, so I sent for him. Everything that I gave him he would save it and say that he was taking it to his 'mom', (his grandmother). Gradually, he began to accept me as his mother." – *Icyline Parker*

"I got married in 1962 and that year I sent for my first child who was eleven years old by then.

> She was late coming because she was sitting her 11+ examinations, so she arrived in February 1963. When my daughter came over I decided to buy a house. I was sending her to music lessons on St. Martin Road and she told the music teacher that I was looking for a house to buy. The teacher informed her that there was a house that was for sale on that street. My husband and I viewed the property and then bought it. Then in 1965, I sent for my baby girl who was six years old. In July of the same year, I had a baby boy. After my second daughter came from Jamaica, life was very hard, but I could not live without my children. I worked full time around the clock just to make ends meet." – *Phyllis Hines*

There were children who were not able to join their parents permanently due to changes in immigration laws or because their parents started having other children in the UK, therefore making it difficult to physically accommodate them. They were never forgotten. Left in the care of capable and loving relatives, the parental responsibilities and bond were maintained through letters, financial support, telephone calls and much later, visits.

The migrant generation was not yet counting the cost of resettlement, they were sure it would be outweighed by the anticipated gain. Over 250,000 Caribbean people flowed into Britain during the 1950s and 1960s, depositing a few thousands in Leeds, and much larger numbers in Manchester, the Midlands and the largest numbers in London. Expectations ran high among the eager immigrants, and those who came before did nothing to dispel the myth of the 'streets paved with gold.' But what they saw and experienced did not match up to the image of the Britain that they learnt about in school.

First Impressions

The vision that many Jamaicans held of Britain was to some extent true. It was indeed one of the wealthiest nations in the world. At one point its history, the wealthiest in the world with an Empire that ruled a quarter of the world's population. It had unfettered access to the resources of its colonies which it exploited for the benefit of its subjects in the United Kingdom. In 1948, Britain was in the final phase of its post war austerity. The arrival of the *Windrush* coincided with an era of stability and increasing prosperity. The proverbial wheels of industry were turning robustly; production was soaring and had created an abundance of employment opportunities. Britain was a revitalised industrial power. Jamaica on the other hand, was still decades away from industrialisation on any scale. However, degrees of poverty and decrepitude lingered in cities and towns across Britain and this would rest uneasily with the Jamaicans. They learnt the hard way that the English houses available to them were no man or woman's castle. For some migrants, their first impressions coincided with their dreams, while others had to quickly erase the postcard image of Britian that was imprinted in their minds.

> "When you lived in the West Indies, England was your Mother Country. You could buy these little books about England in Jamaica and the picture you saw of England was very pretty. When I came I thought it would have been a better country. I was looking for a prettier place." – *Lincoln Cole*

> "When I came to England and I came off the plane and was going up the motorway, I saw a lot of smoke coming out of the chimneys. I said that this place was full of factories and there were jobs all over the place. Then I came to realise it was not so, it was people's homes all that smoke was coming from." – *Lynford Fletcher*

Coming from a warm country like Jamaica, the only buildings that had any use for chimneys were factories. These Jamaicans were unaccustomed to life in a cold country. The weather was another chilling factor which threatened to dampen their dreams and survival in an alien culture.

> "I didn't like it when I came here, it was so cold and foggy. I got lost about three times coming from town: from Marks & Spencer to Harehills Lane to where my sister lived on Avenue Crescent. I was working in town and I caught the bus one Friday night at four o'clock. I did not reach home until eight thirty that night because we decided to walk and I got lost because of the fog." – *Mavis Cole*

> "I didn't like it one bit when I came - the houses, the weather. The weather was really bad - cold - and there was no central heating in the house, you had to make a fire. When you came home from work and there was no heat, you would have to keep your coat on, and sometimes you had to go to bed in your whole trousers and your cardigan." – *Lincoln Cole*

> "The buildings were just so close - very, very close together. I saw all these huge buildings with chimneys which turned out to be houses. I thought they were factories because this peculiar smoke was coming out of the roofs. These were all extremely strange. The nights were quite cold even though it was June. There were a lot of white people and of course, I had never seen that body of white people all together before." – *Bev Lattibeaudiere*

> "I landed in England on December 12, 1960. Unfortunately, there wasn't enough room for my husband and I in London, so the next option was to come to Leeds. We took a coach to Kings

Cross Train Station to get the train to Leeds City Station. On my way to Leeds, it looked so strange to see smoke coming out of the top of some of the houses. I thought they were factories, but when I reached to Leeds I realised that all of the buildings with smoke coming out of the roofs weren't factories. I took a taxi to my sister's house on Grange Avenue. My sister greeted me warmly and I was glad to see her. I was up early the next morning. My sister asked me to go to the shop just across the street in front of her house. Whilst I was in the shop, the sky started to get dark all of a sudden, until it became pitch black. I could not see anything. I was afraid, I started fretting and crying. I said to myself, 'I want to go back to Jamaica if this is how England is going to be.' Then I heard my sister calling me. She had a lamp in her hand and came to take me over to the house." – *Phyllis Hines*

Their arrival in Britain was certainly a demystifying experience. The Jamaicans had to debunk more than just their mental construct of the physical settings but they also had to reassess their notion of the race/class hierarchy that was shaped by growing up in a colony.

"I tell you the first impression that I had of England. When I came off the boat, I noticed all these white men coming along the dock, pushing these wheel barrows and it was a real shock to me. The white people that we have in Jamaica, we had never seen any of them doing that kind of work. So that was the first thing that shocked me really. I got use to it though." – *Finley Wray*

Additionally, they had to come to terms with the fact their precursors were locked in a conspiracy of silence about the stark reality of life in Britain. The news of their day-to-day struggles was never relayed to their families and friends back home.

"When I came I thought more or less it would be much easier for me. At the time that I came, there weren't many black people and some of the white people were frightened of us, especially when I would go to the market. I thought more or less it would have been easier to get more money. I didn't know you have to work so hard." – *Louise Reid*

"When I came my entire impression of what I thought and heard that England was about was certainly the opposite. I had a real shock. We were told England was paved with gold, so I wanted to see this gold. Certainly it wasn't like that. I came and saw how hard my mother had to work, and how early she had to get up in the mornings, which was dark. It was dark going out and dark coming in. I couldn't understand it at all at that time, especially what she was doing. No one explained to you the hardships that they were having. They would say they were working and that was it. My mom never really explained that she had it as hard as she did." – *Yvonne Hylton*

Their silence about life in Britain might have been rooted in the fact that they did not come to stay. Most Jamaicans planned to stay and work in Britain for five to ten years. It slowly dawned on them that their five-year plan had to be abandoned. It was going to take them a lifetime to 'mine gold from the streets of England'. Nonetheless, they were going to make it, they did not come this far to fail. As Jamaican people, they believed in their abilities to overcome hardships. They were proud of their strength, tenacity and perseverance. They were reflecting the essence of their identity and aspects of their social and political heritage. They were descendants of Nanny of the Maroons, the 18th century military chief who led her people successfully in the fight for their freedom against the British in Jamaica. She became 'a symbol of unity and strength for her people during times of crises.' It was in their blood. They were marching to the drums of slaves long gone, like Sam Sharpe, leader of the 1831 slave rebellion in Jamaica who like others before him were engaged in years of struggle to free the Jamaican people from the inhumanity of slavery. Little did they know that the perspectives and experiences that they all had in common would one day draw them closer together as a people. But at this juncture in their history, the only thing that was apparent to the migrant generation was that they would have to draw their strength from the popular Jamaican adage: *'A little hard work nuh kill nobody.'*

BLACK DIAMONDS

Granddad was just another relative to me – I love them, they love me –
come 'round on Sunday and get food for free.
Nothing else. But that was then…

I never understood that every pore on your skin
Had a story embedded as deep as the courage within.

I never knew that then, in ye times of old,
You thought these heat-forsaken streets were paved with gold.

I bet you never knew this nation's invitation would spawn sons, daughters and more next of kin.
You never knew your journey could create doctors, lawyers – losses and wins.

And that's why I love you.

So thanks, for everything. For the plantain and pumpkin and red peas based elation.
For the paraffin heated nights of shared accommodation so that I could go to private school
and get a better education.

So thanks, for everything.

For walking in the paradox of sullen grey streets
Where black and white could never meet.

So thanks, for everything.

For the ackee and saltfish and sorrel based nights.
For when words like 'nigger' really caused a fight.

- just so I could fit in and be alike.
Just so I could walk down the streets in baby blue Nikes.

So thanks, for everything.

For the extra £5 from down in the pit –
Black dark outside toilets only by stars lit.
Just so I can be determined so I never will quit –
Be you train conductor, botanist, unhealthy or fit.

So thanks, Granddad for putting shoes on my feet.
Then, Britain needed you and now it needs me.

By Laurah Pitter, 17
March 9, 2002

2 Leeds, Our home?

The Jamaican community in Leeds began to take shape in the late 1940s. It was comprised mainly of the ex-servicemen and the Windrush passengers. At the onset, these settlers had a sense of community. But it was a community that was being built on unstable foundations. They were the first to learn the hard truth behind Norman Manley's words that "there is a tremendous difference between living in a place and belonging to it". They arrived as holders of British passports, subjects of the Empire with strong allegiance to the Crown. The image that the hundreds of thousands of Jamaicans that followed in the 1950s and 1960s had of the relationship between their country and Britain, would have been shaped by the actions of the Jamaican people who donated ten tons of sugar and bananas, and one ton of coffee to the residents of Lynmouth and Dulverton - areas in Devon that were severely devastated by a storm in August 1952. Such were the notions of goodwill that many thought existed between Jamaica and Britain. The Jamaicans would realise just how wrong their assumptions were, because they were certainly not made to feel welcome by the white indigenous population.

Marcus Garvey had advocated less than two decades earlier that Jamaicans should stop looking to Britain as the Mother Country. In fact, he derided those who did. In the end, his warning was prophetic. There were no laws that prevented their full participation in the society, but the treatment meted out to them when they attempted to settle in towns and cities, was a major deterrent. The social conditions of the Caribbean people in Britain at that time shaped and directed their struggles to achieve a sense of belonging.

The Search for Shelter

> "My journey…the journey that the servicemen took then was relatively easier because we didn't have to think about transport, we didn't have to think where we're going to eat or sleep because all that was taken care of, you were a serviceman and they were looking after you. That was the difference." – *Glen English*

Life outside of the British armed forces was certainly different for the Jamaican ex-servicemen. Once the security of being in uniform had disappeared, they had to face the unsettling reality of being civilians of colour.

> "When I finished in the service, I went to Burtonwood to get my final papers as a civilian and I travelled from Burtonwood to Leeds. When I came to Leeds I went to the YMCA which was on Albion Street then. I remember I was trying to find somewhere to live and I travelled around

Leeds trying to find lodging in any area. It was one of the most difficult time of my life because everyone of them that said: 'Rooms to Let' when I knocked they would say, 'Sorry we are filled up.' Now there would be a telephone box ten yards from the place where you had knocked on and if you go to the telephone box and make a call, they would say: 'Oh yes, we have got vacancy'. You would go and knock again and they would say, 'Sorry it has just been taken.' Finally, bless her, there was one lady from Ireland and this lady's name was McCrum and when I knocked on the door, she said, 'Father God, is not another one of *you* again!' Anyway, we had a little chat and she said that she had a room but I had to share it with someone. I said, 'I don't mind.' Funnily enough, I went into this place and she showed me the room and it was the half size of a toilet with two bed-sits. I was happy to get it because at the time that was how the situation was. Now you wake up in the morning and one of you want to change, one of you had to get out of the room, because it was that small and you couldn't be in the room together." – *Roy Mitchell*

The Windrushians faced the same fate. When the ex-servicemen disembarked from the *SS Empire Windrush* they convinced their travelling partners that they could find accommodation for them in Leeds. But getting a place to stay even temporarily was not easy, the doors were shut even at the places where they once stayed as RAF men and had enjoyed excellent rapport with the owners and their families.

"We just got off the *Windrush*, we got on a train to London and then headed straight to Leeds. We came up to Leeds in the afternoon and I went up to Green Banks hostel and saw the manager. He said, 'Oh, I'm awfully sorry. If I had my way I would have you back. The management says we can't have you here any more.' I went to a house where we used to stop and the woman said, 'Oh I'm sorry but you are not in the RAF anymore and the neighbours won't like it.' So we wound up four of us living in one room.

"We had four beds but the room it wasn't that big. We showered at the public baths. My brother and I left from there and we went down to Coventry Place, but we still had to go to public baths. We didn't have a bath in the house. We paid about fifteen bob a week for rent. When you had to go to the bath, you paid a shilling. The amount of times you bathe per week was up to you. Here in England, it was once-a-week shower. That was the norm. Knowing us, we tried to have more showers. For the average English family, I think it was Thursday or Friday night that was bath night and they all used the same bath water. I can remember this woman, our landlady, she couldn't understand why when we boys came from work we had to get washed before we sat down to eat.

"We left from there and we went up to Clarendon Road after that. It was better because there were two of us to a room. The situation was that no matter where you went nobody wanted to know. They would say, 'I am sorry you know but the neighbours this and the neighbours that'. The neighbours which you knew but you might not know his wife, when you spoke to him, he would say, 'I really cannot do this because of the wife'. You might even be working with him, but he would say, 'I can't'." – *Alford Gardner*

Housing had been critical to the experience of Caribbean people in the UK. The frustrating search for accommodation and the squalid conditions that the immigrants were forced to live in, were indicative of the position Caribbean people were expected to hold in the British social structure. This social problem would later become political ammunition for the Caribbean community when their dreams of returning home began to fade. They were not about to give up on their aspiration for economic prosperity, so they went into survival mode and lived under any conditions necessary to achieve their goals. In essence, they were driven to set up multiple occupancy arrangements, yet the tabloids ran horrendous stories criticising Caribbean people for conditions they did not create.

"When I arrived in England, I didn't know what to expect. Many of us were coming in those days and we were just glad that we were coming to England. I heard about Gloucester but I didn't know where Gloucester was, but I made plans to go there. A friend, he took me to Gloucester and the Lord provided a good mate for me, so when I went to Gloucester I stayed with him. At the time, it was three of us in one room. That was my first experience of living conditions in England. After that, I left Gloucester and went to Birmingham where I lived in a house with fifteen of us. So you can just imagine what it was like when we had to cook in the mornings and you have only one kitchen and everybody was waking up to go to work at the same time! Plus you had to make breakfast and you could not be late for work, because you were supposed to be at work for 8 o'clock. During that time with so many of us living under those conditions you also had very little privacy. But you just had to try and make the best of the situation because then we lived with our own people at the time, and it helped. We were more caring and loving towards each other then than we are now. After twelve months there, I just got fed up with that and I decided to travel around. I had a friend living in Leeds and I wrote to him and asked him if I could come and see what Leeds was like. He said yes and that he would get me accommodation.

"When I arrived in Leeds and I saw my living quarters it was a shock to me. I got a room and in that room I had a bed in the corner. But there was also a cooker in another corner and there

> were two more tenants who were cooking in my room. On a Saturday or Sunday morning when I wanted to have a lie in, these men wanted to come in the room to cook. I was very unhappy about it and intended to go back to Birmingham. But luckily my friend he told me of a West Indian lady who had bought a house in Chapeltown. We went on the Sunday to see this lady and she told us that she had a room to rent. It was a back-to-back house, the room was on the first floor, I went into this room. The room that she offered us, other tenants had to come through that room to go to another room. But in this room there were two beds. It was certainly an improvement to where I was coming from - which was a bed in the kitchen." – *Robert Chrouch*

Overcrowding and scarce accommodation had long since been a critical social factor in Britain and preceded the arrival of the Caribbean people. Throughout the 1940s the Housing Department of the Leeds City Council was constantly faced with the mammoth challenge of re-housing its residents. Each year, it would receive thousands of applications from local residents requesting relocation due to overcrowding and/or unhygienic living conditions. Prior to the war, over 33, 000 slum houses were marked for demolition in Leeds to make way for the rebuilding of new houses with modern facilities. The slum clearance came to a near halt during World War Two and so did the building of new houses, as raw material and labour were scarce. The factors that contributed to the housing crisis continued in the aftermath of the war. A headline in the Yorkshire Evening Post (YEP), February 26, 1957 potently summed up the situation.

40,000 Leeds homes without bathrooms

Unfortunately, the Caribbean people settled in two of the areas identified for slum clearance – Chapeltown and Harehills, which were cluttered with miserable and drab back-to-back and large Victorian terrace houses with no bathroom but an outside toilet. Chapeltown and Harehills would subsequently emerge as the heart of Leeds emerging Caribbean community.

> "When I came to Leeds, I did not know anything but I asked questions. I took a taxi early in the morning to Harehills Terrace. The taxi driver came out and took my case out and I said, 'What do I do?' He said, 'You have to ring the bell.' I asked him, 'Where is the bell?' He rang the bell for me. Somebody came down and opened the door. Anyway, I wanted to go to the toilet and I asked, 'Where is the toilet?' I was told that the toilets were outside. I was so shocked - believe you me! I know back home you have toilet outside, but when I left Jamaica I was in town (the capital city - Kingston), so I was used to indoor toilets. It was horrendous!" – *Mazie Pinnock*

Nonetheless, Leeds was considered to be a city better than most. Leeds Housing Department was praised for its housing record and was held up as a model for others to follow. According to the Yorkshire Post, May 10, 1962: "Few English cities have equalled Leeds record in stripping away this shoddy legacy of the past." But a backlog of persons needing houses remained for many year after the war. In 1975, there were 27,000 people in the city waiting for council houses. However, during those early post war years, Leeds putative reputation for better housing had spread among the Caribbean people.

> "I had a friend who was living in Leeds who was here from 1950. I had never heard about Leeds until he had encouraged me to come. He had friends in Leeds and he said the living conditions were better. So, my friend and I decided to come over to Leeds." – *Samuel Barrett*

The scarcity of accommodation for the Caribbean people bred another disease – Rachmanism. A practice associated with the English landlord Peter Rachman, operating in London who overcharged his tenants while placing them in filthy, overcrowded houses. While Notting Hill was the heart of Rachman country, its tentacles spread into the urban areas where other Caribbean people settled.

> "Before leaving Jamaica, I had arranged to stay with a friend in Nottingham. On arrival at the house, I found out that my friend was already sharing a room with three other men. I joined them in the same room because there was no other alternative. All five of us were from the same district back in Jamaica, so we knew each other very well: one was even my first cousin. The house was vastly overcrowded but we all got along with each other. The landlord was one of the most unscrupulous men I have ever met. One night, we were in the room talking and he knocked on the door and his words were: 'Fellows it is ten o'clock, it is time you were going to bed you are burning too much electricity.' The room had only one light bulb! That really annoyed us. Also in those days the only means of heating your house was by coal fire. All of us in the room would put together to buy our own coal. What I shall never forget is while we were out to work, the landlord and his family were stealing our coal. I watched them doing it one day when I should have been at work. He was getting so much in rent, it was not long before he could buy another house and he and his family moved out of the house." – *Allen Ebanks*

The YEP did one of its first features on the Caribbean community on August 29, 1958, and highlighted the practice of charging inflated rent for sub-standard housing as an inbred practice that was inflicted by the Caribbean people on their own kind: "Certain coloured landlords are known to charge exorbitant rent for cramped accommodations." Evidently, from the Caribbean people's accounts, the Rachmanesque practice was executed by others irrespective of race or ethnicity and was not only carried out by their own people.

> "The houses that were owned by West Indians and the Eastern Europeans were the only places most Caribbean people could get. Things were difficult those times and if you came over and you knew somebody, even if the place was cramped, you liked to be where your mate was. I could not tell if they were overcharging because I wouldn't know the right price when I had just arrived. You just paid what somebody had asked you to pay because when things are difficult to come by, you don't think about prices." – *Samuel Barrett*

The nascent Caribbean community in Leeds did not sit idly by while their fellow island folks suffered the ignominy brought on by scarce housing. Glen English, one of the first Jamaicans, and by extension first Caribbean person to settle in Leeds joined forces with his fellow countryman, Mr. Pennycooke and a local solicitor, Charlie Charlesworth to establish an organisation that would 'free the Caribbean immigrants from housing worries.'

> "We started a Housing Association in the '50s as there was a great demand for accommodation. More and more West Indians started coming in and the problem of accommodation became acute. So we had to try and come up with an answer for it. We started an organisation called the Aggrey Society to help Caribbean immigrants to get accommodation. Aggrey was the name of an African leader who had the saying that 'you can play a tune of sorts on the white parts of a piano and you can play a tune of sorts on the black parts of a piano, but for harmony you need both'. And so we built our organisation based on his philosophy." – *Glen English*

Aggrey Society was one of the first Caribbean organisations in Leeds formed to address the severe housing crisis affecting the community.

With the Aggrey Society along with their own thrift for which Caribbean people are known, Jamaicans were able to own their own houses quickly. They also employed community saving methods, such as *pardner* to help them with such purchases. Pardner is widely practised in Jamaica, it is an informal way of saving whereby a group of people pay a fixed sum of money each week with one member of the group and each member takes turn to 'draw' the total sum. Others brought their money from Jamaica with the expressed intention of purchasing property. A survey taken in the late 1960s, revealed that "there was relatively more owner-occupiers among coloured residents and relatively more Corporation tenants among white residents."

> "Six of us bought this house on Regents Terrace and it was more or less where everybody knew they could go and meet the lads. Each of the six of us had a room. The house had four rooms and two big attics and big cellars. To be quite honest they paid for it and I just paid after. The

other guys, they were all Jamaicans and they were older than me at the time - I was the youngest. They bought it cash. I think they paid £500 for it. Among some English people, buying houses wasn't the done thing in England. In England, you got your house from the Corporation and you lived there and paid Corporation rent until you died. But Jamaicans started buying their own houses and that started causing friction. When I got married and I had my first son, I decided to leave Regents Terrace and to buy my own house. I had it all arranged. When I got this house I decided to strip the wallpaper and re-do it. One day, a policeman said to me, 'Do you know there is a petition going around?' I asked, 'What for?' He said, 'Against you living in this street.' I said, 'How you mean?' He said, 'Do you know that Polish man across the road? He's been going around with a petition because you stripped all your wallpaper.' I told him that the Corporation promised to remove the paper that I had stripped from my wall. Imagine, this man was walking around with a petition to prevent me from living on the street and he didn't even live on the same street." – *Alford Gardner*

"I was throwing a *pardner* at the time. I think it was fifteen of us who were in the *pardner*. We were throwing £5 a hand. At the time, my wife and I were living in one room, then my friend informed me that he would be getting engaged. Now something started to ring in my head. I figured that if he got engaged and then got married, when his wife arrived in England, she was going to need this accommodation for her two children that she was going to bring with her. So I discussed it with my wife, I said, 'Look, now we have to pull every stop out and see what we can do to get our own house'. There wasn't much money in the pot, because at the time I was saving with the view of sending for my children, I wasn't thinking of saving to buy a house yet. I think I had about £170 but I started looking. I was coming from work one afternoon around two o'clock, and I saw this little house which had a note in the window saying that the house was for sale and you should apply within if you were interested in buying it. I went straight to this house, and I rang the bell and the lady came out and I told her what I had come about. She got me to talk to her husband who showed me around. They asked if I liked it, and I said, 'Yes'. Then I said, 'I'll go and get my wife to come and have a look.' We weren't living that far from this house. When my wife came and had a look, she said, 'Yes, it's nice.' It was a three-bedroom house. I managed to scrape what money I could which brought the money up to an extra £100. It was a lot of money to us then." – *Robert Chrouch*

"I first settled in Chapeltown on Reginald Terrace and then I bought a little house in the Hyde Park area, because I didn't have any relatives here at the time. I bought the house about four years after I came to England. I had some money with me and also I had some money in Jamaica. So I asked my mother who was in Jamaica to send me some of that money. The money I had in Jamaica I had earned it in America. It wasn't enough to buy the house but I could use it to make a deposit. The house was cheap anyway; houses were cheap in those days." – *Edley White*

Other Jamaicans in Leeds settled with family members who had bought their own houses. Many of these Caribbean owned houses used to give shelter to new arrivals until they were able to find accommodation that was suitable and salubrious. In whatever accommodation the Caribbean people were able to settle, it was a significant first step. Their accommodation was much more than a place to rest their heads after a hard day's work, it was the beginning of their sense of stability in a foreign country. It was their gradual convergence as a unit that would need to stand together for political and social imperatives. They had demonstrated that they were a force for change. The individuals who walked around knocking from door to door showed courage in the face of rejection, but establishing an economic base was the immediate focus.

A Job for Everyone

Caribbean people settled in the large and medium-sized industrial conurbations across the UK. Leeds would only attract a few thousands over the decades, but they were well placed in the city's major industries - engineering and clothing manufacturing. Others filled key positions in the transport and health sectors. It has long since been acknowledged that without immigrant workers the clothing and engineering industries in Leeds would have closed down. The same applied to the hospitals and the transport services which would not have been able to function at full capacity without immigrant labour. Their presence was invaluable to the extraordinary boom that the industries and key sectors had enjoyed at the time. In a statement to the YEP on August 29, 1958, Caribbean workers were praised for their contribution to the transport sector: "The Leeds City Transport Committee one of the biggest employers of coloured labour in the city found its coloured workers to be most satisfactory in every way."

Jobs were plentiful in the post war period up until the mid 1960s that according to collective memory, 'you could leave one job and find another the next day'. Job conditions were not always favourable, but the Caribbean workers were willing to take almost anything until something better came along. This generation was determined to work very hard, no matter the condition and sometimes the requirements.

> "It was easy to find a job. I think there was job for everybody. My first job was with an engineering firm that made boilers. I can remember it so vividly, because I was teamed up with an older man to collect the castings from the foundries with an electric truck. Not long after I had

started, my workmate, Tom was sick. The foreman told me I would have to do the driving because there was nobody else to do it. I protested that I had never driven the truck before and to drive it in the factory in such closed space would really be difficult. 'You will be OK' was his reply. The first few days were far from OK. The truck was all over the place. It would go anywhere else but where I wanted it to go. It was running into castings, moulding, fittings and all sorts. On the second and third days, the fellow were shouting, 'Oh, he's coming again! He's coming again!' They all stood by their mouldings ready to pull them out of the way as I got closer. By the fourth day, I was no longer a danger to them, so they were able to relax and get on with their jobs." – *Allen Ebanks*

"When I went and asked for the job in chemical work, the manager, he said to me that the job was very dirty and he wasn't sure if I would like it. But I was so desperate to get a job that I said, 'Look, if you give me a chance, I am sure you'll not regret it'. So he said, 'Alright, come the next day.' So, I went on the Wednesday morning and started the job. The wage was so small that I couldn't see how £8 a week would cover my overheads. I discovered that if I worked on shifts, I would get a little more money. You see, I worked where they processed whale oil into the finished product, and then it would go to the other manufacturer that bought it so as to make the ink for ballpoint pens. The whale oil had to go through a very cold stage of pressing; the temperature would be minus five. So just imagine in winter when you go into work in the mornings. It was cold outside and you had to work in a room that was at minus five-degree temperature. You could not put on the heating to bring the temperature up, I was told it could spoil the stuff.

"One morning, I was very cold and I took a bucket in with some hot water to put my fingers in it, and the manager saw me. He nearly blew his top. That was the situation in that factory. But in spite of that you know, I enjoyed the time working among some of the lads, because we were working together as a team. They were very friendly. I eventually went on shift and things were different. I was working with a lot of acids - sulphuric acid and a lot of very dangerous stuff. Then over the years they started making cosmetics and all different sorts. When I first started this job the name of the company was Glovers Chemical. Then they sold the firm to a mining company, who twelve months later sold it out to a brewery company. The brewery kept it for a long while and then they sold it out to a French company. I worked there throughout all the changes until I retired." – *Robert Chrouch*

There were a few who got white-collar jobs but had to work twice as hard to prove they deserved their appointments.

Chapter 2

"I remember the few Jamaicans who were in Leeds in the '40s. They were awesome. They were just freshly out of the RAF and they were looking for work. One guy went to the Post Office service as a civil servant. This other guy, he was a stenographer, another was a radio and television repairman so he started working for a company and eventually started his own company. Most of the others worked for engineering firms in the Leeds area, because Leeds was then a very big engineering centre. The employment rate was very high here in the engineering industry. They were doing machine work like, centre-lathes, batched on milling - those types of skilled jobs. I got a job as a junior draughtsman at a firm in Leeds. I worked at that firm for many years. I wasn't long with them, when they offered me the job of being their planning engineer. I did this along with my design work, so I was pretty well occupied. During that time, I designed a machine, which was a conveyor; they called it a Satra conveyor. The firm began to sell them all over the country.

"I didn't realise it at first, but one day I took a look around and I realised that I was the only black man in a workforce of three hundred. The one problem I found was that I had to work harder than the others because I constantly had to prove myself. I think a lot of them must have thought that I was from Jamaica, what did I know about engineering. That came through a lot of times. In the middle of all that, I got offered a job in Bradford with more money and more prospects, so I left and went to work in Bradford. Whilst I was in Bradford, the Board called me one day and said that they were thinking of starting an apprentice school. They had looked at my qualifications and they thought that I was the guy to run the apprentice school. I took the job and they sent me for a three-week teacher's training course. I worked at the apprentice school for about seven years, until I got another job offer, this time in the Civil Service - teaching my skills as a draughtsman. I became like a lecturer, and I was there for about twenty years until I retired." – *Glen English*

There were a large number of Jamaican women who came to the UK and trained as nurses. They qualified as state registered nurses and went on to specialise in a number of areas.

"I have only had one type of job since I have been here. I went to school and left at seventeen years old and commenced my training in nursing. At present, I work at the Cookridge Hospital which is the oncology centre in Yorkshire. While I specialise in oncology at the moment, I have trained in intensive care, cardiac care, general surgery and other types of nursing, but for the past twenty years it has been oncology. My father on the other hand, worked at the Avon-mouth Docks unloading ships. My mother worked as an ancillary worker for a few years and then because she started having children she did not work for many years until she returned to Jamaica." – *Bev Lattibeaudiere*

"My sister took me to the Labour Exchange to have me registered. I was placed with a clothing factory and I was paid four pounds per week. I only worked there for two weeks because the factory was dusty and dirty. The Labour Exchange sent me to an engineering factory and I worked there for six months. One day I told my sister that I wanted to go into nursing. She told me the names of the hospitals in Leeds and one of them was St. James's Hospital. When I sent in my application, the matron at St. James's accepted my application and called me for an interview. I was sent to the Nursing School for the test for State Registered Nursing. I failed the test because of one question about underground trains, and at that time I didn't know that trains ran underground. So, I was offered the two year training instead. I have enjoyed nursing, it was a respectable job."
– *Phyllis Hines*

The Jamaicans were also coming with specific skills that they were keen on using. But some had trouble securing jobs in the areas for which they were qualified.

"My brother was a cabinetmaker. He was a good cabinetmaker. It was something that he learned to do from he was a little boy. He went to all the cabinet places in Leeds but everyone said the same thing: 'You can't get a job because you're not in the Union and you can't get into the Union because you don't have a job'. He eventually got a job in an engineering firm, as an engine fitter for aircrafts. He never used his skills as a cabinetmaker to earn a living here in England." – *Alford Gardner*

"I landed in England on the 13th day of November 1957. It was just beginning to get cold. I didn't get any work for the first four weeks. I went to the Labour Exchange and I signed up to get a job. They told me that they had temporary work at the General Post Office for the Christmas, and they asked me if I wanted to do it, and I said yes. There were quite a few of us that did that for the Christmas. Right after Christmas, I went out the New Year's morning and the first job site I went to I got a job as a carpenter. That was with the London County Council. I stayed with them for about six months and then I moved on to other companies from there. I used to go around and renovate houses and things like that. I took a break from the trade and I worked in a factory down in Dagenham where they built telephone cables and things like that for about nine years. I left from there and I decided to try another factory, Ford Motor Company.

> I only stayed with Ford for about six months because I couldn't take working indoors. So I went back on the trade. Although the country was so cold, I used to enjoy the outdoor life. Plus I preferred doing carpentry work. You see, I learnt my trade in Jamaica working as an apprentice with a local carpenter. I didn't go to any technical school. You learn it the hard way out there. When you learn a trade in Jamaica, you learn to do everything. In Jamaica, we'd say, 'you start' from the bench'." – *Finley Wray*

They were not only skilled craftsmen, but they were also teachers, policemen and former civil servants who had to contend with doing blue-collar jobs.

> "There was this one guy, he was a policeman from Jamaica where he was a sergeant and he decided to migrate to the UK. He had all the qualifications, but he couldn't get in because the police then didn't have a policy of bringing in black people into the Force, so he didn't get a job. There were teachers amongst them too. Certain job situations were difficult because there was a resistance to having black people in the workplace alongside white people. I remember when I first applied for a job as a draughtsman, one firm in Grid House was quite pleased with my qualifications, but the guy said clearly on the phone that he's got some women working in the office, and he didn't think it would be a good idea to employ me." – *Glen English*

There were so few blacks working in a professional capacity that Roy Mitchell beamed with pride when he saw a fellow Jamaican working in the offices of an engineering firm instead of on the factory floor like the majority of his countryfolks: "While I was at Irwin Bellow I met a man called Glen English and he was the first black man that was a draughtsman that worked in an office there."

When the Canadian recruitment officers came into Leeds offering skilled workers the chance to migrate to Canada, many of the skilled Jamaicans took up the offer fearful of languishing in the gaol of underemployment in Britain.

> "At one stage, Canada had a recruitment drive for workers. Many of the skilled Caribbean migrants took up the offer. Even I got a job offer to work as a chief draughtsman in Montreal. I didn't go because the fact is I didn't want to go. But they recruited right across the country, I think it was '64. The Canadians recruited twice to my knowledge. The second time the recruiters caught even more. They caught those who have been working now in the engineering industry and who had acquired skills and should have been promoted but weren't getting one. Many of the Caribbean migrants were dissatisfied with working in Britain so they decided to try their luck in Canada, so the Canadians had

quite a haul. The Caribbean Cricket Club nearly went under at that time because we lost several of our leading members all in one go and had to build up again from scratch." – *Glen English*

The USA became another option for those with bigger dreams that could not be realised on the factory floors.

"My father was quite sure he wanted to stay in the UK, firstly because his interest was very much in academia. But when he wanted to pursue his career in teaching initially, he found it difficult to do further education. Trying to get into Leeds University at that time was a difficult task for him. When he received an invitation from his older brother to come to the USA to further his education in his area of study, he went. As a result, he is a professor in chemistry and physics. So that paid off for him but it made it difficult for him to remain in the UK with his family. He felt he had a dream and he had the right to pursue those dreams." – *Khadijah Ibrahiim*

"People were going to Canada and America at that time because they were disillusioned with being here. If you look at the situation in the UK, Jamaicans and Caribbean people were doing much better in the US and Canada than here. Let's be straight about it. Colin Powel for example would not have got to the position he has got to if he were in the UK. Look at Grandma Armstrong's two granddaughters, when they were here they were literally thrown on the scrap heap. They went to the US, and one ended up being a doctor and the other a physiotherapist. There are many more like them. Peggy also didn't do well and she did her nursing and wasn't going anywhere as a SCM, and she is now studying medicine in the US, yet she never moved when she was here. She was in a rut." – *Elizabeth Johnson and Nettie White*

The Caribbean workers believed it was blatantly clear to the average white British person that they were making a positive contribution to the economy. Apparently, this was not the case. If it had been, perhaps they would not have been on the receiving end of racial abuse which came hand in hand with their weekly pay cheques. Many felt under appreciated and blamed government laxity for the public's ignorance regarding their presence here.

"I was here for a few weeks before I got the job at Commercial Engineers. Every time I went down to the Labour Exchange the person at the desk changed and all I could hear was: 'Sorry Son, there is nothing for you.' They then said come in the morning or come in the afternoon, and all you got was: 'Sorry, there was nothing for you.' One afternoon when I went in, there were two men, one was standing there at the counter and he said to me, 'Sorry, Son there is nothing.'

But the other man asked me, 'What do you want?' I said, 'I am looking for a job. I know a bit about motor cars.' He said, 'Can you strip an engine?' I said, 'That's the easiest part.' So he turned to the man and he said, 'How many weeks have I been coming here and asking you for a few lads just to do a bit of engine striping?' The man at the counter replied, 'Well, you don't want…' You could tell from his expression what he meant. The man said, 'Look! All I need are men to do some work'." – *Alford Gardner*

"I heard about this job going in Leeds Infirmary kitchen. I went out and I got the job. That's where I started my catering because one day I went in, and the kitchen superintendent asked me, 'Would you like to be a chef?' I said, 'Of course, that will help me out a bit'. So, he put me in a room working with these white men and one white woman. I was glad and not glad. The white chefs were calling me all sorts of names. They were calling me a monkey, they were calling me a baboon and all sorts of names. They were making fun of me but I just ignored them. The white lady chef, her name was Amy, she said to me, 'Francis, don't take any notice of those idiots.' I didn't. Many times I went down into the toilets and I cried and I said, 'Father, I'm just asking you to give me courage'. I prayed and I cried.

"Anyway, the kitchen supervisor sent me to Thomas Danby College on one-day release. During those times, it was rough because there were not a lot of black people in the college: just an African girl and myself. We used to sit together as two blacks and they used to still tease us, because they didn't know black people, black people were a threat to them, I think. They felt black people were going to take their jobs and take all they've got. I just prayed to God to give me strength to carry on. Eventually, I left the private kitchen and went to the diet kitchen. I spent two years in the kitchen diet section. You got the same brushing off but not like before. I spent five years down there; three years in the private patient section and two years in the diet section. I left and I went to Social Services. I started working in the Social Services kitchen on the 8th of March 1970. I spent twenty-four and half years catering for Social Services until I retired and started my own café on Chapeltown Road called the Dunn's River Café." – *Francis Williams*

"Working in the NHS you would also find a lot of racism. Patients called you the odd names and would tell you to go back to your country or go back on your banana boats. Although it hurt, I had to laugh it off and pretend I did not hear them. I gave them the greatest nursing care because it must be difficult for them to see foreigners taking care of them. Some of the staff was prejudiced. They would give us the dirtiest job to do, while they sat around. The atmosphere was tense sometimes." – *Phyllis Hines*

Some bore the racial invectives patiently and courageously taking a personal stance against such abuse when they could, because they believed that it was all for a greater good. Their sacrifice would provide financial security and educational opportunities for themselves and their children. The women survived working full time and looking after their children without the support of the extended family, which they were accustomed to back home.

"I got a job at Neville Reed and I worked there for nine months and then I left there to have my first child, Sandra. Then I said to myself that I have to go and find another job. But first I must go and find someone to look after Sandra. I found a lady two doors from us - an Italian lady, she was a registered nanny so she put my name down. I went to look for work and someone sent me up to a factory and they said they didn't need anybody. That was in 1963. Then one evening, this lady said to me, 'Would you like to work in the hospital?' I said to her, 'I don't mind but when it comes to injection I'm scared of doing it.' She said, 'No, no, nothing like that.' So, she helped me to fill out the application form. I posted the form and in the space of three days, I got an interview. I couldn't believe it! I remember it well, because Sandra was three months old and I had made arrangements for her to be christened. So, I went for the interview and in the space of two days another letter dropped. I had to cry because I couldn't believe it! The letter said, 'Come down at half past eleven and bring your P45'. I went to Mrs Reid the child minder and I asked her to keep Sandra for me. I didn't know I would start work the same day!

"My first Ward was 44 and there was another black nurse there, her name was Tingle Brown. She took me and showed me around and I couldn't believe it! My duty shift that day was from half past eleven until half past eight that night. I was worried because Mrs Reid still had my three month old baby with her and I rushed home to her and I said, 'Oh, Mrs Reid, I'm sorry I didn't know I had to work today.' You see in those days she didn't have a telephone for me to phone and I didn't know I was going to stop.' But she said, 'It's alright' and I said I got the job and I started the job. I worked there for thirty-five years as an auxiliary nurse doing every earthly thing except giving injection. Everything you can think of.

"I tell you something else that I remembered. When I went to Ward 49 this particular patient came in. One night, I was looking after another patient - you know they were like babies they couldn't do anything for themselves, you had to do everything. Some of them were very dirty, so you had to bathe them. Oh! Hospital work is a very dirty job! Anyway, this man he had some dirty clothes on, so I gave him a bath and I put his dirty clothes in the side of the locker. I was doing another patient and his visitors came in and they said to him, 'Oh, you look nice, you got nice clean clothes on. Where's the clothes you came in with?' He said to them, 'Oh, I don't know.

That *nigger* bathe me, you can ask that *nigger*.' I'm telling you, I just put what I was doing down and I said to him, 'Let me tell you something, I have a name. My name is Maizie and I said don't you *ever* call me a *nigger* again!' That's what I told him." – *Maizie Pinnock*

Self-sufficiency was the Jamaicans' personal mandate. In whatever form employment was presented they were going to seize the opportunity. A few tried their hand at self-employment and entrepreneurial ventures which were sometimes borne out of the exigency of redundancy or unemployment.

"I settled on Avenue Crescent. My brother and sister were living there. I came straight to Leeds. I came ten thirty the night and went out in the morning and got a sewing job. I worked in the upholstering trade for nine years. Then I got another job in upholstering and I worked there for nineteen years. In the 1980s there was this big strike and we were all made redundant. About thirty of us put our redundancy pay back into the trade, we started paying ourselves and we were all doing well. Then we got another strike again- the miners' strike and that did us in. So we went bust. We used to do our biggest business with the miners' housewives. Every three months they'd change their suite. The more money their husbands got, the more the wives would spend with us and then that kept us in business. We also used to sell to the shops and that kept us in business too. When we went bust, it affected our lives very badly. The manager was so good because he tried to get us the money that we paid in. We got some money back but some of us didn't get back much. We had to go to the tribunal so that they could sort it out. After that I still worked in the sewing trade again until I retired." – *Mavis Cole*

"My first job was at a place called Kirkstall Forge. I did very well there until they made a lot of us redundant - I was one of them. I was transferred from there to G&H McLaren which did diesel, coach and train engines. At that time, my wage as a qualified engineer was about £15 per week. That was a lot of money in those times. Again, McLaren closed down. But I continued to work in engineering as a bench fitter at Irwin Bellow which made sewing machines. Then Pfaff Sewing Machines took over and they made a lot of people redundant. I said to myself that I would try and find another job. I saw a painting and decorating job being advertised, so I went to this firm for an interview and the interviewer went through me like a dose of salt. At the end of the interview, he said, 'I can't tell you anything about decorating because you seem to know more than me but I want a younger man to climb ladders'. So I got myself a pair of ladder and a pair of steps and set myself up to do my own business until I retired. I did very well on my own. Funnily enough, I started working for the odd black people when they passed and saw me working they would ask, 'Could you do mine?' When I got a job, I did it well. I never advertised; my job advertised itself. Even now people are still asking me about jobs. I remember one day the Councilman was watching me working and he came around and offered me a job as a freelance painter and decorator for the City Council. I was very happy with that." – *Roy Mitchell*

The stories resonate with the pride each worker took in his or her job, it was more than a means to an end. It validated them as human beings in a society that at times stripped them of their dignity. Many of the Jamaicans who came to the UK during the post war period grew up in a Jamaica that was being shaped by the Labour machinery of the late Sir Alexander Bustamante, National Hero, who dedicated the latter part of his life to the cause of the Jamaican worker. He inspired many Jamaicans to strive for prosperity.

Another keen exponent of the Jamaican worker, the Governor General of Jamaica, His Excellency Sir Howard Cooke has eloquently thrown light on the ethos of the Jamaican worker: "One thing you must realise about a Jamaican is that he determines what he wants to do and he is not afraid of anybody - that is one of his outstanding features. He knows his rights and he is prepared to fight for his rights. He shows in all circumstances what he is capable of doing. One of the things that intrigues me, some of these Jamaicans who didn't have any skills, became skilful in a short time and enjoyed the confidence of their employers. I would like the Jamaicans in Britain to know that they are not third class citizens because when it was necessary they had to perform first class work in situations that were different from home and they took advantage of them."

The road to economic independence became entwined with the Jamaicans' struggle for social acceptance and justice. They were challenging racist practices from the factory floors, in the bus aisles and on the hospital wards.

A Community is Born

Prior to the formation of the Jamaica Society (Leeds), the Jamaicans worked for over three decades to create an identifiable Caribbean community. Island boundaries were blurred because the socio-economic problems that affected Caribbean people were not partial to such divisions. The Caribbean community was primarily identified by their patterns of settlement. In Leeds, they settled in and around the Hyde Park, Chapeltown and Harehills areas. However, when one refers to the Caribbean community in Leeds, one automatically thinks of the Chapeltown and Harehills areas. The two are almost interchangeable. Spatially, the Chapeltown and Harehills communities lay side by side. For several years, either of these two communities have been home to the immigrant groups which have settled in Leeds: Jews, Eastern Europeans, Irish, Caribbean, Asians and other ethnic groups. Today, an estimated fifty percent of the Caribbean population in Leeds reside in these areas.

Chapter 2

In light of their multicultural past, Chapeltown and Harehills have evolved into a vibrant, culturally diverse community, but socially and economically, have had more than their fair share of problems. They are nonetheless of geocentric importance to the history and development of the Caribbean community in Leeds. Within these areas, Caribbean people defined their community through the social, political and cultural activities of the clubs, self help and community organisations and agencies that they established.

Notably, Chapeltown and Harehills have been the epicentre of their political and social lobbying campaigns and civil disturbances. The struggle to overcome the economic marginalisation, and the racial and social subordination in a white society steeped in years of class stratification and the belief in its racial supremacy, began with a handful of Jamaicans - initially by the ones who stayed behind after the war and those who came on the *Windrush*. This act of coming together as a people led to the rise of a spirited and recognised Caribbean community.

When it was time to get on with more than just the business of working for a living, the Jamaicans created the Leeds Caribbean Cricket Club along with a very small number of young men from other Caribbean territories. The Caribbean Cricket Club was an organisation that represented entertainment, social interchange, a vehicle for announcing their presence, and for weaving themselves into the social fabric of the Leeds community. It was a game Caribbean people played with their own unique flair and style and they continued in the same tradition of the region's number one pastime. Fifty-five years later, the Caribbean Cricket Club remains the oldest and longest standing Caribbean organisation in Leeds. In the 60s and the 70s, the Caribbean Cricket Club won either the Cup or the Championship within the Yorkshire Central Cricket League.

> "When I was here in '47 living at Horsforth. We bought a bat and a ball and we used to go on the park and have a knock about. So when we came back in '48, the boys got together and formed a Cricket Team. We went to Herbert Sutcliffe, a big sports store and we explained to the store clerk that we were forming a Cricket Team. This man at Herbert Sutcliffe promised to fit us up with a bat and a ball and our gears. We said, 'We won't be able to pay you all the money at once.' The man said, 'Oh, there will be no problem'. So, we got two bats, two balls, two pairs of pads and so on and it came to so much. That was just enough for us. Then we wanted more. The man at Herbert Sutcliffe said no problem again. He told us we could order more gears and that we could pay so much a week. We agreed. We thought it was all arranged. We went in to collect the things and all of a sudden, somebody else came from around the back and say, 'No, no, they can't have it.' He just came out and took one look at us and said we can't have it. There was only one reason. So, we had to go back to the grassroots and buy what we could afford each week. One week, we would buy one thing and the following week, we would buy something else.

"Anyway, we had a Cricket Team and we practised until we played three matches that year against other English Teams. The first team was the Kirkstall Liberal Working Men's Club. The second match we played was the best match. We played a team at Osset. This chap he is still alive, his name is Millington and he was a left hand bowler. When he bowled, I tell you, the ball went right through the wicket. That's all we played that year- just three matches. We were all Jamaicans then with one Trinidadian. We used to have a right good time, because we used to have trips nearly every weekend out in the country areas. We played in the little villages around the area. In 1950, they used to call us the West Indies Cricket Team, you see, because the real West Indies Cricket Team from the West Indies was known by then. No matter where you went they would always say they were looking forward to playing the West Indies Cricket Team. It was an honour to be compared to the West Indies Cricket Team." – *Alford Gardener*

"I was here in Leeds when the entire black population of Leeds were twenty of us. Most of them lived in one house, a big Victorian house at 20 Clarendon Place. We used to go in the cellar and cut each other's hair and some of us used to play dominoes, so it was sort of like a home from home when we went there. When the Caribbean Cricket Club started, it started out of that house. We sat down one day after lunch and said, 'What are we going to do now we're here in England and we've decided to live here?' Then somebody said, 'Well, we could play cricket.' We asked, 'How do we go about it?' Then one thing led to another and we decided that each of us would put fifty shillings a week to buy gears for cricket. When we got enough we bought gears and started to go up to Woodhouse Lane to practise. Whilst we were there playing a practice match somebody told one of the Leagues about us. A representative from the League approached us and asked us if we would like to join the Yorkshire Central League. We joined the Yorkshire Central League and became a force in that League for years. So that was the start of the Leeds Caribbean Cricket Club. It started off just playing cricket on Saturdays and on Sundays. When we met, we used to play friendlies.

"At one stage I was the Secretary and so I had to make arrangements for the matches along with Errol James who was the Chairman for quite some time, he was in the community here since 1944 until he died in 1994. We arranged to play cricket on Saturdays and Sundays and practice matches were on Tuesdays and Thursdays, so we were seeing a lot of each other. When we had to repair or buy new gears, we had to fundraise. We fundraised by having these dances, which actually turned out to be quite big affairs. So it gradually developed into a cricket club instead of just a cricket team. The Cricket Club had a number of guys who were quite interesting. One of them, Cliff Hall went along and formed a pop group and started singing folk songs. He became very, very popular when he joined up with a couple of Liverpool lads and they formed a group called The Spinners and they were popular for years. I remember him because he was always strumming his guitar in the corner when we were all making a lot of noise playing dominoes." – *Glen English*

The Leeds Caribbean Cricket Club was more than just a recreational access point. It took on social welfare roles as Caribbean people began to flow into the area in greater numbers by the 1950s. When the new arrivals were faced with problems the Caribbean Cricket Club would invariably be their closest point of reference.

"For long enough it was the only organisation in this city that was catering to the needs of the black residents. The Cricket Club developed into quite a good social organisation and it remained so for years. It was only much later when other organisations began to spring up that it had to take a back seat to the new groups that the immigrants began to form and to the activities they were involved in." – *Glen English*

Two Jamaicans, the late Errol James and Glen English who were founding members of the Cricket Club, became the city's oldest and longest serving community workers from the Caribbean. Their work on social and community issues has gone a long way into setting the foundation for the myriad of community organisations, agencies and institutions that were formed decades later to serve the Caribbean population. They worked to bridge the widening gap between the Caribbean people and the indigenous people of Leeds. They also worked to maintain links with Jamaican officials at the then Jamaican Mission (which later became the Jamaican High Commission after Jamaica's Independence) and with the Jamaican nationals in the city.

It was the same enterprise and willingness to serve the community that inspired Glen English to join forces with local people to set up Aggrey House in the 50s, the city's first housing association for Caribbean people. Aggrey House was a central meeting point for the community as well. In a 1998 interview, Noel Edwards identified Aggrey House as 'a place where he and his fellow West Indians could congregate for a game of dominoes.' Glen was also a member of the Leeds International Council, a local initiative that looked at the problems affecting the migrant communities. In the 1960s, he spearheaded the 236 Project one of the first summer programmes for children of immigrants in Leeds. Glen English later received an MBE for his work in the community making him the first black person, the first Jamaican and the first Caribbean person in Leeds to receive this honour. His dedication to advancing the quality of life for Caribbean and black people in Leeds often meant being both activist and advocate.

> "Sometimes we would go outside a building carrying placards to demand change. For example, we found out that when young Caribbean people wanted to go into banking, none of the banks wanted to employ them. We forced the issue with the banks and we got a meeting with them and one of the banks (which I won't name) said it was not their policy to employ black people. This bank had big business connections in the Caribbean and our argument to them was this: 'Come on, how can you be saying that when you make a lot of money out of our people back home.' But they didn't budge from there. I think the first bank to have a black teller was the Co-op Bank. On the other hand, I was the Yorkshire representative of the West Indians for an organisation called the National Committee for Commonwealth Immigrants (a precursor to the Commission for Racial Equality), and we used to meet every month at High Wycombe. What we were doing then used to be about changes." – *Glen English*

Equally, Errol James's early involvement in the community has meant he was a forerunner in many respects. Before there were any shops that stocked and sold Caribbean food items, Errol assumed the responsibility of delivering such stock to the Caribbean community in Leeds. After helping to form the Leeds Caribbean Cricket Club, he served as its Chairman for eighteen years. Errol was also one of the founder members of the United Caribbean Association in the 1960s and served as its President. He continued to serve his community by establishing and participating in community-led organisations such as the West Indian Centre of which he was a founding member, and was also instrumental in the lobby for the now closed Chapeltown Community Centre. He also sat on various statutory committees including the Community Relations Council. According to the 1994 Annual Report of the Leeds REC, Errol's venture into race relations in the late 1960s was due to of his own experience with racism. He was in the forefront of the community's struggle to stop Britain from continuing the practice of racialised injustice that was built into the immoral ideology and institution of colonialism.

Errol James became Deputy Chairperson of the Community Relations Council (CRC) in Leeds in 1969. In 1972, he was elected its Chairperson and served in that capacity for over twenty years - throughout the CRC's name change to the Racial Equality Council (REC). He also chaired the first Police Community Liaison Forum that was a sub-committee of the CRC. Those who remember the late Errol James have credited him with being a great negotiator between the statutory and voluntary sectors. Under his leadership, the Leeds CRC broke new grounds in mitigating the atmosphere of suspicion between the police and the younger members of the Caribbean community by initiating and sustaining dialogue between the two. He was awarded an MBE in 1982 for his services to the community and was appointed as a Lay Magistrate in 1984. Both Errol James and Glen English were founding members of the Leeds CRC. Another Jamaican, Ratrica 'Nettie' White served alongside these two on the Committee of the Council for a number of years.

Race and its impact on the social welfare of the new Caribbean immigrants became an issue that still remains on the political agenda today. Consequently, Caribbean communities were constantly in a state of flux. Leeds was no exception. It has been widely acknowledged that the 1958 Notting Hill riots in London, placed race on the forefront of the social and political agenda and made the wider British society take note of its then emergent Caribbean community. Following the explosive situation in Notting Hill, the YEP printed an exploratory article on August 29 on the Caribbean people living in Leeds, which began by outlining the situation across England:

> **Nottingham:** Hundreds of Englishmen and coloured men fought a pitched battle last Saturday. Bottles, knives and razors were used.
> **Sheffield:** A dancehall has imposed a ban on coloured people.
> **Leeds:** Is there a colour problem?"

The Evening Post deduced that "2,500 coloured people in Leeds - and they are happiest here." While the article featured the work being done by the Roscoe Place Methodist Church - " a group of people who devoted their spare time to calling upon coloured folks with the aim of integration and making them feeling at home." However, the Caribbean residents in Leeds were confronted with racial problems on a daily basis.

> "I was one of the first black motorists in the City of Leeds. I remember in the 1950s being stopped three times in one night because the police weren't used to the idea of black people driving cars; they had never seen it before. When I reflected on it later, I could see what their problem was. I was earning relatively good money as a draughtsman and I could afford to run a car, but the police, they were riding bicycles and the idea of a black man being in a better position might not have pleased them at all. Anyway, on that occasion I wrote to the Chief Constable and complained and the harassment stopped". – *Glen English*

> "You got a lot of racism in some of the stores. When you entered a store the first thing one of the sales assistants would do was to come up to you and say, 'Sorry, I haven't got your size.' They wouldn't let you explain what you wanted, or what you were looking for. So all you had to do is just get out of there quickly." – *Phyllis Hines*

Meanwhile, Jamaicans acted on their own accord as individuals, or organised themselves into small, informal groups to challenge the prevailing climate where colour-coded transgressions were permissible. Jamaicans had inherited a long and admirable historical and cultural tradition of struggling for social freedom and equality. Jamaicans embodied the spirit and courage of their forefathers, Paul Bogle and George William Gordon, National Heroes of Jamaica, whose bodies swung defiantly from the gallows in Morant Bay in St. Thomas, Jamaica because they challenged the oppressive status quo of British colonialism. These ancestral memories would serve as moral and spiritual guides in post war Britain.

"In those times, it was very sticky indeed. I was amazed because people used to ask, 'When you sweat and you wipe your face, does the black come off?' Sometimes, you go to some places like a restaurant, they'd refuse to serve you because you were black. Some places used to say: 'Sorry but I don't serve *niggers* here!' I used to turn around and say, 'I'm sorry but when you say that you are insulting me, the correct word is Negro.' If you go into a bar with a friend the landlord would turn around and say, 'Sorry we don't serve blacks'. So we would walk out and we go to another place and if the landlord served us, he would break the glasses that we drank out of and then say, 'You see that, don't come back.' So the following week, if there were three of us we would take another three and make half a dozen. The following week, we would take a few more because we knew that he could not afford to break anymore of those glasses all the time. We sort of tried to break down the barriers then." – *Roy Mitchell*

"In those days we cared for each other. You don't even know the person but as long as he was black and you were passing each other on the same street, you would never pass and don't say hello. Though the colour prejudice was here, I tried in my own way not to let it get me down. You'd get on the bus and you'd sit on the seat and the white people would pull away from you. Sometimes when you try to sit in a seat on the bus, they would just spread out on the seat so that you couldn't get to sit down. Other times you would go to the shop to buy something and you could stay until tomorrow, you wouldn't get serve. Another experience that I had, was when five of us were going out: my wife, my brother and three lads, we said, 'All right, let's stop at this pub and get a drink'. We went in and there was only one man leaning on the counter, so I went to the bar to get a drink and the lady at the counter said, 'Oh! There's no service.' I thought she said she was busy or something else. I didn't quite get what she had said. One of my colleagues he came up and he asked me, 'Didn't you hear what she said? They're not going to serve you'. We left and went to a next pub across the road, and they served us. But the experience that gave me the biggest surprise was at the very church that I attend today. During those times the only person that would greet you was the Minister. I didn't expect that the church would be like that, you know. But as I said I did not let it get me down and I decided to stay put in that church. Today I feel that it has paid off." – *Robert Chrouch*

The 1960s was also a period of legislation for and against the immigrant community. The first bill was the Commonwealth Immigration Act in 1962 which restricted immigration from the former and existing British colonies - a move which shook the confidence of the Caribbean community. The first Race Relations Act came into effect in 1965. The Act was considered weak especially in areas such as discrimination in employment, housing and service delivery. In 1968, a second Race Relations Act was announced which put an end to the practice of barring people of colour from accessing public facilities and addressed discrimination in employment. In Leeds, a small number of Caribbean organisations began to emerge. The United Caribbean Association was formed in 1964. It was an organisation that worked to bring Caribbean people together under one organisation, and carried out groundbreaking work in community development - interfacing with the police and lobbying the Local Authority. It was during this period that the Leeds West Indian Brotherhood - a militant group with over two hundred and fifty members - was most effective. According to a 1962 Guardian report the organisation launched "a vigorous opposition to the new Immigration Bill [by] lobbying Leeds six MPs".

Two of the founding members were Veryl Harriott who came to the UK from Jamaica in 1961 and her brother Ferley Cruise. It was important for Veryl that as a Jamaican she could contribute to a group that represented the entire community which ignored island boundaries and was committed to the welfare of people of African and Caribbean origins in Leeds. The Brotherhood symbolised the attitude of the children of Caribbean immigrants who bore the 'Made in Britain' tag. They were the Black Power generation, politicised by the racial discrimination in the society and were influenced and sustained by reggae music and Rastafarianism. The Brotherhood problematised racism and was responsible for the first Black History classes in Leeds operating initially from the home of Veryl Harriott on Harehills Avenue. In an interview with the YEP June 23, 1973, Veryl Harriott emphasised that "here we have an educational system which allowed the black school children no sense of pride or identity… Cannibals, spear-throwers and cotton-field slaves yes, they heard about that. So the black child goes through school…having nothing of his own race to be proud of."

Veryl Harriott was described by the Yorkshire Evening Post as one of the Caribbean community's leading race workers, she was actively involved in a number of community groups and initiatives - including the Leeds REC and was appointed its Honorary Secretary and Chairperson, some thirty years later. However, in the early 1970s, Veryl initiated the formation of the Chapeltown Citizens' Advice Bureau. She was the first black person to head a Citizens' Advice Bureau (CAB). The Chapeltown CAB dealt with issues that were immediate to the Caribbean community: issues of discrimination, immigration, incidents with the police and the criminal justice system. The Caribbean community could confidently carry out such work, because it was strengthened by the introduction of Race Relations legislation. Another Jamaican involved in the Chapeltown CAB was Travis Johnson who was invited to work as a volunteer by Veryl Harriott.

Travis Johnson like his Jamaican compatriots Glen English, Errol James and Veryl Harriott became an active community worker. His involvement in the community began in 1969 with the establishment of a play scheme. However, he earned his reputation for his work in race relations. Over the next three decades, Travis served in several capacities in the church including the Church of England's governing body, the General Synod. He sat on a number of community-based, regional and national committees and boards, and spearheaded or participated in a number of initiatives to set up key community organisations. In 1977, Travis along with other members of the community, initiated the establishment of Harambee which was a shelter for disaffected and homeless young people mainly of Caribbean descent. His recollection of the formation of Harambee in Leeds came out of a work-related visit to Wolverhampton.

> "I was on a placement in Wolverhampton in 1977 and I came across this organisation called Harambee there and found that what they were doing was useful and very effective. They were providing accommodation mainly for homeless black young people. At that time there was a growing number of black young people who were becoming homeless. So I came back to Leeds and I spoke with a few people about it, we met and agreed that it was something that we could bring to Leeds. Clinton Cameron, Annette Francis and Buelah Mills went with me to Wolverhampton and Birmingham to see the Harambee Projects. We were able to attract funds I think initially from the Commission for Racial Equality and other grant aiding bodies. So, we were able to set up this organisation on Cowper Street. Clinton Cameron, Buelah Mills, Mitch Lewis and Veryl Harriott eventually became employees of Harambee." – *Travis Johnson*

A few years later, he became one of the founding members of Technorth which was set up to serve the young people in the community who had left school with little or no qualifications and wanted a second chance. Technorth offered these young people training in information technology.

> "It was first called the Harehills Information Technology Centre. We realised that it was necessary for young people to have qualifications in information technology and the black community was not benefiting. Again, a group of us got together to set up this centre. The then Leader of the Council, George Mudie was very supportive of the idea, so we were able to acquire a building on Harehills Lane. The Technology Centre was based there for sometime until it was moved to its present location on Harrogate Road. Subsequently, the name was changed to Technorth. It was mainly individuals from the community who were instrumental in setting it up. James Aboaba was the first Chairperson and I also served as Vice Chair. It catered mainly for students who had completed mainstream education and had not achieved much. Most of the students were from

the Chapeltown and Harehills areas. Technorth was very successful, so the Education Department took it over." – *Travis Johnson*

The 1970s can be construed as a period when the Caribbean community in Leeds intensified its lobbying activities. Going home to the Caribbean was no longer the primary issue but building foundations in Britain. The principal elements of these foundations were predicated on the right to be treated with dignity, and recognition of their social, educational and economic needs. Lobbying campaigns were systematically applied with far reaching scope and impact, destabilising the touchstone against which the community had been traditionally measured. The residents took decisive action to form a working relationship with the police, voiced strong concerns about the quality of education their children received from State schools, the deplorable housing conditions in the area and the need for new or improved community facilities.

In 1972, a small but significant creation added to the sonorous voices of the residents of Chapeltown and Harehills - it was the publication of Chapeltown News, which emerged as a militant micro-newspaper known for its no holds barred and unrepentant approach to the coverage of community news. One of its early editors was Clinton Cameron who came to England in 1960 from Jamaica and became a committed community worker.

> "When I got involved in Chapeltown News I became the editor. There were a lot of young people involved like Max Farrar and Leroy Mills. The first issue of Chapeltown News dealt with what was happening at Studley Grange Nursery. Ideally what we were after was to raise awareness about the issues in the area. There were a lot of issues around housing like the proposal to demolish houses and problems with dampness and squatting. We covered problems that young people were having with the police, racism and employment. We also covered action in the community regarding education which was a major issue at the time across Britian. The population in the schools in Chapeltown were predominately African Caribbean and there were always issues around the fact that there were no black teachers. However, Gertrude Paul (a trained teacher from St. Kitts & Nevis) subsequently became the only black headmistress in Leeds. She was very active in raising issues on education as well as setting up a supplementary school for Caribbean children, because there was a lot of organising around Educationally Subnormal Schools (ESN).
>
> "A lot of the Caribbean children who were born in Britain at that time in the 60s began to fail in school. The reason given at that times was that children from Caribbean backgrounds were educationally subnormal, they haven't got the ability to cope with the demands of education. So they ran tests and put these Caribbean children in special schools that were set up by the Local

Authority at that time, which became quite a big issue. I remember meetings were organised at Jubilee Hall on Sundays and hundreds of people came out to listen to Bernard Coard who had written about ESN. He was exposing the system by arguing that it was the schools that were in fact making the children educationally subnormal by putting a high proportion of them into special schools. It was an issue for black people everywhere in Britain.

"Also, there was a kind of stereotype of Caribbean people within the school system. The prevailing opinion was that Caribbean parents were Victorian in their approach to child care and education. Caribbean parents believed that children could not learn unless they were disciplined. I believe that you cannot have a situation in which children in school can treat teachers as they like; they have to behave if they have to learn. But the rule at that time in this country was completely the opposite - children must be free to explore. So there was always that kind of conflict of culture. That was in the 70s, during the time of Chapeltown News, and we covered issues like this one." – *Clinton Cameron*

Chapeltown News also documented during this period of mass mobilisation, the spontaneous action by residents on Sholebroke Avenue about the rubbish problem. This direct action against the 'Rubbish Disgrace' was spearheaded by a well-known community activist Trevor Wynters, a Jamaican who settled in Leeds in the late 1950s.

"I was commissioned to write and perform a selection of my poetry for the Spice of Leeds closing ceremony of 2001. I had just finished performing and was approached by Max Farrar who asked me my name. I mentioned my grandparents' family name, as most people often recognise their names more so, because of their past activities in Chapeltown. Max said he knew my grandfather and proceeded to relate to me a wonderful story about what my grandfather had done some years back. I understand this had to do with a protest where my grandfather had wanted the overflowing refuse removed from the streets of Chapeltown. For some reason this was not being done and from what I understand my grandfather took a stance against the Local Authority along with a number of people from the community, they barricaded Chapeltown Road with the rubbish bags which stopped the flow of traffic. I asked my grandfather if he recalled the event - he gave a smile indicating his memory of the day. The thing about my grandfather, he is very humble, he never ever blows his own trumpet, and when I tell him people want to speak to him about his past activities, he just continues to smile. He doesn't think what he has done is anything extra special, or out of the ordinary. He just considers himself as someone who cares for his community." – *Khadijah Ibrahim*

Chapter 2

Trevor Wynters cared a great deal for his community. He was bold enough to wage a one-man war against the vice of prostitution, whose roots were so firmly planted in Chapeltown that it had become almost impossible to eradicate. Back in April 1968, four hundred residents of Chapeltown protested against prostitution in their community - an area described by the Yorkshire Evening Post on April 5, 1968 as "Vice District Worse Than Soho." Six years later, it was still an issue. The Evening Post, January 31, 1974, ran another story about the problem of prostitution in Chapeltown, labelling the area a "Mecca of Vice: Where prostitutes were just part of the scenery."

> "The point that must be made is that prostitution existed in Chapeltown well before black people settled here. History tells us that it was initially North Street, which is just north of Briggate coming out of the city, where prostitution first started. When the residential accommodation in that area ceased to exist, prostitution moved further north to Chapeltown. I think it is important to emphasise that Caribbean people didn't bring prostitution to Chapeltown. Prostitution found its way into Chapeltown well before the majority of Caribbean people settled here. Also, the majority of Caribbean people have been opposed to the existence of prostitution within the area." – *Travis Johnson*

Trevor Wynters' stance would reinforce the view of the wider community: that Caribbean people neither condoned nor were the main purveyors of the problem of prostitution in Chapeltown.

> "My grandfather Trevor Clifton Wynters was born in 1932 in Jamaica. He used to work for London Public Transport, before moving to Leeds where he worked for Yorkshire Imperial Metal. During 1971, he became quite ill and he was never to able to walk upright again after that. In those days my grandparents were living on Cowper Street in a very large Victorian house, with two tall gateposts in stone, inscribed with the words 'The Villa'. His illness slowly crippled him and he had to walk with the aid of sticks. He was also forced to give up his job permanently. But his illness did not break his spirits, he was a thinker and a doer and would occupy some of his time with community activities. Many people would pass through his home attending many of the meetings and gatherings held at Cowper Street. Some people would just visit and discuss all kinds of affairs while drinking my grandfather's homemade beer or grandma's gooseberry wine.
>
> "I recall one day during the late 70s there was a young white woman who thought she could solicit outside her home opposite my grandparents' home. Now if you've ever met my grandfather, he certainly was not going to have anyone offering herself at a price outside or even near to his home. The woman's activities attracted curb crawlers who often, harassed innocent young

women. This woman's clients would often park outside my grandparent's house, taking his parking spot; this meant that he was forced to walk further to his home which was difficult because of his disability. My grandfather attempted to speak to the woman, asking her not to do her business near his home and that she would be better off if she found a job that was not degrading. The woman became quite angry with him. The upset and anger between both my grandfather and this woman went on for a very long time. He lodged his complaint but the police were not helpful as they did little to take his numerous complaints seriously.

"In one of many heated discussions with this woman, he made his stance to stop this woman's soliciting. I think she had become very tired of this black disabled man 'harassing' her and her clients. She took a swing at him and hit him to the ground. He got up with great difficulty and insisted that he was not going to move from here. He would prevent her from doing her business and he would do this as long as she stayed there. The police were called and their intervention on the occasion brought her activities to a standstill. But my grandfather also had to pay a price as he was found guilty of harassment and was bound over to keep the peace for twelve months – a small price to pay for the good of your community, don't you think?

"Both my grandparents were a shining examples of hope. Trevor Clifton Wynters' voice and actions gave hope to others especially the African Caribbean community. They showed others that you don't have to accept prostitution in your area. You don't have to accept drug pushing in your area. You don't have to accept poor housing in your area. He believed that we have rights as citizens and taxpayers and as people who contribute to the building of the United Kingdom. My grandfather used to say that not because you live in a community that is predominately black and Asian doesn't mean you are of the lowest class. Because once you accept that, then you accept all the negative things that go with this school of thought." – *Khadijah Ibrahim*

As individual Jamaicans stood out in the community, their actions could not be separated from those of their fellow Caribbean community workers and leaders. These community leaders had long since recognised that Chapeltown was a time bomb waiting to explode. It was predicted that the young people born in Britain to migrant parents would fight a race war on the streets, because they would not tolerate the discrimination endured by their parents. On January 23, 1973, the Yorkshire Post (YP) published a feature which echoed these sentiments. The YP had also quoted Glen English three days later, who explained that the young people he worked with "did not bother to apply for jobs because they did not have a chance because of their colour." He attested to the restlessness percolating beneath the surface. But it was Veryl Harriott who openly warned in the YEP, June 27, 1973, that "a simmering discontent has spread among the West Indian community." The racial and social problems that fuelled this discontent took on different forms.

"Yeah, I'd say I grew up with racism. I've experienced some minor things along that line when I was about eighteen years old. That was my first experience. Basically, I was waiting for my girlfriend who worked at a nursing home. I was standing on a patch of grass outside the home. Two police persons came up to me. One was a man. I always remember the male officer because he was a bit more concerned, but it was the female officer who came up and asked, 'Who am I? What am I doing here?' I felt very cross and I said to her, 'You don't approach people that way.' So she got out her baton and went on for a little bit. I wasn't arrested or anything like that. It didn't come as a shock and I wouldn't say I was shaken from it. I was thinking that it was one of those things that happened. Also I was in an area where a lot of black residents wouldn't go into town. When we were younger we would only play in our area but like to go to town, we wouldn't jump on the bus like we do today, and enjoy a day out in the City Centre. It was scary because we were chased and some of us were beaten by white youths. Things were a lot more blatant then. It didn't help that there were a lot of racist programmes on television either." – *Ian Lawrence*

"The police have always given us a hard time. No matter what you did you always found the police was always on the scene. When we lived in Clarendon Place in '48, we were in bed one night, and all of a sudden we heard, Bang! Bang! Then the door was broken down. It was the police. I tell you something, I drew my fist and the first face that came through the door, I went bang! No messing! I didn't know who it was. Apparently, somebody said they heard a carrying on with lots of noise where we were, and the police without asking or listening they just come and broke in the door of the front room where I lived with another lad." – *Alford Gardener*

"I remember in the 70s, there used to be a Youth Club over at Primrose Hill School on Thursday evenings. When the Youth Club finished at 9 o'clock and all the children were going home, they would be boisterous: laughing and carrying on without any threat to anybody. But I can remember seeing several policemen shadowing them as they walked home. There was a lot of intimidating stuff like that." – *Clinton Cameron*

Two explosive situations would occur and would extract the Caribbean community from the shadows of neglect and incognita. They brought Caribbean community workers together with the support of indigenous British people to work tirelessly to close the ruptured wounds. Bonfire Night 1974 marked Caribbean youth's first open confrontation with the police, whom they saw as agents of the repressive white establishment. The confrontation escalated in 1975. The community and race relations workers made it their duty to re-open dialogue with the police and to find ways of preventing a recurrence on Bonfire Night.

They feared the disturbances had ended years of careful and persistent negotiation with the police - shattering what has been lauded as a unique relationship. Errol James as Chairman of the then CRC proposed that one of the solutions to the problem should be a huge bonfire that was heavily supervised by community workers.

> "As the then Community Relations Officer at the Leeds Community Relations Office, I had the responsibility with colleagues and Honorary Officers of the Council of discussing plans for Bonfire Night 1976. The plans included a fireworks display, a community bonfire within the area as well as a more sensitive method of policing the area. Subsequently, very few arrests were made on Bonfire Nights. There were a number of persons from the Community Relations Council who were out on Bonfire Night to co-ordinate the events and to ensure that the disturbances did not recur. There were people like Errol James, Maureen Baker, Veryl Harriott, Nettie White, Ken Glendenning and several others. To a large extent, we were explaining to the youths how best to organise themselves. Some of the young people helped to organise the community bonfire. Similar arrangements were made for bonfire nights up to and including 1980."
> – *Travis Johnson*

One of the positive outcomes of Bonfire Night was the establishment of the Harehills and Chapeltown Law Centre. There were concerns about the affordability of legal representation for the persons who were arrested on Bonfire Night and in general for people in the community with legal problems. Clinton Cameron knew of people who were unlawfully detained by the police because they just happened to be in the wrong place at the time. He felt there was an urgent need for legal facilities within the community: "If you have a Law Centre that gives free legal advice and organised defence for people, that'd be one of the ways to protect them." Members within the community got together and lobbied for a Law Centre.

> "The Harehills and Chapeltown Law Centre was established in the late 1970s. At that time there were certain perceived views held by the community about the Law Enforcing Agencies and the Criminal Justice System. The Law Centre was often the first port of call for a number of persons who were charged with certain types of offences. For many, this was an agency based in the community, therefore they had much more confidence in it. I was involved from Steering Committee days until the Centre was fully established along with a number of persons from the community. Unfortunately, the only names that spring to mind are: the Chairman, Ralph Maynard MBE, James Aboaba MBE, Clinton Cameron MBE, Gary Dore and several others."
> – *Travis Johnson*

Chapter 2

Chapeltown and Harehills would erupt again in the summer of 1981, when many black communities around the country experienced ten consecutive days of violence. When the disorders started in Brixton and spread to areas like Toxteth in Liverpool and Handsworth in Birmingham, race and community workers in Leeds were on the alert. They sensed that Leeds was sure to erupt in a matter of days; it was not *if* Leeds would erupt, it was *when*.

"We had the first of what was first called 'Race Riots' in several towns and cities across the country, in 1981. The Scarman Inquiry referred to them as the 1981 Disorders. It occurred in several places before it happened in Leeds. So the question was not would it, but when would it be Leeds? I recall being in bed on the night it occurred, when I received a call to say that there was a major incident in Chapeltown and Harehills. I got dressed and drove down to Chapeltown to experience a most fearful situation: several cars and buildings were alight, stones, bricks and petrol bombs were being hurled at the police and the police were dressed in riot gear with batons." – *Travis Johnson*

"What I encountered was that some people were standing at their gates in their homes and got arrested. I was working down at Harambee on Cowper Street in the 1981 disorders. People would come from Gipton and all over the place throwing rocks at the police and when the police tried to catch them they would runaway. Any young person who was walking up the street who hadn't been in the disturbances, and he or she saw the police running about, didn't runaway, but got arrested and appeared in court. I worked with a young girl who was about sixteen. She got arrested and locked up for days and she did not appear in Court because there was no evidence against her. It was the same thing, she was walking along and got caught up in it and the police just locked her up. There were a lot of people who were arrested and later released without charge. I was in the building where I worked trying as far as possible to stop the young people I was working with, from going out. I tried to persuade them it was a bad idea to be out on the streets." – *Clinton Cameron*

Again, the community leaders got involved with many of the familiar faces from the Jamaican and wider Caribbean community. It was apparent for sometime that the problems that fuelled the 1974 and 1975 eruptions had not gone away. In many respects they had multiplied. Some of the problems affecting young people during that period were high unemployment, lack of adequate housing and a fragile relationship with the police.

"There were a number of colleagues as well as committee members who were present on the streets on the nights during the disorders. We tried where possible to talk with young people and discouraged them from continuing their action. It could be clearly seen that there were a number of persons, who were instigators, both black and white. We realised that we needed to get to work to prevent recurrence of the three previous nights. We met with several groups of young people, reminded them that it was their community that was being destroyed, that the main instigators did not come from the area. When the instigators returned to the area on the fourth night to continue where they had left off, the young people did not support them. However, it is correct to say that there was a high level of tension in the area following the nights of disorders. It is important to record the fact that the vast majority of young people who lived in the Chapeltown and Harehills areas were not involved in the disorders.

"A lot of work had to be done to try and prevent a recurrence on the fourth night. It was like a miracle. Somehow, it seemed that the young people of the area came to their senses, in realising it was their community that was being destroyed. Those of us who were working for a better relationship between the community at large and the police, were very pleased that within a short period of time, meaningful dialogue recommenced. The dialogue continued over several years and in many ways had positive results. In 1985, there were disturbances in Broadwater Farm, Tottenham and in several other towns and cities, Leeds remained free of any disorders, because the young people refused to be led down such path." – *Travis Johnson*

Travis Johnson recognised and understood the frustrations of the young people in Chapeltown, but felt strongly about the damaging effects that these disturbances had on the physical infrastructure of the community and the long-term social stigmatisation that would follow. He wanted to see young people demonstrate a sense of responsibility for their community. Principles that ran deep for someone who grew up in Jamaica post 1938. The poignant declaration by Sir Alexander Bustamante, first Prime Minister of independent Jamaica, that 'men, women and children have a right to call attention to their condition and to ask of people to fulfil their promises made to them, so as long as they do so without violence' - would have found its way into his consciousness.

The 1981 Civil Disorders temporarily dislodged the Caribbean community from its fragile foundations. They were seen by some people as a transgressive reaction that fell outside any political context. The YEP on July 13, 1981 declared that it was not a race riot but it was stage-managed and hijacked by people from outside including white hooligans. Nonetheless, it was still politically significant to the Caribbean community in Leeds. It had its own internal logic. Once again the Local Authority took notice and money was pumped into the area. The community leaders, race relations workers and young people got to work and created the Chapeltown and Harehills Liaison Committee to bridge the gap between the community, city officials and elected councillors. A suitable cross-section of the community was represented on this committee.

"A number of persons who were active in organisations and generally within the community were concerned about the devastation in the area as a result of the 1981 disorders. There was a need to set up a structure or forum that would facilitate dialogue with the Local Authority and its various departments, the police and other statutory bodies. I have felt that this Committee was one of the most effective forums to have evolved from the community. It was the vehicle for consultation and liaison with the Local Authority and other agencies within the communities of Chapeltown and Harehills. It was during this period that the Leeds City Council established an Equal Opportunities Unit. Some of the members of the committee were Errol James, Veryl Harriott, Maureen Baker, Gertrude Paul, James Aboaba, Gary Dore, Arthur France and Ian Charles and younger people like Derrick Lawrence and Eulalee Williams - both second generation Jamaicans - and several others." – *Travis Johnson*

The actions of this collective meant that Caribbean people were taking control of their lives, they took pride in who they were. They wanted the social, community, political and justice systems and structures to reflect their aspirations as an established group of people. The changes were gradual. During the 1980s, the first set of Jamaicans were being appointed as Justice of the Peace, Travis Johnson was the first Jamaican to be appointed as Lay Magistrate in the city in 1981. He was subsequently followed by George Eubanks, Errol James and Lizette Powell. More Jamaicans have since been appointed to the Bench and to Industrial and Social Security Tribunals, where like magistrates, they serve the whole community of Leeds.

Over the next decade, the Caribbean community had to re-invent itself as its needs changed, a host of organisations were established to deal with the issues affecting the marginalised within the community or those who were not collectively represented. Caribbean people continued to join forces to give greater strength to their desire to effect change. In 1991, Edley White, a Jamaican became one of the foundation members of the Barbadian-led initiative to set up the Leeds Black Elders Association, to represent the interest of the first generation of Caribbean people who had come of age.

The churches played their part in directing the energies of the community towards self-sufficiency. A memorial centre at the Church of God of Prophecy on Chapeltown Road, honours the work of the late Reverend Austin Burke who was the first preacher from Jamaica to serve there. However, on April 4, 1985, Joseph Parker, a Lay Reader in St. Aidan Church, Roundhay, was the first black person in Leeds to receive Maundy gifts from the reigning sovereign, Queen Elizabeth II on Maundy Thursday for Christian service to the church and the community. Joseph Parker's work with the Christian community started in the Anglican Church in Jamaica and continued when he migrated to the UK. His receipt of the Maundy coins was a personal honour that had enormous meaning to the Caribbean community. They remembered feeling uninvited in the established churches in the early years of settling in the UK.

As Caribbean people began to be recognised as a force for change, there was a marked increase in their participation in other areas of mainstream society. Many became involved in the Trade Union Movement. Francis Williams who left Jamaica in 1961 was a shop steward for the National Union for Public Employers (NUPE) for thousands of staff in the catering, kitchen and parks departments at Social Services offices in Leeds. It was a responsibility she welcomed as her memories of her first working experience in Leeds were filled with incidents of racial harassment.

Norma Hutchinson who celebrated her seventeenth birthday on arrival in the UK from Jamaica in 1965, was also an active trade unionist. She started out as a shop steward for NUPE while working at the Meanwood Park Hospital as a nursing assistant. She was the Chairperson of NUPE's Regional and National Race Equality Committee. When the three main unions merged into UNISON she was Co-Chair of the Black Members Group. She was one of the first black women to sit at the head table at the annual conference of the National Trade Union Congress.

"Every year at the conference, when we looked on the top table and there were no black faces up there. So we fought, we lobbied and we talked to anyone who would listen and in the end, I was one of the first black persons who sat up there. We had to lobby the Assistant Secretary first to have black National Officers in the trade unions because we felt that if we wanted to show that this Union is for equality, then we needed to reflect that in the hierarchy. We started seriously to lobby and write to the Branches asking if anyone was interested in being a National Officer, of course we got the training and at the same time, they were doing that, I was asked to stand as local councillor." – *Councillor Norma Hutchinson*

The doors were now opened for Caribbean people to hold positions in local politics, and to assume ceremonial roles in the City of Leeds. In 1991, Norma Hutchinson became the first Jamacan to be elected as a local councillor in Leeds. As a councillor, she has chaired the City Council's Race Advisory Committee and sat on the West Yorkshire Police Authority and Passenger & Transport Authority - other Committees within the Council. She also served on the Social Security Appeals Tribunal, 1995-1998. She implemented projects that were beneficial to the wider community, and specific to the Jamaican community.

"One of the first things I did when I became a councillor, was to set up a project called, CHAMP - Chapeltown and Harehlls Area Motor Project - a car and bike workshop for the young boys in the area. We had a lot of the parents' support. It was going very good, but it had to come to an end. Another thing that I did when I was elected was to form the Friendship Link between the Leeds City Council and the Parish Council of St. Mary in Jamaica. It was a partnership between police, teachers and councillors. Friendship Link was for education; it informed people that there was another world out there. I wanted to put something back into both communities, because I am from St. Mary and also the Jamaican community gets publicity and I wanted them to see that the Jamaican community is not all bad. Another project I started, was the 10 to 2 club for mainly young boys in Chapeltown who are unemployed or not in school." – *Councillor Norma Hutchinson*

In 2000, Susan Pitter was appointed as the first black Lady Mayoress of Leeds and the first of Jamaican descent. Susan's parents were born in Jamaica and came here in the 1960s. She recalls fondly that her parents met here in Leeds while they were both working in the transport sector: "My father was a bus driver and my mother was a conductress, which I think is very romantic". She has been active in the community as a young woman growing up in Chapeltown. Susan has been involved in the Carnival for many years, has done work for BBC Radio Leeds Caribbean Programme, *Calypso* and has organised a number of Caribbean entertainment projects and events in her community. She currently works in public relations. The significance of her appointment was not lost on her and the Jamaican community.

"I was appointed as one of the city's Lady Mayoresses by the then Lord Mayor Bernard Atha, who was choosing a number of women to act in the role at the time as Lady Mayoress. In his words he was choosing women he felt were exemplar role models for people across the city, and I was chosen by him to act in that role. It was a great honour. I think I underestimated its impact on other people, and other groups. I certainly didn't expect a number of things. I didn't expect to welcome Nelson Mandela to the city. I didn't expect to go to Jamaica - my parents' birthplace - and being received as Lady Mayoress there. I was very grateful, touched and very humbled by it all. I was deeply, deeply honoured to be received by my own people, in my own area and in Jamaica." – *Susan Pitter, Lady Mayoress of Leeds, 2000-2001*

In 2002, Celine North became the first Lady Mayoress of Leeds to have been born in Jamaica. She assumed the position when her husband, Councillor Brian North was appointed as Lord Mayor of the city. She migrated to the UK in 1956 at the age of sixteen. She worked in various administrative positions in offices throughout Leeds. In 1982, she joined the NUPE and was a shop steward for the workers in the Home Care Social Services Department. In 1986, she was appointed a Justice of the Peace and served as a Director of the Leeds Hospital Fund from 1996 until 2001. Celine's experience as a Jamaican immigrant to the UK was undoubtedly different from other Jamaicans. It was a matter of being a white Jamaican. She was able to fit into the British society virtually unnoticed. The Jamaican community welcomed her appointment as it reflected Jamaica's multiracial heritage.

> "People are usually astonished when I tell them I am from Jamaica. They cannot understand why I am white because they imagine Jamaicans to be all black people. Jamaica is a very multicultural place; you have Indians, Chinese, Africans and white people. I understand that the people that are related to me came from Germany. My mother's maiden name is 'Kamekas' and my father's name is 'Brown', but it was originally 'Braun' because at that time everybody was changing their German identity. My German ancestors came to Jamaica because the British government was offering the Germans a certain amount of money and a bit of land to start a life in the Caribbean. I grew up in Point Hill, St. Catherine in Jamaica. We had a house on the plantation; it was a massive place. My fondest memories are of disobeying my father and going over to other people's farms to pick strawberries and various fruits. I also remember going to watch the women wash their clothes in the river." – *Celine North, Lady Mayoress of Leeds, 2002-2003*

Since their arrival in the City of Leeds in the late 1940s, Jamaicans and equally, their fellow Caribbean counterparts have given their time, energy and dedication to building a strong and influential community. Their contributions have been largely positive, but they did not stop there. It was in the late 70s that six individuals took the step to form an organisation that focused specifically on addressing the needs of the Jamaican community in Leeds. It was one of the ways that Jamaicans believed they could contribute to the improvement of community life in Leeds as a collective. Jamaicans were in danger of being fragmented as a community, because its leaders were shouldering the weight and responsibility of the issues affecting Caribbean people as a whole. Though Jamaicans recognised the need for a unified front by peoples of the Caribbean region - with whom they share a similar history and cross cultural reference points - they were of the view that there were precise aspects of Jamaican culture and socio-political welfare that had to be preserved and tackled by an organisation for and by Jamaicans. Their responsibility extended beyond the Jamaican community in Leeds and to Jamaicans living in Jamaica.

The economic advantage they had as Jamaicans living in the Caribbean Diaspora meant they were in a position to provide financial support for their families back in Jamaica, which in turn benefited the Jamaican economy. The sense of purpose that the Jamaican community had acquired, was previously articulated by Norman Manley who believed that "no amount of economic good will make our people a real unity." Unless they established a sense of belonging and unity in the UK, their economic gains, though significant, would just be another hollow badge of achievement. The Jamaica Society (Leeds) became the catalyst that re-activated and stimulated the Jamaican people's sense of pride in their country of origin, and the value of their historical and cultural heritage.

CHRISTMAS COME

Each December
Creating Christmas
From memory
My mouth waters and
My heart aches
For home…

Talk triggers thoughts
Opening half closed doors
Once more -
It's Kingston,
Nineteen Sixty-Four…
I hear again the stomping feet
Of crowds running from
Jonkonoo jumping in the street
Bellywoman, Pitchy-Patchy, Devil and Horsehead
On my last bus journey back home from Parade
I sit watching the passing masquerade.

Standing
In a steamed up kitchen
Galvanising goodwill
In
Tottenham…
Stockwell.
Devouring coconut drops
Drinking sweet cold sorrel,
Warmed with ginger,
This deep midwinter, I remember
Christmas in Thornton Heath
The feeling?
Not quite complete!

Home
What it was
Has gone forever.
In England
Fireworks are let off in November.
Starlight and thunderbolts
Only ignite in the mind…
Kindling smells of, roast breadfruit -
(Oven-baked in aluminium foil)
Bammy real chocolate tea,
Saltfish and ackee (without the coconut oil)
Stove signals start Christmas day festivities…
Stoking traces of a past left behind.

Now, for some,
Christmas only ever come
In supermarket hamper
And tradition
Like a rush of wind from forty-eight
Read the sign, again 'UNWELCOME'!
And decide before it evaporates
Like fruit soaked in too little rum
To repatriate to fi him setting sun
In a corner of Jamaica

Leaving us
This second generation
Reliving a new old situation,
Adjusting to migration
Seeking to answer the who me? -
Identity in England…
Jamaican, African, Caribbean …All three!

And find it!

POEM

Revolved 360 degree...
Downstairs in a Chapeltown kitchen
Where women were cooking
And gentlemen were serving up the essence
Of a Christmas thought missing.
Hybrid and unique -
Like an ortanique!

Old, young and in-between people
Milling around or seated at tables - set to eat
Sights, smells and sounds surround me
Telling our story, sour sweet...
Capturing a part of our history
The warmth of used to be
Embraces me
My feet touch ground ...
Finally!
I take a seat.

MarvaB © 2003

3 THE FORMATION OF THE JAMAICA SOCIETY [LEEDS]

When the Jamaica Society (Leeds) was formed in 1977, Chapeltown's identity was being re-shaped in respect of the problems that its denizens encountered on a daily basis. A number of community organisations and initiatives were established and under their ambit residents were lobbying for change. The Barbados Association which tackled the issues that Caribbean migrants from that island faced, was already in operation. However, there was no organisation that specifically addressed the needs of the Jamaican community in Leeds. The Jamaica Alliance was formed in the late 1960s and was disbanded by the early 1970s. There was a gap waiting to be filled and a community responsibility that could not be ignored. The missing element was a unifying system. One of the ways this unity could become a reality, was passionately expressed by Norman Manley during Jamaica's struggle towards nationhood: 'It is out of our minds, out of our faith in ourselves, out of our own convictions about the future that the spirit of national unity can be built.' Those individuals who shared the same convictions about the Jamaican community, were the ones who would assume the responsibilities of starting the Jamaica Society (Leeds).

The formation of a Jamaica Society in Leeds started as an idea that was banded about by Ratrica 'Nettie' White, Committee member of the Racial Equality Council and registered nurse. She tried relentlessly to engage her compatriots, who already had huge responsibilities in the community, into taking decisive steps towards this end.

> "For years we didn't have anything in Leeds for Jamaicans. From 1973, I used to say this to Errol James who was the Chairman of the Racial Equality Council for many years - I used to go to meetings with him, as I was a member of the Racial Equality Council too - that we needed something in Leeds for our people. He went, 'Oh yes, we do, oh yes, we do.' I never gave up on the matter because nothing would stop me." – *Nettie White*

Two subsequent events would demonstrate to the Jamaican community the practicality of forming such an organisation. The first was the arrival of Louise Bennett in Leeds on a special tour of the UK. The Honourable Louise Bennett-Coverley, OJ, affectionately known as Miss Lou - a poet, storyteller, actress and authority on Jamaican folklore - performed at the Polythenic Hall in 1977.

> "Louise Bennett came to Leeds in early 1977. When her show ended that night, she and the cast were hungry and they wanted something to eat. They asked if there was anywhere they could go for this purpose. Now it was very late when the show ended, but we managed to get them into

a Chinese restaurant that was about to close. After that a few of us talked among ourselves. We were very concerned that here it is that a prominent Jamaican was in Leeds and there was nowhere we could host them with Jamaican cuisine, instead we had to finish up at a Chinese restaurant. We felt that if we had an organisation for Jamaicans we could have done something about it. That was what prompted six of us to get together and establish the Jamaica Society (Leeds)." – *Travis Johnson*

Nettie White's wishes were granted. She seized the moment to move the process along by seeking advice from Roy White at the Jamaican Consulate in Manchester.

"I said to myself, 'Well that's very sad. Same thing I've been saying all along'. I went to Manchester to see Roy White who was our Jamaican Consul there. I spent a day with Roy putting together ideas of how we could start something in Leeds and the various ways we could go about setting up a Society and what we would call it. He said that there was a Society in Manchester called, 'Jamaica Society (Manchester)' and said that we could call our Society the 'Jamaica Society (Leeds)'. I came back to Leeds and we decided to have a meeting to explore starting this organisation." – *Nettie White*

The second event was the founding members' awareness of the impending closure of the Jamaican Consulate in Manchester. By 1979, the Consulate wrapped up its northern operations and all its business was done from the High Commission in London.

"At the time the High Commission was closing its office in the north, therefore it was important that we had somewhere where we could have a voice and our people could get advice. This was very necessary because Jamaica had gained its Independence. Most persons who were here at the time came over when we were still British subjects. Now our country had gained independence, much had changed, especially laws relating to immigration. We needed assistance from the High Commission, and if the nearest one to Leeds was Manchester and that was to be closed leaving us only with the London office, then a Jamaica Society in Leeds was even more important." – *Elizabeth Johnson*

From Core Group to First General Meeting

The six founding members, the late Errol James, Nettie White, Elizabeth Johnson, Lizette Powell, Yvonne English (formerly Bovell) and Travis Johnson, sat down and discussed the structure and function of this new organisation.

> "As founding members, three of us were all working as nurses on this particular ward: Nettie White, Lizette Powell and myself. The others, namely Travis Johnson and Errol James worked in Race Relations, and Betsy is Travis's wife. We decided from there that we needed somewhere that Jamaican people could go to and be at home rather than wandering around Leeds to find somewhere. We had our first meeting at Nettie White's house, and it all started from there." – *Yvonne English*

A number of meetings were held before the Society had its first public meeting. Roy White, the Jamaican Consul was invited to one of these exploratory meetings. He proved a valuable mentor to the group of six - transferring his knowledge of, and his experience with other Jamaican associations and societies in the region. Both Elizabeth Johnson and Yvonne English recall his most indispensable advice.

> "Roy White advised us that the Society should not only be for Jamaicans but it should include non-Jamaicans married to Jamaicans. We couldn't say it is only for Jamaicans. Hence, in the Constitution it says Jamaica Society (Leeds) and Friends." – *Yvonne English and Elizabeth Johnson*

The founding members had a collective vision of the type of organisation they wanted to create. The pursuit of excellence was a key factor. They wanted an organisation which reflected the best attributes of their country and their people. They also wanted an organisation with the authority to intervene on behalf of the Jamaican people in Leeds.

> "One of the driving forces behind me wanting to see the formation of the Jamaica Society in Leeds was that it would provide information and education about things that affected our community and us as Jamaican people. Persons were sometimes unaware of certain developments and the action that they could take. You saw and met with people in the workplace and in the community, but we were not united. I remember reading an article about Jamaica in what was then the Midwife and Health Visitors magazine and I was really upset about some of the things that were written in that publication. I felt helpless that I could not do anything by myself."
> – *Elizabeth Johnson*

> "The idea of establishing the Jamaica Society was that we could deal with issues pertaining to Jamaicans. We recognised the need to work closely with the Jamaican High Commission, to receive Jamaican guests and dignitaries when they visit Leeds, to provide an advice service for our members and the wider Jamaican community, and to organise social events for them as well."
> – *Travis Johnson*

Chapter 3

The founding members wanted to build an organisation that was credible and sound. The Society would be rooted essentially in constituted principles and rules. The first task they set for themselves was to draft a Constitution. They opened up the core group to other Jamaicans in the community including the late Joseph Parker, retired Public Inspector and Lay Preacher in the Anglican Church. His experience and seniority were essential to a process that had tremendous potential. Joseph Parker along with Errol James and Travis Johnson were the architects of the Constitution. Starting in a constituted manner meant that the Society was being built on very firm foundations, and would steadily guide the members and the Executive Committee in achieving the organisation's goals. The core group would present the Constitution to the wider membership for approval which clarified the objectives of the organisation.

> "When we decided to draft the Constitution, we decided to bring in other people to help to set up the organisation. People such as Percy Francis, George Eubanks, Barry Cain, Florizel Lee, Joseph Parker's son - Junior Parker, Pansy Patterson, Thelma Thomas, Peggy Lunn and Ruby Lewis. I think that the initial group was of people who had the skills to help with forming the organisation." – *Yvonne English*

The next stage was the recruitment of more members to the Society. Recruitment was done mainly by word of mouth - true to their Jamaican tradition - especially in light of the costs and availability of other forms of communication. The members of the expanded core group were relentless in their recruitment drive.

> "Informing the community of the formation of the Jamaica Society (Leeds) was mostly done by word of mouth. It was a very effective way of communicating, because it took us awhile before people would give us their names and addresses. Wherever there was a group meeting we would go and announce it. Most of us were working in hospitals then and we would tell others that we were having meetings. We met them in the market, in the streets and in the shops and we'd say we were having a meeting. I think it was even better that way because when you stood up before someone and they would ask why should they come, then you got the opportunity to bring over your position. The good thing about that also was that one person would tell six persons, those six persons would tell a further two or three. So, it was effective." – *Yvonne English and Elizabeth Johnson*

> "It was not difficult recruiting members. The six of us had several friends and associates, we used the 'each-one-tells-one' method of recruiting and in a very short time interest and membership grew. I cannot remember us having to mount any campaign to recruit members. Once people learned of our proposals to set up the Society, they wanted to be a part of it." – *Travis Johnson*

> "I joined the Jamaica Society sometime in the '70s, I'm sure. I can't remember the exact year, but I was introduced to it by Mrs. Johnson. She approached me one evening while I was at Harehills Primary School on some other venture. She asked me if I ever heard of the Jamaica Society, and proceeded to explain what it was all about. She informed me that it was a charitable organisation, and said some good things that got me interested. It was about Jamaicans getting together and keeping our culture alive. So, I became a member." – *Florence Williams*

> "When the Society used to meet at the West Indian Centre, I was there one Sunday afternoon on some other occasion and I had a word with Mrs. Powell. She said to me, 'Why don't you come to the meeting one Sunday afternoon? You'll then find out what it is all about.' Of course, I came to the meeting and I really enjoyed it and at the second meeting I became a member, and I have been ever since." – *Roy Mitchell*

> "George Eubanks told me about the Society. He also told me that it was for Jamaicans and that it would be good for us to get together to share our views." – *Allen Ebanks*

The Society went ahead and had its first General Meeting and outlined the objectives of the organisation to the prospective members in attendance. This first meeting adopted the Constitution and the Jamaica Society (Leeds) was firmly established and had a significant number of supporters. Over the next twenty-five years, the Society's membership would grow to over 350 registered members, an exceptional achievement for an organisation that started with only six discerning men and women. The Society appointed its first Chairperson, Lizette Powell and its first Executive Committee at this introductory meeting.

An urgent challenge that the Society faced was to have a financial base. Prior to the General Meeting, the six founding members made an initial contribution of £5 each from their pockets towards starting the Society's fund. As the core group expanded to a further twelve, they too made personal donations of cash and kind. During the first few years of the Society's existence, fundraising social events were funded primarily from the personal resources of these committed members.

> "When we first started there was no such thing as money to buy things. I remember for Socials we took ingredients from home, because the Society had no money to purchase the ingredients. One person brought the rice, one the peas, one the oil, one the meat and another the pots - that's how we got started and the profit went back into the Society's fund." – *Elizabeth Johnson and Nettie White*

Personal sacrifice and unswerving commitment would become the hallmark of the Society's membership. The example set by the founding members and the core group would become the ethos of the Jamaica Society (Leeds).

CHAPTER 3

Early Activities

The first act of charity that the Jamaica Society (Leeds) as a newly formed organisation carried out, was fundraising for the 'Jamaica Flood Appeal Fund'. In 1977, parts of the island of Jamaica were severely damaged by floodwaters. When this crisis arose, the six founding members were the only ones who were meeting. Equipped only with limited financial and human resources, they set about to accomplish their task and to test their mettle as a new organisation that aimed to have an impact on the wider community. They tried their hand at their first jumble sale which turned out to be more of a comic adventure than a rewarding financial venture.

> "The first fundraising activity of the Jamaica Society was the Jumble Sale at Clayton Hall at St. Aidan. The first money we raised was about £25 and that was just selling people's unwanted clothes, shoes and all sorts. We raised £25 and that went into the funds." – *Yvonne English*

> "It was the time we borrowed this little old van - Yvonne and I - from someone to collect things for the sale and to take them to the church, only to find that the van had brakes that weren't very good. There was Yvonne and I with this little van that we weren't sure would even stop but it did. We collected our 'jumble' and took it to the church. We didn't do much in terms of sales, so we had to cart it back off again. But that didn't stop us because we had done some hair brain things just to get this Society started." – *Elizabeth Johnson*

It was not a total failure as they eventually raised a substantial amount of money for the Emergency Fund. In order to cement themselves in the consciousness of the Jamaicans in Leeds and the wider community, the Society staged its first public event which was a dinner and invited members of the Jamaican community to attend. After that event, the Society went into overdrive, staging at least six fundraising socials each year and a series of bring-and-buy sales. They harnessed the skills of the growing membership to sew, crochet, knit, and to make Jamaican pastries for these sales.

> "I can remember Ruby Lewis, she used to do a lot of cooking and baking for our bring-and-buy sales. Persons like Mrs. English, Mrs. Powell, Mrs. Patterson and I used to sew then - I'm not so sure where I found the hours in those days - but we made a lot of things for the sales. In those early days, we also held fundraising socials or just plain get-togethers. That was how we built up the Society's savings." – *Elizabeth Johnson*

The Formation of The Jamaica Society [Leeds]

"The most frequent thing we used to do in those days was what we called a Social, where you bought a ticket and that ticket entitled you to come in and dance and eat all night at one price. In those days, we used to sell all the tickets before we even opened our doors. So before the Social started we knew whether the event was going to be a success or not, and that went down very, very well. I remember we used to have some of those Socials at Harambee House." – *Glen English*

"At the Socials we used to charge £2 and that would include rum punch on arrival and then you had your meal which would be rice and peas, curried goat, fried dumplings and yams, sometimes. I remember at the first Social, we served yam, bananas, dumplings and roasted breadfruit and that went down well. Everybody wanted another. So, we started having more and more and then the price went up to £2.50 and then it escalated from there onwards. The Socials continued to be well attended because people felt the food was excellent and the price was reasonable and there was nowhere else to go. Some of the people who used to help and were members of the Society were Rita, Dougie, Peggy, Elsie, Ruby, Vena and a few more people whose names I cannot remember. At that time, I was co-ordinator of the Social and Fundraising Sub-committee. We had lots of fun, although it was hard work, we had an aim that we were working towards." – *Yvonne English*

Prior to the formation of the Jamaica Society (Leeds), the founding members would take their children to learn Jamaican folklore and songs with an elderly Jamaican woman, Mother Armstrong. This event was later incorporated into the Society's programme as its first children's activity. The provision of cultural activities would become a part of the Society's community outreach programme.

"When the children were small, we used to take them to Mother Armstrong. Yvonne and I would collect all the children and drive them to her house and she would teach them folk songs. The first time that they sang publicly was during the visit of Cindy Breakspeare - Miss Jamaica (World) and Miss World - at the Dewsbury cinema. They were known as 'Mother and her Children'. Our children were like only four, five, six and seven and we had about twelve children. Mother Amstrong taught them, *Bruk 'em one by one* and *Carry Mi Ackee Go A Linstead Market*. We were trying to hold on to our culture. The children enjoyed it, they thought it was so funny then, because they dressed in costumes that we made. The costumes were made out of calico and had a crinoline underneath, and were trimmed with strips of bandana. We still have ours and Catherine, (Yvonne's eldest daughter) she still holds on to hers." – *Yvonne English and Elizabeth Johnson*

The Jamaica Society (Leeds) was formed post the Bonfire Night disturbances. The problems the community had with the police, racism, poor housing and other legal and social issues persisted. In 1980, concern about the Caribbean community's relationship with the police was on the agendas of both the Society and Jamaica Northern Regional Committee. At the 1981 Annual General Meeting of the Society, the Chairperson brought attention to the number of racial attacks against the black community in Leeds, and pledged support for the Action Committee set up to review the problem. As a result, the Society then organised surgeries for its members with representatives from the Racial Equality Council (REC)-formerly the Community Relations Council (CRC), the Chapeltown Citizens' Advice Bureau, the police and other agencies.

> "The period pre-1981 disorders and post the Bonfire Night incidents were fairly tense within the Chapeltown and Harehills areas. Relationship between the police and a section of the young people of the area was very strained. Unfortunately, at that time there was a marked absence of black people within the Police Service in Leeds. The Community Relations Council was the main agency with responsibility for fostering good relations between the police and the community. Three members of the Society were part of the CRC. Errol James was the Chairman, Nettie White was a member of the Executive Committee, and I was an employee of the CRC. The Society held a number of surgeries during this period, drawing on the expertise of members of the community. Some of the issues that were dealt with included police community relations, education, immigration and other matters. Some of our members were able to lead on these issues." – *Travis Johnson*

In 1983 following the Scarman Report, the Society received an invitation from the West Yorkshire Police to participate in the establishment of a Police Forum within the Chapeltown community. When the Forum was set up, a member represented the Society at the meetings.

On the lighter side of the community and race relations initiatives, the Society participated in cross-cultural events with other nationalities in Leeds. They did their part to foster an integrated multicultural society that was built on understanding and mutual respect for other people's culture and way of life. The Society was helping its own members with problems they had experienced personally, or collectively as Caribbean people. Networking with another migrant group demonstrated a commitment to building a harmonious society.

> "We used to organise an event called the Jewish/West Indian Evening. Initially, they were held at Scotthall Middle School. It was felt that as two minority ethnic groups, we were poles apart. The events were organised through the Leeds Community Relations Council. They were held annually over a period of four years. They were well attended with significant contribution from both communities. From our end, we had Mother Armstrong and her children performing, art & craft exhibi-

tions and typical West Indian dishes. The observation that I would make about the Jewish/West Indian evenings was that they were a success." – *Elizabeth Johnson*

One of the most vital tasks of the Society since its formation, has been the provision of some of the services that the Jamaican Consulate in Manchester used to perform. In its absence, the Society played the role of facilitator, while not actually offering the services of a Consulate. The Society became a focal point for Jamaicans in Leeds and the surrounding areas who needed help with documents pertaining to their personal and business holdings in Jamaica, and assistance with passport applications and similar documents. During that period after Jamaica's Independence, Jamaicans who wanted to remain in the UK could apply for British citizenship. The Society held surgeries for its members to inform them of the application process.

> "Jamaicans in Leeds needed assistance from the High Commission. They had to make applications for birth certificates and passports. At the time they were required to apply for British citizens, the forms that they had to complete were not simple. So they needed advice from relevant agencies. With the existence of the Jamaica Society, we were able to invite persons to speak to our members. I remember we used to hold surgeries at Barrack Road on Saturday mornings where persons could attend for help and advice." – *Elizabeth Johnson*

The Society continued to organise and facilitate surgeries on important issues in the community: from the adoption and fostering of black children, to the importance of being screened for Sickle Cell by inviting established organisations and experts in their fields, while being mindful not to duplicate the activities of existing agencies. It acted as a referral point for its members. The Society's early activities reflected the needs of its members at the time. However, it would expand its programme of activities as the community changed, and its influence and reputation grew. The members of the Society also recognised the potential and scope of the organisation, and the power of organising oneself within a community. As a Society of Jamaicans, they affirmed Marcus Garvey 's belief that "organisation is a great power in directing the affairs of a race or nation toward a given goal." The Jamaican community in Leeds acknowledged that as a united force they were far more effective than as far-flung individuals striving to do and figure out things on their own.

Educational and Cultural Events

At the 1980 Annual General Meeting, the guest speaker the late Reverend Kenneth Glendenning remarked that "the future lies in groups such as ours, doing the things that are important to us." He recognised the

Society for the charitable contributions it had made to the community and encouraged it to continue to explore new ways of serving its target public.

One of the Jamaica Society (Leeds) main objectives is the advancement of education. In fulfilling this mandate, the Society has been involved in promoting and educating the general public about the culture of Jamaica, facilitating cultural exchange programmes and in some instances, providing supplementary education. The Society's major educational and cultural activity was the launch in 1998 of the Windrush exhibition, *Had We Not Come*. The exhibition was part of the 50th celebration of the arrival of the *SS Empire Windrush* from Jamaica to the UK. A Windrush Sub-committee was formed to plan and supervise activities during this period; the exhibition was one of them. A Jamaican artist and graphic designer, Paul Aiken, designed *Had We Not Come*: a Leeds perspective on Caribbean people's experiences and achievements since their arrival in the UK. The exhibition has become a permanent educational resource for the Society which promotes understanding of Caribbean immigration to the UK. *Had We Not Come* has been used in schools, community and cultural activities particularly during Black History Month events.

Nine years earlier in 1987, the Society had put on an exhibition to celebrate the centenary of Marcus Garvey, Jamaica's first National Hero, with information provided by the Jamaica Information Service Office in London.

> "We did our first exhibition at Primrose Hill High School. It was an exhibition of the life and work of Marcus Garvey. At the time we were celebrating the centenary of his birth. The exhibition ran for two weeks in the foyer of the Primrose Hill School. We got various articles and items from the High Commission and the Tourist Board. It was a very big exhibition. Enid Edwards and I took turns to man this exhibition. Mind you, we worked some nights and we slept during the days and then spent some time at the exhibition." – *Elizabeth Johnson*

At the 1988 Annual General Meeting, former Chairperson, Lizette Powell paid tribute to the memory of Marcus Garvey by highlighting the significance of his work to Caribbean people and people of colour around the world:

> "This year the 25th anniversary of Jamaica's Independence coincided with the centenary of the birth of Jamaica's first National Hero, the Rt. Excellent Marcus Mosiah Garvey. His life not only mirrors the early struggles and triumphs of our Jamaican nation but inspires us to even greater efforts, commensurate with his own achievements in the fight for universal liberation for African peoples."

Both the Marcus Garvey centenary celebrations in 1987 and the Windrush celebrations in 1998 were of tremendous significance to Caribbean people in the UK. As part of the official Windrush celebrations, the

Society organised its first Children's Activity Day. The children from the community were invited to learn about traditional Jamaican artistry such as sculpting, woodcarving, storytelling and drumming. The Children's Activity Day was so successful that the Society hosted the event again in 1999 and 2000: it was a cultural vehicle to reach to the third generation of Caribbean children. The event attracted as many as one hundred and fifty children and their parents.

Other cultural activities that the Society fostered included facilitating the cultural exchange between a Jamaican dancer and Primrose Hill School. Local students were introduced to traditional Jamaican dances such as the quadrille, dinki mini and kumina. Two similar workshops were held in 2000 and 2002 with a Jamaican student from the Northern Contemporary Dance School in Leeds, and with visiting dancers from the National Dance Theatre Company of Jamaica.

During the early 1980s, a programme called 'Friends of Talent' was launched to assist young people in the community with further education. Under the banner *Give them a Chance*, the Society raised funds and donated money to deserving candidates. After the Society acquired its building, Glen English began to conduct supplementary maths classes for the children and grandchildren of the Society's members and the wider community. It has been a long term desire of his to contribute to the Society in this way.

> "After I retired, I started running classes on Saturday mornings to help the youngsters who were having problems with Maths. I asked the Executive if it was alright and they said that it was ok. So, I did some flyers and passed them around. A few youngsters used to come along and we got a class going. I was sad but in the end, it didn't sustain itself well enough, not enough students came. I was disappointed about that because, here was something that was for free and they appeared not to want it with the same enthusiasm with which I was giving it. I used to do these classes in the early 90s, about 1993." – *Glen English*

However, the Society successfully supported educational initiatives in Jamaica. In 1988, the Jamaica High Commission contacted the Society to inform them of the Jamaican Government's Adopt-A-School Scheme through the Programme for the Advancement of Early Childhood Education (PACE).

Organisations were asked to adopt one or more basic schools in Jamaica and provide cash or inkind support. The Society formed the PACE Sub-committee, chaired by the late Errol James and adopted the Breadnut Basic School near Ipswich, St. Elizabeth. Over the period of the adoption, the Society supplied the school with books, pencils, chalks and crayons, and liased with teachers. Members who went on vacation to Jamaica would visit the school to assess the impact of their donations. By 1993, the Society had raised close to £1,000 in cash for the Breadnut School through various fundraising ventures.

Over the years, the Society has been involved in a number of cultural activities. Errol James was in charge of the Society's Cultural Evenings from 1981 which also doubled as a fundraiser. Since the Society's involvement with the CRC in the Jewish/West Indian Evenings, requests from a number of schools in the area started to pour in.

> "We were invited by various schools such as Harehills County Primary School and Allerton Grange to do West Indian Evenings, because of what we had done over the years. At Allerton Grange, we were invited to participate in an International Evening. We had a full house with others like the Jews and the Asians. We continued to get a lot of requests from schools and we wondered what we had got ourselves into. One headmaster or headmistress after another was telling each other about us. The teachers at those schools were interested in the West Indian Community." – *Yvonne English*

In 1993, the Society set up a small library at Jamaica House. Patricia Dennis (née Thomas) was assigned the task of acquiring the first set of books and later, Yvonne English during her travels to Jamaica purchased books for the Society's catalogue. The late Gertrude Paul also contributed a substantial number of books to the library.

The Society has never wavered in its personal pledge to provide cultural opportunities and facilities for the community. Its past and present activities stand as testament to this fact.

Funeral Rites, Lost Relatives and the Care Group

In 1981, a member of staff from the St. James's Hospital informed the Society that Nathan Jarrett, a Jamaican had died on April 30. He had lived in isolation and very few Jamaicans knew him. He had no immediate relatives in the UK and no one knew how to contact any living relative he might have had. The Jamaican High Commission was contacted to help with the search.

> "This was the first time the Society was asked to help when a person died who had no relative in the UK. I remember we got a call from St. James's Hospital informing us that a Jamaican had died and if we knew how to reach any surviving relatives. We tried to find the relatives for the deceased with the help of the High Commission and other organisations. We managed to find a relative but he was unable to travel. So the Society organised the burial of that person." – *Elizabeth Johnson*

With the Society's involvement, this man though unknown to many, could be sent off with dignity. The downside of migration is that people sometimes lose touch with their family members. The members of the Society felt this incident affirmed the need for the Jamaican community to stick together. But it happened again - twice.

The following year, Clarence Inverity, another Jamaican immigrant died in his flat alone with no known relatives. The Society was once again contacted. The Society's first intervention was to contact the Department of Social Services to prevent the deceased from being given a pauper's funeral. The members contacted the Jamaican High Commission to launch a search for any living relative. This time the result was less propitious, no relative was found. Consequently, the Society arranged the funeral and organised a small repast for Clarence Inverity at the St. Aidan Church in Roundhay. About five or six years ago, a third Jamaican man, Dermot Clarke was found dead in his flat by his co-workers.

> "Probably the most difficult case we dealt with occurred a few years ago. We were informed of a Jamaican who had been found dead at home. A couple from another Caribbean country passed on the information to us. They were friends of his but did not know how to contact relatives of the deceased. They were also concerned about funds for his funeral. We discussed at length all they knew about him. Some of us could remember that he was someone who we had seen around Leeds over the years. He was not very communicative: he kept himself to himself. We embarked on a course of trying to find people who had known the deceased and whether he had family in the UK or Jamaica. We learned of a fellow Jamaican, Wesley Simpson who probably could help. With Wesley's assistance, we were able to make contact with members of the deceased family in Jamaica. The contact resulted in seven members of his family journeying to the UK from Jamaica, the Cayman Islands and the USA to help plan and execute his funeral. It was most heartening to know that members of the deceased family were prepared to journey here within a few days of being informed of his death. They had not seen or heard from him for several years. However, they arrived, financially equipped, to give their deceased family member a good funeral. We were pleased and indeed grateful for the assistance received from John Tempest Funeral Services. After all necessary funeral expenses were met, the balance of the deceased's estate was forwarded to Jamaica to his mother and his daughter." – *Travis Johnson*

In 1986, a Jamaican man came to join the Society because he feared that he might die alone.

Locating lost relatives has become one of the special services that the Society offers. A number of requests have come in over the years and they have been dealt with appropriately. Such incidents had prompted the then Chairperson, Lizette Powell to voice her concern at a March 1985 meeting about the number of elderly Caribbean persons in isolation. It was therefore suggested that a group should meet on

April 14th of the same year to examine the issue and devise a possible solution. On that day, the Jamaica Society (Leeds) Care Group was formed with Doreen Eubanks as its first co-ordinator. Other members who have taken up the mantle of co-ordinating the Care Group have been Winston James, Finley Wray and Theresa Condor. The Care Group regularly visits the sick, elderly, house-bound, distressed and bereaved in hospitals, hospices and at home, and arranges activities and excursions for the Senior Citizens. By 2000, the Care Group was carrying out over five hundred visits per year.

> "I was elected to the Executive Committee and I worked with the members and I found it very interesting. I was there until they had formed the Care Group that goes around and visits sick, elderly and lonely people. I was a part of that group. After awhile, the co-ordinator of that group resigned and they asked me to become the co-ordinator of it. I was a bit reluctant at first but I took it on and everybody was very helpful. I was lucky to have a group of members that volunteered to work with me and they used to make my job very easy. We used to do a lot of travelling around the community, it was about ten or twelve of us. We usually took turns - two people at a time. We had this rule that if we were going to visit someone's home, we should always go in twos. But with hospital visits you could always go alone. I really enjoyed being the co-ordinator of that group." – *Finley Wray, former Co-ordinator of the Care Group in the early 1990s.*

> "One of my roles at the Jamaica Society is to be a part of the Care Group. It is one of the things that I do enjoy, because I enjoy looking after people and caring for people. At the moment, I have about twenty Care Group members, who go out and visit members within our community. You feel very good when you actually go and see someone, and they are so pleased to see you when you go to have a chat with them. Their excitement gives me the faith to go on. The people we visit are not just members, they are people within the community as well. At the Society's General Meetings, the members let the Care Group know the persons who are ill. When we visit, we take a card, flowers or a basket of fruits" – *Theresa Condor, Care Group Co-ordinator*

Funeral rites for the deceased within the community have always been solemnly observed by the Society. Prior to acquiring Jamaica House, the Society supported its members during times of bereavement, by sending wreaths and paying them visits. After acquiring its own building, the Jamaica Society (Leeds) was able to provide a place for the holding of funeral repasts. It was upholding a Jamaican tradition of according the dead a proper burial. Its genesis lay in rites of passages ceremonies such as Kumina, Dinki Mini and Nine-Night.

Kumina is an ancestor worship religion originating from Africa. It is based on the belief that a dead person must be given a proper burial to prevent his or her spirit from wandering and haunting others. Like the

Kumina ceremonies, the Nine-Night custom is a community affair; friends and family gather to sing and provide comfort to the relatives of the deceased. This is called a 'set up' which sometimes go on for nine nights until the funeral, the most important night being after the burial. In the parishes of St. Mary, St. Ann, St. Andrew and Portland in Jamaica, Dinki Mini singing and dancing are observed for eight days prior to the Nine-Night ceremony. Dinki Mini is a African Caribbean tradition where lively and joyous music and dance are performed to cheer up the family of the dead. Though not strictly observed in their full traditional forms, elements of these rituals are still observed. The service that the Society has provided for its members and the community during times of bereavement has meant a great deal to the beneficiaries. Some become tearful when they recall the level of support.

"The support that members gets from the Society should you find yourself in crisis is so encouraging. For instance, not long ago I lost my mother and it was amazing the support that I got before I went to Jamaica and after I came back. There were so many cards. People were so kind with such words of sympathy. Before I left, there were twelve or thirteen people who visited me at home, even though it happened so quickly. They had like a short service for me and that was really, really so heartening. That took me through my travels home until the funeral. They used a booklet of hymns as part of the wake and that booklet was used in the service as well. I shared the cards that I got with my immediate family. It was very, very good. The support from the Society is always there to see the bereaved right through to the end." – *Irene Henry*

"I think there's a lot of respect for the Society. If somebody has a relative who has passed away, the first thing that they do is to look to the Society to ease the burden by doing the catering and organising things in general for them. People think that if there is a disaster or a problem, they can always come and get help from the Society. I think this is why a lot of people support the Society because they know it will be there to help them when they are in need. I was helped when my daughter died. She was murdered at home, by her boyfriend, six years ago." – *Florence Williams*

"Before my husband died, Mrs. Powell was something else. The members of the Society were all nice, but Mrs. Powell, she went out of her way. When I had to dash off to town to get my shopping done and rushed back home, it was Mrs. Powell who would stay there with my husband. When you leave your sick husband and you go shopping, you're always wondering if he's alright. When you get home and you see somebody there with him, it makes you feel really good to know that if anything goes wrong, somebody is there with him, which I was really pleased about. I thought it was a good job I was a member of the Society." – *Elma Davis*

"After my husband died, I didn't think I could make it, because we were together for so long - since childhood days. I haven't even got over it now to be truthful. At that point, my sister had died, my brother-in-law had died and a close friend of mine had also died. It was the Society that helped me. Mr. Johnson asked me what I wanted them to do for me. So, I said that I would like to have the reception for some of my husband's friends from Birmingham, London and Doncaster, after the service. Mr. Johnson and Mrs. Powell were of great help. They helped me with the well-wishers and with arranging the service. They also arranged for the choir to sing at the service. They were really helpful and I'm grateful for it." – *Phyllis Hines*

Social Welfare Activities for the Community

"For a start, the Society is more welcoming to older people because more places cater for younger people. If it were not for the Jamaica Society it would have been a lonely life. I know it has been an excellent organisation to a lot of people. Most of us remember what the social scene was like for us back in the early days. So, we know how good it is to have the Society." – *Samuel Barrett*

In addition to the activities of the Care Group, the Society implements a number of social welfare programmes for the young and the senior citizens within the community. The Senior Citizens' Christmas Dinner is one such event that takes place yearly. The event is of no cost to the participants and has attracted over one hundred persons including people who have had long-term illnesses and are being nursed at home.

"Although the name is the Jamaica Society it is for the community. One of the time when we had the third Senior Citizens' Christmas dinner, the Society sent an invitation to the Baptist church, and I think it was twenty-one of the white people from my church who came to the Christmas dinner. I know they have looked back and have said this was something that Jamaica Society has brought to the community. If people went to something like that at other places think how much money it would cost them! To say that the Jamaicans have come here and have invited the community into their environment, so that many different people can enjoy an event like that - it is a good thing. Each time I talk about the Society in my church they say, 'Oh yes, that is something for the community'." – *Robert Chrouch*

The Senior Citizens' Trip is another activity that targets the same group of people. Each summer, the trips have been to seaside resorts in Blackpool, Bridlington, Skegness and Hartlepool. The Society also organised trips for the wider membership to other destinations: Preston, Wolverhampton, Westminster and the Caribbean Expos in London.

> "On the trips from Jamaica House to the seaside, it is always somebody's birthday. The meal is prepared from Jamaica House and when they go, oooh! - there is one massive party on the bus."
> – *Maizie Pinnock*

The Children's Christmas Party has been going since the 1980s. But in 1986, the Society thought seriously about pulling the plug on this event because only a handful of youngsters turned up the previous year. However, this did not happen and today over eighty to one hundred children are in attendance, with members or friends of the Society playing Santa Clause. One person who has been Santa for a number of years is Edley White who recalls: "At Christmas time when the kids come, I used to play Father Christmas. I played it because my two grandchildren used to attend the event, so I decided to do it. I played Father Christmas for about three or four years."

The Society also started its Meals-On-Wheels activity in 2002. Under the umbrella of the Care Group, members of the Society prepare meals for house-bound senior citizens of Caribbean descent. The meals are fixed to their dietary and cultural requirements and taste.

Opening up its facilities and programme of activities to a section of the community that is sometimes forgotten, is a primary focus of the Society. Many of the Society's members could remember that when they first arrived in UK, many facilities were closed to them. The Society therefore has an obligation to this section of the community.

Community Initiatives

From early on in the Society's history, the formation of a Sickle Cell Support Group was on its agenda. A few members met towards the end of the 70s but the initiative did not get off the ground until 1983. Initially, very little information and medical support were available in the UK for persons with the Sickle Cell condition. Consequently, members of the Society set about trying find ways to redress this oversight and they liased with representatives from other Caribbean organisations and the health sector. Sickle Cell affects mainly people of African and Mediterranean descent; by extension this includes members of the Caribbean community.

> "In the late 70s, Liz, Travis and Jasmine Comrie had tried to set up a Sickle Cell Group in Leeds but it did not gain momentum until this case gained national attention. A pregnant woman had a Sickle Cell crisis and died as a result. Liz Powell (a Health Visitor) and I (a midwife) discussed the case many times, because we were aware of persons with the Sickle Cell condition through our jobs.
>
> "A Jamaican Health Visitor working in Manchester spoke at one of the Society's meetings. She invited us to visit her clinic. The outcome was that the Sickle Cell Support Group was formed

with participation from some of the Society's members and from the wider community. A core group used to meet at the Barrack Road Clinic. We also went to lectures and conferences which were held nationally in order to get additional information. It was important to find out how many persons within our community knew about Sickle Cell. We carried out a small survey within the community and we discovered that not many persons knew about Sickle Cell and its effects on their lives. Some said that they were tested but were not sure of the outcome.

"By then in Leeds, the Health Service was testing people if they had to have operations because the anaesthetist needed to know if they were Sickle Cell carriers. Even those people who had the trait still didn't know much about Sickle Cell. They were told it didn't matter. When in fact it mattered. If two people who had the Sickle Cell trait are married, one in four of their children would get the Sickle Cell condition and some would carry on the trait. We got a grant to employ a Health Visitor to do the screenings to counteract the misinformation that they were getting elsewhere and to communicate the right information to the community." – *Elizabeth Johnson*

In 1983, representatives from the Jamaica Society (Leeds) went to a meeting at the St. James's Hospital to discuss illnesses specific to the minority ethnic community. Following this meeting, the Society formally co-ordinated the establishment of the Leeds Sickle Cell Support Group which was set up as an independent body.

The Society has been instrumental in helping to establish another community organisation, the Community Action & Support Against Crime (CASAC) that was developed into a community partnership for dealing with crime and its effects on Chapeltown and Harehills areas. As early as 1985, the then Chairperson raised the issue at the General Meeting that members of the Society were concerned about young boys in the area congregating outside a well known pub selling drugs. On July 2, 1990, the question was raised at another meeting asking: 'what is the Society doing about the drug problem?' However, it was in 1992 that the Society would strongly encourage the other community organisations to join them in doing something concrete about the problem. In a letter dated March 27, 1992, the Society highlighted the reasons why the problem needed urgent attention:

> There is a growing number of young people from our community who are appearing before the courts, charged especially with taking without owners consent, robbery, burglary and drugs… 1990 statistical information produced by the Home Office disclosed that over 17% of the male prison population is black and over 28% of the female prison population.

After an initial meeting with representatives from the community, the first public meeting of the newly formed CASAC was held in 1993 attracting over two hundred and fifty persons.

"The Jamaica Society (Leeds) was one of the lead organisations in the setting up of CASAC. This came about when some members of the Society became increasingly concerned about the level of crime within the Chapeltown and Harehills areas. Four of us were involved in the Criminal Justice System as magistrates, and we were also sitting in Youth Courts. We were particularly concerned that we often saw young people of African Caribbean origin appearing in courts, some of them barely above the age of criminal responsibility. We questioned ourselves that if young people of such tender age were getting involved in criminal activities then we needed to find out what was happening to our community.

"After discussing the issue among ourselves, we wrote to other Caribbean organisations and Black Majority Churches to see how we as a community could address what was becoming a grave problem in our community. At the first meeting there were members from the Barbados Association, the St. Kitts and Nevis Association, the United Caribbean Association, the Church of God of Prophecy, Roscoe Methodist Church and the New Testament Church of God. Most churches in the area were represented. The organisations and churches were at one about the issue and the decision was reached to form a group to stem the tide of criminal activities within the community. A lunchtime meeting was held with members of the clergy from the churches within Chapeltown and Harehills. They were most supportive of our intended action and CASAC was established. The organisations and churches donated funds to CASAC to facilitate administrative expenses. A number of interested individuals joined the organisation also.

"We conducted a survey on residents' views about crime in the area. The questionnaire was devised, executed and analysed by members of CASAC. Public meetings were arranged and they were well attended. We were well supported by the police and certain departments of the Local Authority, but above all, the community was fully behind CASAC in its initiative. There was a noticeable reduction of certain criminal activities within the area." – *Travis Johnson has been a former Chairperson of CASAC*

In 2002, the Society launched another joint community effort, the Community Health Awareness Project to work with people in the community to promote changes in lifestyle in order to bring about improvement in health. It has also lent its support to a group raising funds in Leeds for the Diabetic Association of Jamaica.

The Jamaica Society (Leeds) has also supported social issues that it did not initiate. In 1981, it supported and contributed to the fund set up by the Leeds Action Group for the thirteen Caribbean young people who died in the Deptford Fire. Members of the Black British communities were very disturbed that the wider public expressed little sympathy for the young people who perished in the fire. The Society also liased with the Action Group set up to probe the case of the Jamaican woman, Joy Gardner who died while allegedly being manhandled by immigration officers during an attempt to deport her.

Celebrating Jamaica's Independence

A principal event on the calendar of the Jamaica Society (Leeds) is the annual celebrations to mark Jamaica's Independence. The service is significant on many levels for the Jamaican community in the UK. Many of them were not in Jamaica when the country gained Independence, and were probably not in a position in 1962 to effectively organise themselves to participate in the celebrations. Every year in August, the Society and members of the community commemorate this special occasion. Special services have been held to observe the 21st, 25th and 40th anniversaries of Jamaica's Independence as momentous milestones for the nation. Over two hundred worshippers and well wishers join in the Thanksgiving Service each year.

> "The first Service put on by the Society to recognise the Independence of Jamaica was at St. Aidan Church in 1981. For two subsequent years, this recognition was integrated in the Main Mass. In 1984 and 1985, the Service of Thanksgiving for the Independence of Jamaica was held at the New Testament Church of God. There were difficulties experienced trying to rotate the Service to different churches. The general membership decided that all future Services would be held at St. Aidan Church. Since 1986, the Service returned to St. Aidan and has been held mostly on the first Sunday in August at 6pm. Annually, we give careful consideration to the person we invite to deliver the main address.
>
> "Over the many years, we have tried to vary the invitation between ministers of different denominations. We were fortunate in 1988 and 1998 to have had the Bishop of Jamaica The Right Reverend Neville DeSouza. He also blessed Jamaica House in 1988. We are conscious of the need to give God thanks for all the many blessings He has bestowed on us as a people and country. Most of us were born and brought up in colonial Jamaica and looked forward to the day when Jamaicans would be responsible for their own destiny. We are indeed most appreciative of the support we receive from members of the other Caribbean communities and members of the indigenous community." – *Travis Johsnon*

> "The celebration of Jamaica's Independence is a time to reflect on where we as Jamaicans living in the UK are coming from. We should always keep that, and be proud of our heritage and culture. It makes us stronger. It is also an important event for those who were born here, because

they should know where they are coming from and who they are. They should always keep that intact." – *Irene Henry*

Celebrating Jamaica's Independence does not mean members do not cherish the opportunity that they have had to live in their adopted country. Many have recognised that the best way of showing their appreciation is by contributing to the community they currently reside in, and living as model citizens.

"I cherish both my British and my Jamaican citizenships. I can hold up my hand and say I have lived in this country for so many years and my record is clean. I have lived in Jamaica and I can say the same. Although, I have spent so many years in Britain, I still love Jamaica. I remain a Jamaican." – *Lynford Fletcher*

"We believe it is important to play our part and participate in every possible way in the life of our adopted country, but equally we are committed to the land of our birth." – *Travis Johnson*

The Independence celebrations usually begin or end with social events. The extraordinary popularity and enthusiasm displayed during the Independence celebrations led to the creation of the Jamaica Society (Leeds) Choir. Formed in 1989, the Choir has performed at many community functions and participated in other celebrations held by other Jamaican associations around the country. But the formation of the Choir had a rather interesting start.

"Early on in the Society's life, we decided to form a Choir. We got together to practise folk and spiritual songs. The first song that we practised, did not meet everyone's approval. The Society's Choir was asked to sing at an Easter event at the West Indian Centre, but our Choir had not practised and could not perform. We came up with this bright idea that the Jamaica Society Junior Choir would sing, because Samantha, Liz's daughter and Melanie, Vena's daughter used to come along and sing along with us. So the Jamaica Society Junior Choir made up of only these two young girls sang at this event and they sang their hearts out. They got a loud applause and they were invited to come back many times. After that the Jamaica Society (Leeds) Choir had to get its act together." – *Elizabeth Johnson*

"I used to be the choir director, organising the various practices and conducting the choir whenever they performed. I was already a member of the Choir of the Society and there was a time in the Choir's life when it did not have a director. I was asked to do it and I was so delighted to do so. I chose to co-ordinate the Choir because it is something that I love. I've always loved music and loved to sing. I know how to harmonise and arrange voices together. I've been singing since I was twelve years old in Jamaica. I'd go around the island singing at different schools, concerts and festivals and things. Then I came to the UK and I sang with various groups in the community and once or twice further a field. Singing with the Jamaica Society (Leeds) Choir was a natural step. The Choir is something that I put a lot of energy into and it's been great each time we've performed, especially since we have been working together for years." – *Yvonne Hylton, former Choir Co-ordinator*

"We come to Choir practice every Wednesday and we sing!!!. When the time comes for the Jamaica Society's Independence Service, we all look forward to dressing up in our uniforms, and we look very nice. One of the uniform that we have had was full black with the scarf made in the colours of Jamaican flag. But the highlight for me is singing in front of loads of people in the church and guests such as the Lord Mayor and Lady Mayoress. It's just wonderful. I love it!!!" – *Francis Williams*

The Choir's repertoire includes gospel, Jamaican folksongs, revivalist songs, African songs and traditional church hymns. It has been a requisite feature at activities such as the Senior Citizens' Dinner, gospel concerts, church services and Easter variety concerts. The first Choir co-ordinators were Michael and Nessa Nedd, who drilled both the Choir and members into singing the Jamaican national anthem correctly, when a visitor from Jamaica pointed out that they had got it wrong. An easy mistake, since most of the members had not resided in Jamaica prior to Independence, but they enterprisingly set about doing it on their own.

Visiting Dignitaries, VIPs and Celebrities

When the Jamaica Society (Leeds) was formed one of the major concerns was that they did not have an organised body or a place to receive VIP guests from Jamaica. The visit of Louise Bennett highlighted this shortcoming. Since the Society's inception, the members have played host to a number of dignitaries and VIPs - local and Jamaican. The Society meticulously prepares a reception, sometimes complete with a three or five course Jamaican meal to ward off any longings that the guests may have for Jamaican cuisine. The welcome is elaborate and members turn out to greet and welcome them. Over the years, they have received famous Jamaican actors, Oliver Samuels and Audrey Reid, as well as the Area Youth Project Drama Group from a Kingston innercity community and members of the West Indian Cricket Team. Much to the delight of the Society they have also received in 2000 the incumbent Jamaican Prime Minister, the Right Honourable P.J. Patterson, ON, PC, QC, MP and assisted the High Commission in organising for him to speak at a public meeting at the Northern School of Contemporary Dance. In 1994 and again in 2002, the Society welcomed the Governor General of Jamaica, His Excellency the Most Honourable Sir Howard Cooke, ON, GCMG, GCVO, CD who holds the highest office in the country as the Queen's representative. On both occasions the Governor General paid a courtesy call on the Lord Mayor of Leeds, toured facilities in Chapeltown and met with members of the community. On his last visit to Leeds, the Governor General shared his impressions of the Jamaica Society (Leeds).

> "Eight years ago, I visited Leeds. It was remarkable to see the sort of upward social mobility of the people here. I saw a Society that was anxious to be identified. I saw a Society that wanted to do all it could to help each other. Here was an association that wanted to improve not just the social but the intellectual and the spiritual situations of its people. That time it was a Society that truly was not impaired because they didn't have a desire. In fact, they had a will and they wanted to improve those people who were not fortunate to be affluent. They were trying to help them and when they met it wasn't just a social event where they sang hurrahs; it was a gathering where they were talking with one another and trying to help each other to improve." – *His Excellency the Most Hon. Sir Howard Cooke, ON, GCMG, GCVO, CD*

The Society has also rolled out the welcome mat for a number of High Commissioners, Deputy High Commissioners, First Secretaries, Information Attaches, and Community Relations Officers from the Jamaican High Commission. Since the appointment of the first Jamaican High Commissioner to UK, Dr. Arthur Wint, every appointee has paid a visit to the Jamaican community in Leeds: Ernest Peart, Herbert Walker, Ellen Bogle, Derek Heaven and David Murihead. The Society works closely with the High Commission; members of the Society are often contacted for advice or help and to sit on working committees. The current Chairperson, Travis Johnson is a consultant to the High Commission on community development issues. The Society takes seriously the links it has maintained with the High Commission and the enormous value this relationship has been to the Jamaican community.

> "The Jamaica High Commission's relationship with the Jamaica Society (Leeds) is similar to the relationship with several organisations around the UK that are comprised mainly of Jamaicans and are concerned with the welfare of Jamaicans in the UK as well as matters affecting Jamaicans in Jamaica. In so far as Jamaica itself is concerned, the relationship is one of interchange. They are concerned with improving the prospects in the field of education and the medical field and

they do provide substantial assistance in those areas: basic school education, helping to repair schools and providing equipment for hospitals. They also help in the area of fishing - providing safety equipment for fishermen and they help to carry out training programmes where they see the need exists. In so far as the Society in dealing with their own community, it provides an opportunity for them to meet at Jamaica House, it provides inspiration and leadership; it assists the members to access all the various organisations here, and at the same it acts as centre to which the Jamaican High Commission sends materials. We have a Community Relations Officer who directly engages in interchange and activities with the Jamaica Society." – *Hon. David Muirhead, OJ, QC, Jamaican High Commissioner to the UK, 1999-2002*

"The Jamaica Society (Leeds) is one of the really progressive Jamaican organisations in the UK. We get information from them and we also transmit information to them on changes in policies in Jamaica. We in turn update them on information from the Government of Jamaica. Through organisations like the Jamaica Society, we receive feedback from the Jamaican community on a wide range of issues, and this information is sent back to the Jamaican government.

"My first contact with the Jamaica Society Leeds was in 1999. I had reported to work in January 1999 and in February, we had a visiting government minister who wished to have a community meeting in Leeds. I called the Chairman of the Jamaica Society (Leeds), I gave him the information that the minister was coming and asked him if he could possibly get a community meeting together for me. 'No problem,' he said. I didn't even have to go to Leeds to assist with the arrangements. When we got to Leeds with the visiting minister and the High Commissioner, everything was organised - a full hall, refreshment and even hotel accommodation had been arranged. I was truly impressed.

"I can also remember we had a Jamaican student who needed money urgently - the student was in Leeds. The parents had contacted us at the High Commission and said they would like to send the money to their child who needed it urgently. We said, 'Oh, no problem.' They handed over the money at our Mission in Miami. I picked up the phone and I dialled the Chairman of the Jamaica Society (Leeds) and I said, 'Travis, we need you to please take a certain amount of money to this young lady who is studying in Leeds, she is at this address and she needs it urgently'. Within an hour, I got a call back saying, 'It's been done, no problem'. We reimbursed the Society back when we got the money here. So these are things that hold such special memories.

"I am very pleased to say that the Chairman of the Jamaica Society (Leeds) is a also consultant to the Jamaican High Commission on all matters relating to community development. The support of organisations such as the Jamaica Society is critical to the development of Jamaica, because they encourage Jamaicans in the UK to invest in Jamaica's development. Jamaicans abroad send remittances back to Jamaica to support their families and provide much needed foreign exchange inflows to the country. They promote Jamaica's rich cultural heritage by staging special events for descendants of Jamaicans and the wider community, and promote the island as a tourist destination for family celebrations and other events. They are definitely good ambassadors for their country: promoting Jamaica as a viable investment destination when they play host to Jamaican financial institutions that hold community meetings. Over the years, they have supported a number of health and educational projects in Jamaica and always respond positively to Special Appeals, for example, Flood Relief. " – *Delores Cooper, Community Relations Officer, Jamaican High Commission*

The members appreciate the facilitating role that the Society plays between the High Commission and the local community. The maintenance of political and social links with Jamaica, gives Jamaicans in Leeds a chance to contribute financially to their homeland which is still experiencing the growing pains of nationhood. Forty years is not a long time in the life of a country. They are painfully aware that their country still has some way to go until it can achieve the comfortable standard of living that they have experienced while living in the UK. It is therefore, their patriotic duty to assist with its development.

"The best experience I have had with the Jamaica Society (Leeds) is when people like the High Commissioners and the Prime Minister from Jamaica visit. If I were back in Jamaica there was no way I would meet the Prime Minister. I have been here donkey's years and I never knew any of these representatives until I came to Jamaica House." – *Samuel Barrett*

"I remember when the Prime Minister came to Jamaica House. He went around and shook everybody's hand. After he shook everyone's hand, he came back to me and was talking to me. That made me feel really, really good. He asked me how long have I been here in this country. So I told him. I said I came up in December 1960 and he said that was the same time he was in Leeds doing his studies. It was good to see him come over to Jamaica House and I was the first one he came up to and had a chat with. It was good." – *Phyllis Hines*

The Society does not forget its local dignitaries. At the end of the appointment of the city's first black Lady Mayoress, Susan Pitter and the first of Jamaican descent, the Society hosted a soirée on her behalf to reflect the pride the Jamaican and Caribbean community felt at such an achievement.

"My most memorable event with the Jamaica Society (Leeds) was the special reception that was thrown for me when I was Lady Mayoress. That was very touching for me. I didn't think it would have been such a moving affair. I had my family around me, people I cared about and the people of the Jamaica Society. I was really moved when members of the Jamaica Society and in particular the senior citizens came up to me and hugged me and said, 'Oh I'm so proud of you'. Some were in tears and that really, really moved me. That's when I realised what the appointment meant to the Jamaican community. The Lord Mayor also came along and representatives from the High Commission, National Commercial Bank of Jamaica, and there was also a message from the High Commissioner. I felt honoured and I was very humbled by it. So for me, the atmosphere at the reception was like being at home. Also I thought it was fitting that my very last engagement as Lady Mayoress was in Chapeltown with the Jamaica Society and with my family and friends around me." – *Susan Pitter*

The Society extends its good relations to members of the Jamaican business community in the UK. It has received support for its fundraising events from J. Wray & Nephew, Grace Kennedy, D&G, Air Jamaica, Jamaica National Commercial Bank, Jamaica National Building Society and Victoria Mutual Finance. The Society provides space for Jamaican financial institutions to have open days or surgeries on its property. The law firm Cook & Partner Solicitors and the Registrar General of Jamaica have also held surgeries at Jamaica House: the former focusing on legal problems with property in Jamaica and the latter with the application of birth and marriage certificates and other legal documents. It is evidently a two-way relationship because the businesses get the opportunity to promote their products and services to the Jamaicans in the area.

"Initially, I worked with the Jamaica Society (Leeds) in terms of just merely renting the main room they have, and that would give me an opportunity to meet with the Jamaican community in Leeds. This was however, when I worked as UK representative of Jamaica National Commercial Bank. Thereafter, it developed into a stronger relationship where we did joint projects together. The Jamaica Society (Leeds) is considered one of the leading Jamaican societies in the UK and it also set an example for other societies to follow. It has, over the years, had strong leadership and an extremely effective Executive Team and that has led to its success." – *Paulette Simpson, chief representative of Jamaican National Building Society*

In 1999, the transitory Millennium Sub-committee wanted to stage a series of outstanding events to celebrate the year 2000. One of the special events for the year was the invitation of the Hands in Praise Choir from the Caribbean Christian Centre for the Deaf (CCCD). The Society joined forces with the Yorkshire

Baptist Association to secure sponsorship for this visit. Six children with hearing impairment arrived in the UK with their chaperones for a three-week stay. The Society organised a tour for the group and they performed in Leeds, Bradford, Sheffield, Wakefield, Hull, Doncaster and Bolton. The members provided accommodation, warm clothes, transport and of course, a first-class reception at Jamaica House.

> "I give a lot to charity. I give to the Caribbean Christian Centre for the Deaf in Jamaica. I sponsor one of their children. I use to give £5 a month for five years. Then I changed it and now I give £7 a month for three years - £7 without fail, I give it. When the children came here, I raised £300 to buy warm clothes by putting on a fashion show. Also, I hosted three of the children at my home. It was very nice. I feel I should do something to make them feel happy." – *Louise Reid*

The CCCD Choir returned in April 2003 to the same generous reception. The Society's members made large donations of clothes, shoes, toys and books to the visitors and to their fellow residents at the CCCD Centre in Knockpatrick, Jamaica. These are the channels that the Society explores in order to effectively serve both the Jamaican communities in Leeds and Jamaica.

Women's Group

The Women's Group started in 1989 and evolved out of the Society's observation of International Women's Day in March. The aims of the Women's Group are to create an awareness of women's health issues, particularly those affecting women of African Caribbean origin; to bring together women of Caribbean origin who are interested in their history and culture, and to identify and develop Caribbean women's talents through art, drama, folksongs and culinary skills. In 1986, the Society organised its first International Women's Day activity which highlighted the achievements of black women. There was a photographic display of leading Caribbean and African women. Over two hundred persons attended including Tessa Sanderson OBE, the javelin gold medallist.

> "When we used to have the first sets of International Women's Day functions, the Society didn't have a women's group then. There also weren't so many activities to commemorate the day. I remember the Society got involved in an International Women's Day event which was held at the Harehills CP School on Shepherd's Lane (which no longer exists). We had a good turn out. At that time, the Executive did the organising. Lizette Powell and I did most of it. I used to go over to Liz's when the children were in bed and I would be leaving her house, two or three o' clock in the morning driving back home as the saying goes, even *when dog 'fraid* to get things like

International Women's Day sorted out. For other International Women's Day events, we organised sessions and seminars around other women's issues. In 1988, we did a seminar on PMS and Menopause. I worked with an obstetrician who recommended a gynecologist who specialised in PMS to join us in organising and delivering that seminar at the Harehills Community Centre. The Society's Women's Group grew out of the observation of International Women's Day. " – *Elizabeth Johnson*

Over the years, the different co-ordinators of the Women's Group brought their own remit. With several of the women in the Society having worked in the health sector, the promotion of, and education around health issues have been paramount. Under the leadership of the late Cynthia Samuels in the early 1990s, the Health Club was formed. The women participated in keep fit classes and made use of the exercise machine donated by the City Council. She also arranged fundraising summer barbecues and handicraft activities, preserving the sewing skills the women learnt in Jamaica which was useful to many who worked in the clothing factories around Leeds. Subsequent co-ordinators like Nettie White and Yvonne Hylton have organised a diverse number of events which were not necessarily health focussed but were culturally relevant to the members. Currently, the sphere of activity is health and lifestyle focussed. However, the group invites guest speakers from the community which are good exemplars to women.

"My remit for the Society's Women's Group is health. Because I am a nurse, I have always taken on the role of co-ordinating an event around an health issue. I try to get speakers in - not just for the women, but for the general members, so that all the Society including the men can share in the health issues. I've invited one of the Consultants from my workplace, he is a radiologist and a specialist in prostate cancer. I feel that our Caribbean men may not know enough to seek the advice they need to maintain their health or to seek early advice for prostate cancer. I also have other things in the pipeline for health, a project that works to improve people's health by changing their lifestyle. My long term goal is for the project to become part of the institution of the Society. Since I've been co-ordinator, we have had International Women's Day events. The first one I co-ordinated dealt with women's contribution to society and we ended the day with complementary therapy. The next Women's Day we were given the theme that was 'Campaigning Women', and we looked at the future of our daughters and granddaughters." – *Bev Lattibeaudiere, Co-ordinator of the Women's Group*

"Within the Society, there is the Women's Group and I think that has been very beneficial,

because we usually invite speakers to come and speak on issues like childcare and health problems. A speaker who stood out for me was a young police constable who was invited to speak at the General Meeting. I felt very proud because she was black, she was a woman, and she was the daughter of one of our members. I thought that was great. I remember that very well."
– *Florence Williams*

Drama and Domino Groups

Throughout the early 1990s, members of the Society participated in the plays written by the Society's own self-appointed playwright, Edley White. He penned Jamaican-styled dramas such as *Hen Peck*, *Sammy Dead* and *Miss Lou* along with the Nativity play and The Trial at Easter. The Society's Drama Group (SDA) was formed in 1989, which coincided with the completion of Jamaica House. This meant that the group had a steady base to rehearse. The Society had always wanted to form a drama group and attempted to do so in the early days.

> "When we started to meet at the school, we talked about having a drama group as another way for fundraising. We wanted to hold a good old fashioned concert, so we decided to do a play. I remember Lizette Powell writing that first play. But we could never decide on who would do what. We met on a number of occasions but that particular play didn't come off." – *Elizabeth Johnson*

Perhaps they were a little ahead of their time, because the drama group was certainly ready to take off in 1989. The greatest challenge would not be finding an audience for the plays - that was the easy part. It was finding willing volunteers to become actors. After Edley's persistent cajoling, members began to join the SDA. The Drama Group eventually had a troupe of twenty players. When the curtains went up on the SDA's first public performance, they received excellent reviews and the audience could not get enough of them. They performed at least three plays per year.

> "Every time the Society wanted to raise money they would put on a dance. So, I said, 'Let's put on a concert.' Mrs. Johnson said to me, 'You *gwaan* and put on your concert'. I scraped the bottom of the barrel to get these people together. When I put on the concert, it came off pretty good. So, they started calling us the Jamaica Society Drama Group. We did quite a few plays. We put on one at Mrs. Reid's church and another at St. Aidan church. We used to put on a play after a certain time had elapsed, or if someone said it was time to put on a play." – *Edley White*

The SDA forged alliances with the Choir to put on a number of variety concerts to raise funds. The Drama Group became purveyors of Jamaican culture; they were a cultural vehicle for the promotion of the Jamaican language and the preservation of their heritage. Sadly, in the mid 1990s the curtains came down on the drama group's run. Ill health prevented the co-ordinator and only playwright from continuing in this post. Even though SDA hired an independent drama tutor, it was not enough to keep it going. The spark that lit its flame had died.

The Domino Group met a similiar fate. The group has been functional since the early days of the Society and was co-ordinated by Mr. Watson, Allen Ebanks, Mr. Franklyn and Winston James. The early years of the Domino Group was plagued by the lack of a firm base to meet in order to prepare for matches, until the Society acquired its own building. Like the general membership, the Domino Group moved around a lot. It played a few friendly matches with the Barbados Association. The members of the Domino Group also helped to raise money for the Society's various fundraising events by staging matches until the Group was disbanded in the mid 1990s.

Fundraising

Fundraising accounts for the largest number of activities put on by the Society in any given year. Although the regular dues paid by the members are sufficient to cover the upkeep of Jamaica House and its grounds, extra funds are needed to support all the charitable events and causes to which the Society is committed. The Society has contributed to funds and appeals launched by other agencies or individuals in Jamaica and the UK. In 1984, it responded favourably to the Stephen Cain Fund, (a young paraplegic in the community who needed assistance to participate in the Para-Olympics), and to the Lord Mayors' Ethiopian Fund. Money was raised to help a Jamaican child with heart surgery in 1986 and the following year, the Society gave generously to the 'Give for Life' Appeal. In the same year, the Society purchased and donated heart valves to the Heart Hospital in Jamaica. It responded once again to the 1986 Flood Appeal in Jamaica and committed to raise £8,000 for the Jamaica Hurricane Appeal in 1988. This was a mammoth task and every possible method of raising the funds was explored.

> "I can remember going out to collect money for Hurricane Gilbert. Liz and I went to many places trying to raise funds. We had rang up this place and got official tins so we can go around with some credibility. One night, Liz and I went off with the tins and we drove past a pub in the Bayswater area. We asked ourselves, 'Should we go in?' Now a pub is not a place I go to, neither did Liz. But we pulled up in the car park and we got out this tin along with our letter. We spoke to this little man at the door and explained why we were there and he shouted to someone inside

and then he shouted back to us, 'Come on in luvs.' We walked in and collected some money and when we came out we asked ourselves, 'Did we just go into that place?' But for Gilbert Fund Appeal we went to places that we would never have considered before." – *Elizabeth Johnson*

In order to fund the Senior Citizens' Trip, a Fundraising Social is held in June each year. In order for the Senior Citizens' Dinner and the Children's Christmas Party to take place another Fundraising Social is held in November. A large number of events are held and serve the dual purpose of providing entertainment for the community and maintain a solid financial base for the Society. Over the years, the Society has arranged the following events: Variety Concerts, Christmas Socials, Dinner & Dances, Valentines Socials, New Year's Eve Socials, Family Day, Gospel Concerts, Plays, Barbecues, Independence Socials, Carnival Stalls and Carnival Socials. Most of these events have been attached to charitable causes.

"I became the co-ordinator for the Social and Fundraising Sub-committee, which I did for about nine years and I enjoyed it very much. Whenever we are having any kind of social event, the Social and Fundraising Sub-committee would organise the buying of the food, the arranging of the menus, and the entertainment. We put on these events not just for financial gain, but also to encourage people to continue to be a part of the Society and to support it. It helps to keep people together, as much as it offers people a nice time. Then, of course, if the financial side has paid off, we have had our bonus. A lot of our people find there are not many places for them to socialise and Jamaica House caters for them. Because of that, when the Society has these social events, people seem to take great pride in coming out and enjoying themselves and meeting other people." – *Florence Williams*

Keeping track of the finances from these events is a full time job for Lynford Fletcher, the Treasurer. He has remarked that it has been a quite a challenge "to put the little bits in place, especially when you are going to the auditor. You have to know where you put every cent. Every penny must be in its place. Sometimes, I have to work out how every penny is spent before I put it on paper. I don't keep a great account of my own finances as I do the Jamaica Society's. Because when you handle other people's money you have got to be careful." When Jamaica House was being renovated and the Society had to manage approximately £250,000 worth of funds, Lynford Fletcher kept such accurate accounts that the Government Task Force said there was no need to audit the accounts because of the quality of record keeping. Each member who has filled the post of Treasurer has always been devoted to safeguarding the Society's financial future and ensuring sound financial management.

The grandest social event in the Society's history has been the 25th Anniversary Ball in July 2002. It surpassed all the other social events in terms of its splendour. Over two hundred guests were in attendance. The Ball was held in the Lord Mayor's Banqueting Suite at the Civic Hall under the patronage of the Lord Mayor Councillor Brian North and his Jamaican wife, Lady Mayoress Celine North. Members of Parliament, local councillors, Jamaican dignitaries, representatives from the Jamaican High Commission and from Jamaican financial institutions attended the event. One of the achievements on that night's event was that over £2,000 was raised for the Spanish Town Hospital in Jamaica. Of equal worth was the commemorative meaning of the night. It was a salute to the past and present members of the Society who have given countless time and sacrificed their personal resources to build an organisation that stands as one of the pillars of the Jamaican and Caribbean community. The sentiment that reverberated all night throughout the hall was that the Society could look forward to another twenty-five years of existence. The Anniversary Ball has now become an annual event in the Society's social and fundraising calendar.

One member, Louise Reid, has created her own space within the Society to fundraise for various charities. Her medium for fundraising is a fashion show which she has been staging since 1991. Louise raises additional money by selling the clothes on display. She also involves other members like Audrey Reid as models for her fashion show: "I modelled for Mrs. Reid Charity Show. But the clothes that I modelled were what she'd already made for me. She made them for me to go to a wedding reception. She also made about three more dresses for me when I was going on holidays." Mrs. Reid's Charity Fashion Shows also demonstrate how one can still contribute to one's community even after retirement, by learning a new skill and putting it to work for charity.

> "One day I went to Jamaica House and there was a lecture there. The speaker said the government would give anyone of us senior citizens £50 to do something to help ourselves. I said I'll do something; I'll do some dressmaking. At that time, I did not know I had the potential in me to do it, but I said I would do it. When I came home, I filled out the form and they called me for an interview. When I was interviewed, they liked what they saw because I brought down some dresses and suits that I had sewn and they were impressed. A week later, they wrote me and told me that I qualified for the £50. They had asked me a lot of questions at the interview like 'what would I do with the £50 if I got it?' I said, 'I'll go into Leeds City Market and buy some materials and sew some dresses for women over sixty. I'll try to show it off by getting people to model them. I'll do that at Jamaica House, and the patrons have to give a donation. I'll charge £4 to £5 per person to come in.' The first venue was so full that the next time when I had arranged it, I was in all the papers. That was in 1992. I felt good to have done something to help the Jamaica Society because when I keep my fashion shows I make a donation to the Society. I also give money to other causes because I always do the fashion shows for charity." – *Louise Reid*

The preservation of one's culture takes on different forms; the retention of culinary traditions is one of them. Providing the best in Jamaican food is a cultural mantle the Jamaica Society (Leeds) holds up high. The Society's social events have become a showcase for demonstrating the best in Jamaican cuisine. A great deal of care and creativity go into the preparation of each meal, which have been described as 'sumptuous' and 'delectable' - the descriptions often surpass the superlative. According to Paulette Simpson, Jamaica National Building Society, chief representative: "Everybody knows if you want good food you go to Leeds and you go downstairs in the kitchen of Jamaica House and in fact some of us have our stools down there." Others share this sentiment.

> "The kitchen at the Jamaica Society (Leeds) is one of my favourite places. I have my own stool there. It's always the highlight of my evening when once we are finished with the formalities upstairs, then I run down to my stool to partake in some nicely prepared Jamaican food. It's like being back in Jamaica." – *Delores Cooper*

> "The Society can pride itself on the cuisine that it provides at Jamaica House. I would be bold enough to suggest, that it is second to none. Every effort is made to ensure that it is authentic Jamaican food. Over the many years, the Society has received compliments from fellow Jamaicans and other nationals about the quality of meals served at Jamaica House. Probably, our biggest weakness is that we always over cater. There is always an abundance of food at Jamaica House." – *Travis Johnson*

The Jamaica Society (Leeds) culinary reputation has spread beyond the community. In the winter of 2000, when Frigid, a television production company was shooting in Chapeltown, the Society was asked to do the catering. A core group of women work tirelessly and ceaselessly catering for these events, assisted of course, by an equally dedicated cadre of men. Over the years, there have been a number of women have laboured away in the kitchen for an incalculable number of hours: Thelma Bucknor, Lydia Cunningham, Elma Davis, Enid Edwards, Yvonne English, Doreen Eubanks, Phyllis Hines, Dorothy James, Lizette Powell, Louise Reid, Constance Taylor, Pat Thomas-Dennis, Cynthia Samuels, Florence and Vena Williams, supported ably by Zephaniah Cunningham, George Eubanks, Winston James, Roy Mitchell, Edley White and Finley Wray. Today, the women that one would invariably spot in the kitchen are Joyce Baxter, Norma Fletcher, Audrey Henry, Irene Henry, Betsy Johnson, Rheta Macdonald, Icyline Parker, Pansy Patterson, Maizie Pinnock and Nettie White. Sometimes they are joined by Samuel Barrett, Robert Chrouch and Lincoln Cole. One is guaranteed to see Allen Ebanks, Lynford Fletcher and Travis Johnson, making arrangements for the beverages.

CHAPTER 3

Our Biggest Event Yet – Jamaica Day 2000

On August 12, 2000, over one thousand five hundred people streamed into the grounds of the Civil Service Sports Club in Chapeltown to participate in a free all day event, Jamaica Day 2000. This event was staged to celebrate the millennium and it brought Jamaicans from all over the country to share in this occasion. Coach loads of Jamaicans, friends and their offsprings rolled into the park from Sheffield, Leicester, London, Manchester, Huddersfield, Bradford, Birmingham and other towns and cities. People from all over Leeds, Jamaicans and non-Jamaicans alike, turned out for this huge cultural spectacle.

The event kicked off on a perfect English summer's day with domino tournaments, races and football. The highlight of the day was the playing of Jamaican games. This took many back to their school days in Jamaica: lime & spoon, three-legged and sack races and a very competitive game of tug-o-war. Leeds Carnival 2000 made an appearance, showing off the costumes for that year. The only thing that rivalled the resplendence of the Carnival costumes was the huge spread of Jamaican food, all of which was free. In attendance were representatives from the High Commission, the Jamaica Tourist Board, the Jamaican business community and city officials - the Lord Mayor, Councillor Bernard Atha officially opened the day with an Executive from the National Commercial Bank. After a Jamaican style variety show and dancing, the day ended at midnight.

Jamaica Day 2000 was the brainchild of Paulette Simpson, former manager of the National Commercial Bank of Jamaica, UK. Other Jamaican sponsors came on board to make the event possible notably, Air Jamaica and Grace Kennedy. The Society's members put in hundreds of hours of planning and preparation. The women and men worked in the kitchen non-stop for weeks to cater for approximately two thousand revellers.

> "The most memorable project that I have done with the Jamaica Society (Leeds) is that of Jamaica Day 2000. I came up with the idea of celebrating the year 2000 in a way that could involve a lot of people. The idea was to create and restore a positive image of Jamaica and the Jamaican family structure. There had been lots of activities all over the country and we tend not to concentrate a lot of them in the North of England. I met with Travis Johnson and his team at the Jamaica Society (Leeds) and suggested that we put on Jamaica Day 2000 together. So, NCB which I worked for at the time, Air Jamaica and Grace Kennedy came together alongside the Society to organise Jamaica Day 2000.
>
> "It was an excellent day. In fact, it is something that we still speak about even now. It was a bright sunny day and we had over 2,000 people. The format was that we would invite people from the community and the surrounding areas. We had two coaches from London, we

had people from Sheffield, Manchester and Nottingham. We tried to get as many people as possible to come and join in from all over the country. On the day, we tried to include the wider community. We had participation from community Netball teams from around the UK. We had football matches which were geared towards the under 16s. We also included a family element to the event. We had the field events that parents and children could participate in together.

"The message it sent to the wider community is that Jamaicans can all get together and have a really good time and it helped to dispel some of the negative images that people have of us. In fact, the wider community has recognised that but it was important for the descendants of Jamaicans, their children and their children's children to see this. People met together and made new friends out of this event. The Jamaica Society went all out for the event. The only sad thing was that some of the members were too tired to enjoy the event because they worked so hard at organising it. They had to put so much effort into preparing the food that they did not get to enjoy themselves. When we sat down at the end of the event, we all felt that we had a good day. It is something we would like to do in Leeds again." – *Paulette Simpson, chief representative of the Jamaica National Building Society*

"Jamaica Day 2000 was really inspiring. With sponsorship from the National Commercial Bank and other Jamaican companies, the Jamaica Society (Leeds) organised this event for the thousands of people who attended from across the UK. They cooked all the food, they arranged the marquees coordinated the officials for the games and the security at the gate: everything was tightly organised by the members. Jamaica Day 2000 was like going home to Jamaica. That was an event that Jamaicans still speak about to this day." – *Delores Cooper, Community Relations Officer, Jamaican High Commission*

Members of the Society share similar reflections of Jamaica Day 2000 and often refer to it as the most memorable event that the Society has put on in its twenty-five year history.

"The most memorable day would be for me, the Jamaica Day 2000. We had a full day of activities because it was the millennium year. The preparation for it was enormous. A lot of work went into that but it was thoroughly enjoyable." – *Bev Lattibeaudiere*

"Jamaica Day was most memorable. A lot of really, really hard work went into it. Most of the members really pulled together for that. It took about three to four weeks of preparation. Then on the day, we had to entertain the many coaches of Jamaicans who came from all over the country. The park was also packed with different people from other Caribbean countries: for example, St. Kitts, Barbados and Trinidad…just to hear the comments that people were making about the day; how enjoyable it was and that this should happen more often." – *Irene Henry*

"When we had Jamaica Day, people of all sorts gathered there. It was of some significance. We were doing something in the community and for the community. I think it was a good thing. Things like these help the reputation of the Jamaica Society." – *Edley White*

"Jamaica Day was a beautiful day. I made hats - crocheted, cloth and fur ones and I went down there to sell them. I sold £80 worth of hats. I would have done more but I was in a bad spot up on the hill. A lot of people have been looking forward to it happening again." – *Mavis Cole*

"I enjoyed the Jamaica Day 2000. It was a big event down by the park, and it was really good. It was a beautiful day, everybody took part in it. It was brilliant!!! The games they had on the day, it was like being back in school in Jamaica, and the kids were running for prizes and things like that. It was good." – *Francis Williams*

"Jamaica Day 2000, nobody has ever seen anything like that except for the Carnival. It is like the best thing that ever happened to us. I think the Society benefited from the publicity of this event." – *Samuel Barrett*

Jamaica Day 2000 was about putting the Jamaican culture on display - a tribute to Jamaican people's talent and creativity.

A Dedicated Membership

Each recollection is a testament to the steadfastness of the Society's members, and demonstrates that there is no limit to their generosity and their commitment to building a better community for themselves and for future generations. A member of the community who has been supportive of the work of the Society, Father Alan Taylor, city councillor and Canon of the St. Aidan Anglican Church in Roundhay, believes that the Society's contribution to the community has been enormous.

"Through particular individuals [such as] Travis Johnson [and others]… there's quite a list of very able people in the Jamaican community who have enriched the life not only in the church, but enriched the life of the city. Collectively, Jamaica Society has done an enormous amount of good. It's given a lot of Jamaicans and nationals from other countries, a place where they feel they can belong. They are very much linked to the community through pastoral visiting and linked to so many other organisations throughout the city - it is remarkable - and that is at every level, which is very, very pleasing." – *Father Alan Taylor*

Veryl Harriott thinks the Society reflects its name by linking effectively the Jamaican people living overseas to do voluntary work to help people here in Leeds and in Jamaica. The Society is equally aware that the road to progress has had its challenges.

In her report to the 1988 Annual General Meeting, past Chairperson Lizette Powell described the road that the Society has travelled: "The Jamaica Society (Leeds) is a prime example of achievements in a variety of pursuits and activities, but this is not to say we have not had our share of problems and perplexities but we faced them with strength and confidence in the future." For some members being a well constituted organisation is one of its achievements, having never contravened any of its laws and principles. The Society has never failed to have its Annual General Meeting around May each year. Paulette Simpson in her years of working with the Society as a member of the Jamaican business community has made the following observation about the Society: "It is of vital importance to reiterate that where a lot of organisations struggle is on strong leadership, and having a good vibrant Executive Committee and the Jamaica Society (Leeds) does not have that sort of problem."

The Society kept charting a progressive course, because each person who has held its highest office has served unstintingly and commendably. They have been able to marshal the energies and talents of its members towards the common good of the Society to the extent that it has had enormous meaning to each one.

"The Jamaica Society is very important because I can always get information from here about stuff that is happening in Jamaica. I feel comfortable because I am among my own people. When I come here it feels like home. I am happy being among my people. It contributes a lot to my life really, it makes me feel at home." – *Jerome Brown*

"With the Jamaica Society (Leeds), you feel as though you belong. It is a good place to be and whenever it's possible, I'll do what I can for it." – *Allen Ebanks*

"You know you can come to the Society and meet your own people. You know you are welcome. You don't have the feeling like when you walk into a pub that you have never been to, you start to look around you to see if you know anyone. But with the Society, you know you are among your own and you are among your family. I have made so many friends there." – *Samuel Barrett*

"The Jamaica Society (Leeds) is for any Jamaican or any West Indian in the area (and I just don't want to single out Jamaicans), who want to be involved in a social way with other West Indians, share their problems and to be in their company. I think that this is what the Jamaica Society does and does very well." – *Glen English*

"Jamaica Society (Leeds) have a lovely set of people; they are very warm and they are willing to share information with you. I find there are benefits when we come together as one people who share a common culture. We are able to find out what is happening here and in Jamaica. The Society adds to the social aspects of my life. There is a positive feeling. We are involved with issues about black people and knowledge of our rights. It builds your confidence up as well. It's all about community relations, really." – *June Wood*

"I think that the Society is a pillar of the community. Within Chapeltown they liase with the police, Social Services and with others." – *Yvonne English*

"I have got to know new people and made new friends. Officials come from Jamaica and we get to see and chat to them. If we were in Jamaica we would not have the chance to meet with them. We get to go places which if we weren't in the Jamaica Society we would not have got to go there. We get to hear them talk about what is going on in Jamaica." – *Lynford and Norma Fletcher*

"The Jamaica Society (Leeds) is the happy circulation of people. You meet people and you can talk to people and you feel like you are at home again. So therefore, it is very comforting. Once you get involved in it is very hard to get out of it. It is like a postage stamp sticking to an envelope. I enjoy it very much." – *Roy Mitchell*

"The Jamaica Society (Leeds) has been part of my life for the past twenty-five years. I think at times, I get very emotional when speaking about the Society. Certainly, because we came from Jamaica or are of Jamaican origin and we are able to share in a common way of life and history. We are afforded the opportunity of receiving Jamaican visitors, dignitaries and friends. The thing that has truly inspired me over the years, is the loyalty and commitment of our members, ensuring that the Jamaica Society (Leeds) is an organisation, of which one can be justly proud." – *Travis Johnson*

"As a single person, I see the organisation as supporting you if you are ill and if you pass away you are guaranteed a decent burial. It also brings people together. We also have a place where we can sit down and reminisce. If you want to have a decent social there is somewhere you can go, because at the moment there are not a lot of places in the area where people of a certain age can go and relax and don't feel threatened." – *Councillor Norma Hutchinson*

"The importance of being a member of the Jamaica Society is the companionship between all the Society's members especially the women, and finding people who are likeminded to be in contact with, to discuss light hearted matters or to talk about a problem. You also gain other knowledge and skills that you never had before. The more I have found out about the Society, the more grateful I have felt towards the founding members. Because they had the foresight to have the concept of the Jamaica Society and to work so hard to get this present building and to bring the Society to what it is today." – *Bev Lattibeaudiere*

"I've always been proud of where I have come from and who I am. I'm a Jamaican. Being a member of the Society has helped me to reinforce that. The best experience of being a part of this Society is seeing it grow, meeting many people and sharing in the different experiences over the years." – *Elizabeth Johnson*

"Because of my involvement with so many different West Indian people, I didn't want to join something that says, 'I am a Jamaican, I belong to the Jamaica Society'. I was trying to say we should form something together as West Indians. But over the years I sat and listened and started to read between the lines and I realised it was the right thing to join the Society. I believe the Society is like a security for us as Jamaicans. The first place that I would think of getting a reference would be from the Jamaica Society. One of the things I'm proud to know is that I am a member. I try to encourage people to come and to be a part of it." – *Robert Chrouch*

"I say suppose there wasn't a Jamaica Society what would happen to me? I hardly go anywhere now. I find the Society useful in that I can go there and meet a few friends and have a good meal. When I first came to England in the 50s, there was no such thing as a Jamaica Society where you can go to find a few friends… It serves a good purpose, the Jamaica Society as it is now, because you go there and you explain that you are a stranger and you just come, they would help you and give you advice. *I tell yuh something fi nothing*, I think the Jamaica Society has one of the best set of people that ever came to England, the amount they contribute each time at the meetings because they like the Jamaica Society and they want to keep it going - is a lot." – *Edley White*

"The Society has opened up my mind to many things. It has allowed me to speak up and to express myself, which I wouldn't normally have the chance to do. Before that, when I wasn't a member, I wasn't too outgoing. I think the Society has done a great deal for me in that way. It gives me confidence." – *Florence Williams*

"It's a very good organisation. It's definitely where we black people can come and have a talk with someone who will listen to us. The Society has helped many people in the community as well. There aren't many black organisations that cater for you but you can depend on the Jamaica Society for their help." – *Icyline Parker*

"I think that the Jamaica Society has played a very positive role in developing the image of Jamaica and Jamaicans. The Society presents an image and an identity that is very strong. It is very organised and is very caring of its community and its surroundings. I do think that one thing that people do expect when it comes to the Jamaica Society, whether it's an event, whether it's general meetings, is a certain degree of quality. The Society is homely and welcoming. They have good food, their intentions are well meaning. Another word that I'd use to describe the Society is developmental." – *Susan Pitter*

"The benefits of being a member of the Jamaica Society is that as Jamaicans, we are giving something back that can help people from my country and also people within the community. By doing so, it gives me extra sense of self-fulfilment. I also get to share experiences with the members and to listen to what they've gone through over the years. So I feel that it is more like a family than a Society, because of the things that we do when we do get together, which is very family oriented. When I think of the Jamaica Society the words that come to mind is that the members are very proud, very active, very conscientious, very hard working people who are willing to pursue the goals we want to attain." – *Theresa Condor*

"I have gained a lot of experience from being a member of the Society. I got the chance to meet a lot of people through the Jamaica Society when I was there. Even though I live in the US, I try and still keep in touch with them. When it is coming up to Independence Day, I always get in touch with the Society, if I don't get them I always leave a message there. I contact them every New Year, they can always expect my phone call." – *Finley Wray*

Close associates of the Society share similar views to that of its membership.

"The relationship that the Society has is that of a family. The Society always delivers and when Jamaican government ministers visit the UK, they always come to Leeds. We have a set of people in Leeds who contribute to their community." – *Paulette Simpson*

The Jamaica Society (Leeds) has earned the reputation as being family oriented and family like because of the types of assistance it gives to its communities in the UK and Jamaica. It caters for people without families in the UK and the elderly, and it provides many with a sense of security that there is someone looking out for their welfare and interest. The maintenance of cultural links through its activities ranks high among its members who take pride in their Jamaican heritage and culture - creating an atmosphere where people can meet new friends and achieve a sense of belonging. The Society provides the unique opportunity to interact with Jamaican dignitaries, exposing its community to public figures they would not have had the chance to meet under normal circumstances.

Such interactions and diversity of activities have aided members in their personal development and have opened their minds to bigger and better possibilities. Members have acquired skills that they have not had before through their involvement. The Society is important to the members as a source of information for news and developments in Jamaica and to disseminate information on issues affecting the Caribbean community in the UK. It stands out as a pillar of the community and the dedication of its hardworking membership is an inspiration to many.

Two eminent Jamaican historians, Sir Philip Sherlock and Hilary Bennett wrote that a cultural transformation and a national movement were the revolutionary forces that shaped independent Jamaica. For the members of the Jamaican Society (Leeds), their revolutionary forces were their national and cultural identity, spiritual values and "ancestral memories", which were used to transform their community. These cultural elements worked as a combined buffer against the race and class-conscious society that has become their adopted home. But with the Jamaica Society (Leeds), the boundaries of race and class cease to be self-conscious factors. The Society has become a symbolic refuge from the larger pressures of otherness that have coloured the Jamaicans' experiences since their arrival in the UK.

At the heart of the membership of the Jamaica Society (Leeds) is a spirit of collectiveness and dedication. They have put into practice Norman Manley's belief that 'collective effort and involvement are absolutely necessary to turn personal values and beliefs into realities.'

But the Society had a bigger achievement to celebrate.

Chapter 3

Tributes to the Society's First Chairperson

Lizette Powell, JP, SRN, SCM, HV

"I first met Lizette Powell in 1964, when I worked for the same organisation. This was the start of over thirty-five years of close association. I was never sure if it was because we both had freckles, why a lot of people thought we were actually siblings. The many years of close working relationship and understanding of each other, probably made getting together with our fellow co-founders a fairly easy preposition in setting up the Jamaica Society (Leeds). She was a devoted Chairperson of the Society for twenty-two years, therefore she was involved in all aspects of the Society's development. Lizette was very keen to see the Society have a home of its own and she worked tirelessly to ensure that Jamaica House was firmly established. As Chairperson, she ensured that the business of the Society was conducted in accordance with the Constitution. Lizette was also a founding member of the Leeds Sickle Cell Society and Community Action and Support Against Crime (CASAC)." – *Travis Johnson*

"Mrs. Powell has worked tremendously hard especially on Jamaica House. When she started as the Chairperson it was so hard for her that time, because that time there was no building. She and Mrs. Johnson lost sleep minutely and hourly to raise money for this building." – *Louise Reid*

"Mrs. Powell was a very nice person to me, I miss her very much. She started with this Society when there were a few people. I want to send greetings to her in St. Elizabeth. She helped me with my passport and other little things." – *Neville Atkins*

"Mrs. Powell was part of the backbone of the Society. But the thing that touched me the most about her is the calm and loving way that she was able to bring people together, and the love that she showed to people throughout the time that she was here. Also, she really worked especially in the early days on this building. The way she worked in this place was one of the things that touched me. She rolled up her sleeves and worked like everybody else – that made me join the Society just to support her. Plus she had insisted that I had to be a part of the Society. I have to mention the unity between her, Travis and Betsy Johnson and Nettie White, it was something else. We are proud that we have these people leading us. It has really strengthened my faith in this Society. Although she is not here now I still respect her. I feel she is still a part of the Society. She is not here in body but she is here in spirit." – *Robert Chrouch*

"My impression of Mrs. Powell is that she was very hardworking and a very conscientious lady. She has given a lot of her time to the Society and other people in the community as well. Her major contribution to the Society was working to develop it in the early years. I have listened to stories that people have told how she had helped them in their distress and was always the first one there." – *Irene Henry*

"Mrs. Powell always had nice and kind words to say to me. The day when my husband passed on she came to the house and sat with me, and the next day she came with a bouquet. She was always pleasant." – *Francis Williams*

"Mrs. Powell is a very nice lady to talk to. She was always there for you anything you wanted you could talk to her. When my husband died she was right beside me all the time. We miss her."
– *Phyllis Hines*

"I say Mrs. Powell's name over and over because when my husband was sick, she was there when I really needed somebody to be there for me. The thing is, I didn't ask her to be there. It just happened automatically. When I rushed out to do my shopping and came back and saw her sitting there with my husband, I would say, 'Well there is somebody up there looking after me'."
– *Elma Davis*

"Liz and I used to work closely together. We used to meet a lot at each other's homes and worked late throughout the night. I used to go over to her house and I would be leaving her house sometimes at 1am. Liz was very hardworking and she took what she needed to do seriously. She would put her all into it and she believed in the Society. So whatever it took, she did it. She didn't just devote her time and energy but her finances as well; we used our phones, our cars and anything to get the job done. Before we got Jamaica House and we would use other places to hold our meetings, sometimes we would have to roll up our sleeves and scrub the facilities before the meetings started. But we did it joyfully. We used to meet a lot of time at Nettie or Ruby Lewis's house after we had a function. I remember how we would sit around on the floor and count the pennies we made from the functions and balance our expenditure. We had some good times." – *Elizabeth Johnson*

Remembering the late Errol James MBE, JP
Founding Member

Errol James arrived in the United Kingdom in 1944, as a member of the Royal Air Force and therefore served in the Second World War. I first met Errol in the late 1960s. He served on a number of Boards, Councils and Committees. He served as Chairman of the Leeds Community Relations Council (later known as Leeds Racial Equality Council) for over 20 years. Errol was an experienced and skilled negotiator, a splendid Chairperson, one who was most knowledgeable of procedures in the conduct of meetings. Errol was a founding member of the Jamaica Society (Leeds) and was involved in the drafting of its Constitution. He was also a founding member of the Leeds Caribbean Cricket Club, United Caribbean Association, Leeds West Indian Centre and Community Action and Support Against Crime, and was instrumental in the setting up of the Leeds Equipment Service. He was appointed Governor of approximately six Central Middle Schools and Park Lane College. In 1977, Errol was awarded the Queen's Silver Jubilee Medal for services to the community. He served as a Justice of the Peace in Leeds, and was awarded an MBE for his services to the Community and Race Relations. In 1986, he was appointed to the Lord Chancellor Advisory Committee, the body which interviewed and recommended appointments to the Bench. Errol liked and adhered to punctuality. He believed that agendas of business should be transacted and presented in reasonable time before meetings. Errol could be described as one who committed his life to helping individuals and the community at large. He was a jovial person and enjoyed social events and occasions. The community at large mourned his untimely death in 1994.

Errol James

Tribute by Travis Johnson, Chairman and Founding Member

A Journey Through Our History

Robert Chrouch spent 36 years working in the chemical industry in Leeds.

Francis Williams owner of Dunns River Cafe has received a number of awards for her business endeavour.

Glen English as an RAF Serviceman in 1944

Samuel Barrett was encouraged by his friends to abandon his farming endeavours in Jamaica for more lucrative prospects in the UK, and he did so in 1956.

Allen Ebanks as a transport sector worker, a field he worked in for over 30 years.

Elizabeth Johnson like scores of other Jamaican women made an invaluable contribution to the UK Health Sector.

Ratrica 'Nettie' White arrived from Jamaica in 1958, and later trained as a nurse at Killingbeck Hospital.

Councillor Norma Hutchinson, the first Jamaican city councillor.

Joseph Parker, Lay Preacher at St. Aidan Church in Leeds: A significant appointment for Caribbean people. Initially rejected by the mainstream churches, they formed their own black majority churches.

Susan Pitter, the city's first Lady Mayoress of colour and of Jamaican descent, 2000-01.

Founding Members: *[above] Four of six founding members [l-r] Travis Johnson, Nettie White, Elizabeth Johnson and Yvonne English. Absent are Lizette Powell [resident in Jamaica] and Errol James [deceased].*

Early Members: *[above] Early Executive Committee members of the Jamaica Society (Leeds) and the Choir [below].*

Travis Johnson (left), chairperson of the Society with Jamaican Prime Minister the Honourable PJ Patterson, ON, PC, QC, MP (centre) and High Commissioner, the Hon. David Muirhead, OJ, QC, 1999 to 2002 on the PM's first visit to Leeds.

His Excellency the Most Honourable Sir Howard Cooke, ON, GCMG, GCVO, CD on his second visit to Leeds in 2002 with the Society's oldest living member, Edley White.

High Commissioner Ellen Bogle 1989 to 1994 on her first visit to the Jamaica Society (Leeds)

High Commissioner Derek Heaven 1994 to 1999 (centre) at the presentation of the Deeds to Jamaica House with Fabian Hamilton, MP (left) and Roy Mitchell, member (right).

Three of the Society's most dedicated members: Icyline Parker (left), Maisie Pinnock (centre) and Audrey Henry (right) at the 25th Anniversary Ball, one of the fundraising events they can enjoy without working tirelessly in the kitchen.

Two of the Society's most loyal supporters: Paulette Simpson (left), chief representative of Jamaica National Building Society and Delores Cooper (right), community relations officer at the Jamaican High Commission.

Jamaica Day 2000: Children's Tug-O-War event.

The treasurer, Lynford Fletcher serves up an excellent Jamaican brew to one of the thousands of patrons at Jamaica Day 2000.

Photo Spread

The late Egbert Williams (centre) Jamaican workman speaks to HRH Prince Charles on his visit to Jamaica House on December 2, 1987 during the renovation periods

The Hon Louise Bennett-Coverley, OJ (Miss Lou) visits Jamaica House in 1991. Her visit to Leeds in 1977 kicked started the initiative to start the Jamaica Society (Leeds).

Four Generations of Jamaicans at Jamaica House: *Yvonne Hylton (left) with daughter Marcia (second left), grandson, Dean (second from right) and her great grandson, Jahmai held by his mother Lola (right).*

Ann Elliot, one of the Society's young members.

Lincoln Cole volunteers to tend to the gardens at the Jamaica House along with Allen Ebanks.

Members of the Jamaica Society (Leeds) 1998: Committed, dedicated and hardworking.

ANCESTRAL ARCHITECTS

The first man walked into the building
Looked up and saw the stars.
He read them
As ancestors - The Dogon
The Cosmos spoke from afar

The woman's eyes sublime
Beheld a future monument...
A visionary's living proof;
While water cascaded down the walls
She saw the flag flying from the roof.

Like Imhotep
Creating Saqqara
The temple of many steps
These men and women
Did not see ruins as they stood
It was already home
Though not quite yet.
This was the start
Of a place to be shaped
From their tears, blood and sweat.

They called out to their village
The response came in throngs
Steeped in day work tradition
Donating muscle, food and songs

Disbelievers lay unreasonable conditions
Stipulations rained like hailstones
But culture well versed in adversity
Has stubbornness soaked in its bones

The village worked
With odds stacked against them
They used brains when money ran out
From pardner, bring and buy to dances
Till, my dear,

When you hear from the shout…
Those very same said nay sayers
Haffe tek han' an' kibber dem mout'!

For rising like the phoenix from ashes
Three storeys high with a nice piece of land
They came and saw what we had conquered
Those officials middle, low and grand…

Hands shook with such energy at the Opening
Congratulations flowed like a spending spree
Everyone had a story to tell how this venture started
And their part in how it came to be

Silently watching
The ancestral architects
Let the building speak for itself
The plumbing, the plaster, the painting
Each door knob, window sill and shelf
Polished…
Every speck of dust removed
Standing totem to their burning desires
They knew they had not a thing to prove

They watched as their place was opened
Fit to burst with a national pride
Planned from discipline and determination
Prayed the walls be Eternally blessed
Both in and outside

Honouring well-planted footsteps
Staking claim to this piece of soil
Erected on grounds of independence
Fierce pride and good honest toil

With hands and hearts of conviction
These architects and builders point the way
To what it takes to lay a foundation
What it truly means to pave the way.

MarvaB © 2003

REFLECTIONS OF A JAMAICAN ELDER

Time past...

We look back with nostalgia that we hope to recall

    Time future...

We look forward with anticipation that may never be

        Time present ...

It is the only opportune moment for me around here

            Time in reality...

It creates a place like Jamaica House for the community;

Jamaica House creates entertainment for everybody; the most enjoyable dinners, dances and outings.

Edley White, 81
© 2001

4 A Place of Our Own

The history of Jamaica House is a remarkable account of cooperation and community spirit. The members of the Jamaica Society (Leeds) renovated Jamaica House on the firm foundation of their national cultural heritage. The process by which the members of the Society acquired and renovated the building, can be seen as a wonderful tribute to the energy of solidarity and teamwork behind the institution of free villages that marked post emancipation Jamaica. The freedmen and women of Jamaica got together and helped each other to build free villages across the island in order to retain their independence from the plantation owners. Sherlock and Bennett's assessment of this period in Jamaica's history reveals its significance to the Jamaican community in Leeds: "In these early years are to be found the source of empowerment and ennoblement…and efforts … to triumph over what appeared to be insuperable obstacles."

Though the members of the Society were unwittingly paying homage to this system, what is certain, is that the struggle for self-reliance and self-progress is deeply rooted in the national character of the Jamaican people. Many of the members of the Jamaica Society (Leeds) grew up in Jamaica when the ethos of the Jamaican worker was being defined by Labour Movement Leader, Sir Alexander Bustamante. The words he spoke in 1938 still echo in the bones of Jamaican people today.

> "…what I preach to you is love and unity and fellowship. Work for a better Jamaica and a prosperous people." *(Speech: Race Course - June 22, 1938)*

They were no longer on the shores of Jamaica, but Bustamante's words were relevant to this set of Jamaicans whose individual quest for prosperity was transformed into a collective vision to ensure their success as a community.

The Jamaica Society (Leeds) started with the six founding members meeting in the front room of Nettie White's home. As the organisation gained considerable support from the Jamaican community, their stability rested not on securing a firm membership base (three years after its inception they had one hundred members), but on acquiring a headquarters from which the Society could operate. For the first twelve years of the Society's life, their meetings and social events were held at a number of venues in and around the Chapeltown and Harehills areas. They met or socialised in the "little cabin" at the Harehills County Primary School, the Harehills Nursery, Barrack Road Centre, St. Martin's Institute, Harambee House, the West Indian Centre and other community amenities. The lack of a permanent operation base did not curtail the Society's activities, in fact, as an organisation dedicated to community service the Jamaica Society (Leeds) was and still is, exemplary. But the years of moving from one location to the next, took its toll. It was very clear that new and existing community facilities were not enough. Indisputably, their principal goal was to find a place of their own.

Chapter 4

Laying the Foundations

By 1982, the Society had identified a building at 190 Chapeltown Road and entered into negotiations with the City Council to rent or acquire the building. If their application was considered favourably, the Society requested that the City Council should first renovate the building that was in a desperate state of disrepair. The identification of the building came after Executive members had viewed more than their fair share of dilapidated buildings. Between 1982 and 1983, a flurry of letters were sent to the City Council, during which time the Society was assured that it would get the building. On one occasion, Lizette Powell and Elizabeth Johnson attended a meeting only to discover that other community organisations were bidding for the building. It was clearly a disheartening moment, while other groups were declaring how much funds they had, the Society could not, because it did not have that kind of cash outlay. But that information was closely guarded.

> "Lizette and I used to actually drive around and look for big empty buildings. There was one on Grange Avenue and one on Louis Street that we looked at and considered. We saw this empty building on Chapeltown Road and we rang up and asked if it were available. They invited us to collect the key in order to take a look at the building. We collected the key and tramped around this dusty old building and we said, 'Yes, the possibility is here'. So, we came back and met with the members who basically said, 'Yes, we would love to have the building'. We asked the Council if we could have it at peppercorn rent with a view to buy because we had no money.
>
> "While we were waiting to hear if we had this building, we got this letter to meet with councillors at Chapeltown Community Centre. We thought we were just going to be meeting with these people to finalise things. When we got to the meeting, the hall was basically full. Different community groups were present, and it was quite a formal meeting. We sat down to listen to what was happening. We suddenly felt like we were all bidding for this building. One of the things they said was that each person was supposed to get up and talk about their group and talk about what their finances were like. People got up and did that. But we said there is no way we are going to publicly discuss our financial situation, because the letter that we received did not indicate that this was what we were attending the meeting for. Basically, we felt we were being pitted against each other and it wasn't nice. I think we left the meeting before it was finished."
> – *Elizabeth Johnson*

On September 9, 1984, the Society's frustration was further compounded by an incident that made it very clear to all its members that they needed to purchase their own building. It was no longer a desire but an imperative.

"When one looks back over the years at the number of venues that we used to have meetings, it was to a certain extent bouncing from pillar to post and we were told we could meet here but you had to leave at a certain time. There was a situation where a group of our members, mainly Executive members, were meeting for another organisation which the Jamaica Society was instrumental in setting up, the Sickle Cell Society, and a member of a certain organisation turned the light off and asked the members to leave. That was a painful experience. As Jamaicans, we are proud people, and that sort of behaviour is not the one we would tolerate. I remember when the Executive and the General Meeting met, we told ourselves that had we had our own building, nobody could have done that to us. I think in many ways that is one of the things that pushed us to get our own place." – *Travis Johnson*

"We were using the Local Authority premises by the Harehills CP School and another premises in Leeds that was there for the Caribbean people to use. Once we went to a meeting there and the light was turned off on us from the main switch. We said that would never happen to us again, we made sure that we had something of our own, not only our own but for other people to share." – *Yvonne English*

According to the General Meeting minutes for September 9, 1984, the Sickle Cell meeting took place at the venue in question just hours before the monthly General Meeting. The person who turned off the light said he had had his 'bellyful of Jamaicans coming here to burn the lights and not supporting the club.' The Society sent a letter of complaint, and the Management Committee of the venue expressed its apologies and promised to take disciplinary action against the person who exhibited the malicious behaviour.

This incident led to a serious discussion about purchasing a building and particularly, how many fundraising events the Society would need in order to raise enough money. There were suggestions that members could make interest free loans to the Society or donations of £50 each. The annual membership fee was raised to £2.50 as another way of getting as much money as possible.

And if the year could not have got any worse, the November General Meeting was informed that they had lost the bid for the building at 190 Chapeltown Road: the Council needed it for another more urgent project. This was a blow to the Society. The disappointing news came after two years of continuous dialogue with the Council and of sending letters back and forth. What seemed like firm assurances eventually turned out to be empty promises. The Society was back at the beginning. Nonetheless, the Society members felt that if they were serious about acquiring a building they needed a core group of individuals who would commit their time to finding one. A number of individuals volunteered to form a Building Project Sub-committee: Travis Johnson (as the co-ordinator), George Eubanks, Alburn Patterson, Yvonne Bovell-English,

Lizette Powell, Lynford Fletcher, Roy Powell and Nettie White. They were to work closely with the Fundraising Sub-committee on all financial matters pertaining to the purchase of a building. The plan at this stage was to send letters to all the councillors and the Housing Authorities to inform them that the Society was interested in purchasing any available property on Louis Street or Chapeltown Road.

The New Year began with good news. At the General Meeting on January 20, 1985, Lizette Powell reported that the Society had received a letter from the Housing Department indicating that a building on 277 Chapeltown Road was for sale and viewing permission was granted. The Chairperson told the members that the building had "ten rooms, a basement, a stone built frontage, large garden but the roof had tiles missing". The news was received enthusiastically. In the spirit of unity and generosity, a number of members made on-the-spot donations which totalled £49. They were Roy and Lizette Powell, Errol James, Yvonne Bovell- English, Kenneth Robinson, Alva Heron and Ashley Johnson - they knew that *one, one coco full basket*. This Jamaican proverb sustained the Society throughout the fundraising efforts for the building. It was the Building Project's official motto. At the meeting, it was also agreed that all subsequent funds that had been raised from social events, a substantial portion should go towards the Building Project.

As more and more members viewed the property, it became clear that they had purchased a building that required a great deal of work.

> "Having earlier failed to purchase and gain ownership of 190 Chapeltown Road, we were still trying hard to find a property that would meet our requirements. We were informed that the property at 277 Chapeltown Road, owned by the Local Authority was available for sale. We viewed the building which was in a very poor state of repair. It was obvious when we viewed the building, that only two floors of it had been used in recent years, the basement and second floors had been sealed off. The building was viewed by a substantial number of our members. Some felt that it was dilapidated and would cost far too much to make good. Others felt that because we needed a building of our own, we should purchase it and make good the repairs. A majority of our members were in favour of us acquiring the building, so we entered into negotiations with the Local Authority to secure the building. There were other factors to take into consideration. We had limited finances and to purchase a building in better state of repair would require a substantial layout that we could not afford. A fair number of our members were trades persons and could help with the repairs of the building. Also, if the repairs were to be financed over a number of years, it would be easier for our members to provide the necessary finance." – *Travis Johnson*

"When we didn't have any place to meet we met in a caravan in the Harehills CP School and then at the West Indian Centre. And lo and behold, the Jamaica Society purchased a place at 277 Chapeltown Road. It was one big decision that the Jamaica Society had taken. Coming to the meeting and hearing this and hearing that, we all decided like one big family to buy this place. Before that, when they got this place, it was really in shambles; it wasn't fit to put hens in, it was just one broken down place." – *Roy Mitchell*

"The first Saturday we came to look at the building, we had never seen so much muck in all our lives. God help us! The muck! Every time we look at the wall in the hall – we can still remember the green mark we saw coming down the side of the wall that day. There was no front door, there was no thoroughfare, and there was certainly no second floor. Only the men could climb up to what is now the second floor. They went up through a small hole to see what was up there. We tried to peep up through this hole in the ceiling, but we could not go any further than the top of the ladder." – *Nettie White and Elizabeth Johnson*

"I remember we were meeting in a wooden building at Harehills CP School and it was then that they had bought this building. When we came here to work on the building, I couldn't believe what I was seeing because you could look up and you could see all the stars and I thought they must be mad to purchase a building like this." – *Allen Ebanks*

"What I remember is that we had a look round at a number of places and this place was vacant, 277 Chapeltown Road. When we came up to look at the property and saw the state that it was in, my personal feeling was that it's going take us years to put right. But one of the gentlemen said, 'Once we've got this far, we'll make it.' We started pulling down and getting rid of all the old bits that were there. To see the work that had gone into putting it right and then to see that we've got this far - we've got a place of our own - it was just incredible. Everybody started talking about what different activities they would like to see there and that sort of thing."
– *Yvonne English*

With the majority of the members in favour of purchasing the building, the Executive members went ahead to negotiate the cost of the building. During the process of negotiation, the Society had to bear in mind that though they were promised the building it was still not certain that they would get it. The asking price was £17,000 and the Society's bank balance was still nowhere close to that amount.

"The building was like a hux (hollow structure) for when we went there water was coming down through the ceiling. People had stolen the tiles from off the building. God was good because it was pouring with rain when we went there with the Council. They wanted the same price for it and we told them, 'No! We couldn't pay that price for it because look at it!' So, we got it for less than the asking price." – *Lynford Fletcher*

"I recall during the time when we were negotiating the price for the building, we met a representative of the Local Authority at the building, luck was certainly on our side. It was raining heavily, water was pouring in because the roof was in such a poor state of repair. Interestingly, that strengthened our hand in negotiating the price downwards. We eventually agreed on a price - £9,000 - which was accepted by Leeds City Council. Although we had hoped to pay less for the building, we agreed on £9,000 in the confidence and belief in the ability of the membership of the Society to acquire the necessary funds to repair the building." – *Travis Johnson*

A Force of Unity

The fundraising machinery of the Society went into overdrive to raise the £9,000. A fundraising dinner at Harambee House raised about £300. A domino match at Harehills School, a fashion show with the young people, a coffee evening, a bazaar, the Carnival stall and Mrs. Reid's dinners and cake sales, all contributed to the fundraising effort for the Building Project that year. Nettie White, an Executive member began approaching financial institutions for loans, and the rejection from these institutions came fast and furious. At one of the General Meetings, a representative from a Jamaican owned financial institution in London gave a presentation to the members and also assured the Society that it was no problem getting a loan from his company. Sadly, that was an empty promise; the loan never materialised. Some members made good their word and offered interest free loans to the Society.

"When we decided to purchase the building, some members were willing to make loans available to the Society to facilitate the purchase. Those members who actually provided loans, were repaid shortly after the Society acquired the building." – *Travis Johnson*

"I was very much part of the development of this building. In fact, I remember that I was one of the first persons who said I would put my money up front to buy it, when we were talking about whether we should buy it or not. It was £200. They gave it back to me after." – *Glen English*

"We had asked the membership if they would loan us some money and some did. Some gave

> £250 or £300. The people who offered us the most was Rita and Dougie, their offer was substantial." – *Yvonne English*

A Building Fund was launched and the members suggested that as many members of the Jamaican community as possible should be asked to give a minimum of 50p towards the purchasing of the building. At each General Meeting leading up to the final purchase date, the Society collected between £100 to £300 because members were assiduously raising money from all quarters and putting money from their own resources into the kitty. Members started donating 50p per week or £2 per month.

Between January and August of 1985, the Society had numerous meetings with the Department of Industries and Estates to negotiate the purchase of 277 Chapeltown Road. The Deed of Trust was drawn up by the Society's solicitors and to ensure that the Council did not renege on its promise as with 190 Chapeltown Road, lobbying letters were sent to the city councillors to ensure that the Society would get the opportunity to purchase the building. What clinched the deal was a visit to the Society's own bank by Nettie White and Lizette Powell.

> "Mrs. Powell and I decided to go to Yorkshire Bank in town to see the manager and we got a loan. After all the rejections that we got, we went to the Yorkshire Bank, we explained what we wanted the loan for and they lent us. Just like that we got about £6,000." – *Nettie White*

> "We made the decision to purchase the building. We approached a number of finance companies for a loan to make the purchase. There were times when we had what appeared to be positive responses, only to be eventually disappointed, because we had not got any track record. At one of our meetings, Nettie White reminded us that we had not made an approach to our bank and suggested that we did so. Nettie White and Lizette Powell were the two officers who secured and kept the appointment with the bank. They returned with the joyful news that the bank had agreed to the advance of a loan to the Society. At the following monthly General Meeting, members were informed. The matter of repayment of the loan and cost of refurbishment of the building were discussed. Some members put forward the idea of a monthly donation. The suggestion was unanimously supported and agreed by members present at the meeting. It was agreed that each member would donate £2 monthly or what they could afford. It was agreed that it was a donation, and not a levy and should only be made if members wanted to do so. Some time later at the suggestion of members, the donation was increased to £4 monthly. When the loan was repaid, members suggested we continue the payment of the donation for the upkeep of Jamaica House." – *Travis Johnson*

Chapter 4

In November 1985, the membership was informed that the building was theirs. The final deal was closed in mid October. In the Building Sub-committee report to the General Meeting, the co-ordinator announced that the Society had hired an architect Barrie Fernandez, a Trinidadian who had been engaged and invited to submit plans for alterations She was able to get approval for the plans within record time; she was professional in her execution of tasks and efficient in her delivery of services.

With the building finally purchased, there was clearing up work to be done on site. This was the commencement of the Society's first sets of free work days. The partitions and chimney breast needed to be removed, the chimney stacks capped, and rubble and debris were to be cleared away. The members turned out in their numbers on Saturdays to assist free of cost with such work. As time went by, a few would turn up to do work in the evenings. Alburn Patterson volunteered to do the plastering and another member submitted estimates for the door and window frames repairs.

> "I didn't realise that we would have say reached to the stage we are today, but I still remember when we managed to get Jamaica House, we all knew that we would need a lot of hands on deck. In the beginning when they started working on the building, they would say there is going to be a work day, I arranged whenever time that was possible that I would participate in the work. I was ready, because I have a bit of experience in doing joinery and I knew then I could contribute my skills. At first we were digging, removing stuff, climbing on ladders to drill, you name it." – *Robert Chrouch*

> "I was the first man to shed blood in that place when it was being refurbished, and maybe the only one. I fell and cut on my leg when I was digging down the chimney." – *Lynford Fletcher*

> "We decided that we could do a lot of the work. We organised work days to remove partition walls and to clear rubbish. We were of the view that if we got the roof repaired and the windows made good, we could start using the building. We were able to secure a grant of £6,000, which enabled us to repair the roof. We agreed a price with a local joiner to repair the windows. He made a very poor job of the repairs. As a result, we had workdays on most Saturdays, both male and female members, trying to see how we could get the building to a stage where we would be able to use it." – *Travis Johnson*

However, it would not be until January 1986 that free work days would be held regularly. The work days that the Society had instituted were very much a Jamaican tradition called Day Work. It is a system whereby members within a community get together to complete a specific task such as digging, clearing a field or building a house. Sometimes, it is accompanied by singing and it has been said that many Jamaican folk songs originated from this tradition. Minus the folk songs, the members came out and did many of the tasks expected during a traditional Day Work.

With the roof and the balcony completed, and new windows and door frames fitted, the Society was faced with the monumental task of raising sufficient funds to complete the total refurbishment of the building. The Society began to look for grants. The first application was to the Yorkshire County Council which awarded the Society £15,000. Other grant options presented themselves, but the Society had to finish preparatory work on the building by March 31, 1987 in order to qualify for these grants.

> "We were given an estimate of £90,000 to renovate the building. Our next approach for financial assistance was to the Local Authority. We secured an appointment with the Leader of Leeds City Council. We told him what was the estimated cost of making the building good. I remember him saying to us: 'Well, that's a lot of money. Why do you want to spend all that money on that building? We could let you have one not much further up the road at peppercorn rent'. Our response to him was: 'You know, Mr. Mudie (who was the Leader of Leeds City Council), in Jamaica, where we come from, there is a saying which goes, *Mother has, Father has, God blesses the child that has its own*. We were after a building that we could call our own.' He told us that the Local Authority could not help with that amount of money. However, if they were able to help, it could only be done within a partnership.
>
> "At the same time, Sight & Sound, a City Centre based training centre was interested in establishing an annexe in the Chapeltown area. I was approached and asked if I knew of any suitable accommodation for the project. We approached the Government Task Force Office and informed them that we would be prepared to provide accommodation to Sight & Sound, if they would assist us with funds to refurbish the building at 277 Chapeltown Road. After a lengthy discussion, the Government Task Force agreed that they would be prepared to fund the refurbishment, jointly with another funding body. We remembered what the Leader of City Council had said, so we went back to him with the Task Force proposal. A partnership was firmly established between the Government Task Force, Leeds City Council and the Jamaica Society (Leeds). The grants from these funding bodies, along with the generous donations from our members, provided the required amount of funds to refurbish the building." – *Travis Johnson*

A letter dated October 16, 1986 outlines the Society's proposal to the Task Force regarding the operation of the Sight & Sound annexe in the Chapeltown area.

> Although Sight & Sound operates from the City Centre, unfortunately it does not attract trainees from the Harehills and Chapeltown area. Drawing on the Toxteth, Liverpool experience, it is not only desirable but essential that a branch of the college be established in Chapeltown/Harehills... As no doubt, you are aware Harehills/Chapeltown is an economically deprived area, with deepening unemployment. A substantial number of parents have been made redundant over the years, therefore they are not in a position to finance their offspring in this type of training. Indeed, this type of training would enhance the employment prospect of young people from this area.

The Task Force was set up as an innercity initiative by the Department of Trade and Industry to stimulate growth, to create business enterprise and employment in economically disadvantaged areas such as Chapeltown and Harehills. The Society wanted to ensure that the building that they had acquired would become part of this developmental scheme. Also at the root of the desire to own their own building was the need to contribute to the advancement of their community. Their building along with their charitable endeavours would serve that purpose.

It was not all smooth sailing after the meeting with the Leader of the City Council. Their application for the £90,000 that was promised to the Society under the Urban Programme was refused, even after having secured the funding with the Task Force. The Society took up the matter with elected members of the Council so that their application could be reviewed. On account of the Executive members' dogged persistence, the sum was eventually allocated. But a great deal of energy had gone in to ensuring that an approval was secured. Clinton Cameron who worked the Urban Programme proved to be an invaluable ally during that bleak period.

> "There was resentment from some organisations about the Government Task Force being in Chapeltown. Somehow there appeared to be a stigma attached to the Task Force. Some held the view that projects should not be funded via Task Force. We saw nothing wrong with this method of funding. As taxpayers, our members were contributing to the Exchequer's Purse and had been afforded the opportunity of benefiting through the Government Task Force. We had never regretted going into partnership with the Government Task Force and the Leeds City Council. We firmly believe that the community has benefited from that partnership." – *Travis Johnson*

In February 1987, the Society reached an agreement with the Task Force. In April of that year the contracts were signed. Though the Society wanted a Community Programme from the Chapeltown/ Harehills areas to undertake the job of refurbishment, the Task Force recommended another contractor to carry out the work. The Task Force also promised that local labourers from the Chapeltown/Harehills area would be engaged as well.

> "Following the 1981 disorders and the Scarman Inquiry, it was decided that the government would put some money into Chapeltown to create work. They created this Community Programme - the idea being that any work done in Chapeltown under the Task Force would be by local labourers. When work was supposed to be done on this building, big contractors were brought in from outside along with their labourers and very little work was given to the people of Chapeltown." – *Elizabeth Johnson*

Going along with this decision would later prove to be regrettable. The refurbishing work on the building commenced on June 1, 1987. The Building Project Sub-committee took a hands on approach - making numerous site visits and ordering materials. 1987 would be the year when the Chairperson would declare that "the Society had more meetings than hot dinners." Unfortunately, many more meetings were to come.

As work on the premises seemed to progress, the Society became disheartened by the shoddy workmanship. The situation on the site became tense when members of the Society started to discover the cover up. The architect backed the Society in their formal protest to the Task Force about their 'highly recommended' building contractors. In a report to the General Meeting, the Building Sub-committee stated that 'the poor quality of workmanship carried out by the agency was disastrous. This was due to improper supervision of staff and lack of co-operation between the [contractors] and its workers with the Society. Most of all, there was a 33% wastage on the job.'

> "When work on the building finally got started, it was under the Community Programme Scheme. Task Force introduced us to Teamwork, who in turn introduced us to a company based in Barnsley. Shortly after they commenced the contract, we realised that the standard of work they produced, fell far below the standard we expected. They often tried to cover up the poor workmanship. We were fortunate that one of our members, Egbert Williams was employed by Teamwork as a site labourer and kept a watching brief on what was happening. (Unfortunately, Egbert passed away a few years ago.) Whenever, Lizette or myself turned up on the site, he would meet us at the gate and would say for example, 'you need to look at X window sill or such and such an area'. We would then point it out to the foreman. They wondered how we were able to find out where their shoddy work was. It was so good that we had a member like him on site. Interestingly, they were not aware of how we could find out about their shoddy work. Eventually, we managed and were glad to see the back of these contractors because members of the Society knew better and were not willing to accept shoddy workmanship. Eventually, the project was completed by the Society engaging skilled tradesmen from the Chapeltown/Harehills area; men who were willing to provide good workmanship." – *Travis Johnson*

Once again, the members came to the rescue. All the men who had skills in the relevant areas gave their advice and their time to rectify the problems. The free work days activities were intensified. On any one of those days as many as twenty members or more, turned out to assist. Three members who were skilled craftsmen were contracted to complete aspects of the work.

"The thing is this, Mr. Johnson and Mrs. Powell, they decided to get rid of the people who were doing it and bring in our own Jamaican and Caribbean workmen to do the refurbishing: carpentry, joinery, the masonry, plastering and painting. So it is our own Jamaicans with a few other West Indians who put Jamaica House where it is now! If we were depending on the people who were doing it first that building would be have been down already. Their plan was that after a few years that building would be gone and we would not have Jamaica House standing here today". – *Lynford Fletcher*

"I know when we got the building at the time, I was working on my own as a painter and decorator. The members of the Jamaica Society asked me to give them an estimate for painting the place. I came, had a look around and I went back and I made an estimate. It was accepted and so I started to work. As a painter and decorator, I did all the work myself - inside and outside. I was the only one who decorated this place, top to bottom. I did it on my own. I had no help. That was my best experience with the Jamaica Society" – *Roy Mitchell*

"Getting the building was only half of it. The other half involved having to apply for the grants, meeting with different people within the community to secure the grant, and to inform them of what the building would be used for. There were many meetings where we had to discuss just how to move forward with the building. We had lots of difficulties with workmen trying to take short cuts and not doing things properly. But the main things which I thought was absolutely wonderful, was when we had organised work days. Every one of us, members and friends came to give a hand to get everything cleared up and ready to look more like a finished building." – *Theresa Condor*

"The ladies, we used to do the cooking on a Saturday when we had the workdays. We had to first cook from our houses because we didn't have a kitchen there yet. So each member would cook and take the food there, or the food would be picked up from their house. It was really interesting to do, and we really enjoyed it. It was hard work but still we did it." – *Norma Fletcher*

"The bigger work like the paid work was given out to contract workers. I remember I helped out with the toilets by putting up the bits and pieces. In the storeroom downstairs, you cannot imagine the amount of work we had to do to clear that place out and to make it useable. I can say that Mr. McDonald, Mr. Johnson, some others, and myself worked as a team to make that place usable. We were able to work together as a team to get that place sorted." – *Robert Chrouch*

"We had plenty of free work days. The ladies spent a lot of time cooking and feeding all the men as they dug and humped dirt and all sorts of things while the building took shape. Mr. Mitchell, Mr. Philips, Mr. Wray, Mr. Hines, Mr. Patterson - persons like those spent an awful lot of time, doing an awful lot of work and the hours were long. When the landscaper did the garden in order to reduce the overall cost, members volunteered to assist him. I remember the day they were putting the tarmac over the car park area, we had another work day for that."
– *Elizabeth Johnson*

"The Free Work Days! Oh yes! We used to gather up as many tradesmen as we could, that could do everything so they can work on the building. One thing I know is that everybody was doing something. We had professionals who knew what they were doing, but most of the labourers were members of the Society. We didn't have enough money to give a contractor to come in and do it, so they did it all ourselves. I was the one who was in charge of installing the kitchen. In fact, I am the one who installed the kitchen. I had two carpenters with me. But I tell you something, Travis Johnson did a lot of work on that kitchen as well: the engineering work and the plumbing. I also built the cabinet in the library. Then the ladies always made sure to cook! It used to be fun! Yeah, everybody used to enjoy it because they'd come to realise that they were building a house for themselves. One day, they were going to own it." – *Finley Wray*

"I remember one time when I was in the hospital because I had had four heart attacks. When I came out of the hospital, I understood that they were having a free work day, I decided to go up there and do my bit, because other people were up there giving free labour. So I went up to Jamaica House and I pushed a wheelbarrow time and time again taking out rubbish. I tell you something, it was a trying day for me because I was not feeling well and I didn't tell anyone because I wanted to put in my share. When it was finished I felt like a champion!" – *Edley White*

"When there is work to be done at Jamaica House and as long as there are members who can provide the necessary skills, the work is normally done in-house. There has never been any difficulty arranging workdays, members are always ready and willing to play their part. Workdays have continued well beyond the refurbishment of the building. Recently, the land next to Jamaica House, which is earmarked to be developed for use as a car park was cleaned up, by arranging a workday. The officers and members of the Executive Committee are elected annually to manage the business of the Society, but over the many years, officers have been able to call on a substantial proportion of the wider membership, when there is work to be done." – *Travis Johnson*

The extent to which members would give up their time, braving the elements, and in some instances risking their health to build something that would become a community property showed a remarkable sense of commitment and dedication. Unknown to the men and women labouring diligently away, their enterprise and co-operative effort would have a huge impact on a young apprentice architect of Jamaican descent. It would remain for him the most notable moment in the history of the Jamaican community in Leeds.

"I joined the Jamaica Society about 1998. But my first encounter with the Jamaica Society was some years before that. I was working for an architectural practice and had just started as a junior architect and one of my tasks was to oversee this structure being developed. I remember sort of standing and saying: 'Boy! Look at all these black people working together!' It kind of shook me in a sense. It was really encouraging for us as a people. Actually seeing some of my black people, men, women and trades people working on this building, which later became Jamaica House, it encouraged me to continue doing my studies. I'd never seen anything like that happening before to black people. So many black people involved in a project like that!" – *Ian Lawrence*

In their design to give the Jamaican community their own building, the Jamaica Society (Leeds) has achieved much more than they set out to accomplish, these achievements are difficult to quantify but the legacy is far-reaching. They became a symbol of black pride and a stellar example of what a community could accomplish by pulling together. They proved to themselves and to others that they could achieve the goals they had set for themselves. This joining of forces to get the best possible results for their dream they had, is reminiscent of a quote from Norman Manley: "I had a real capacity to work hard for what I wanted, and an unquenchable belief in excellence. The only superiority I accepted was the superiority of excellence". That was the Society's aim all along.

The Royal Seal of Approval

Though the spectre of Teamwork and its contractors would continue to hang over the Society like a dark storm cloud for a few more months, the Society would experience other more rewarding moments that took place during the period of refurbishment. On December 2, 1987, HRH The Prince of Wales visited and toured the facilities at Jamaica House. He unveiled a plaque to commemorate his visit and gave the project his Royal Seal of Approval. His visit to Jamaica House was part of his official tour of selected projects in the Chapeltown and Harehills areas that were funded under the Government Task Force Scheme. The then Chairperson, Lizette Powell would declare that the visit was " a historic day not only for Jamaicans and members of the Society but for the entire Harehills and Chapeltown community."

> "The Prince of Wales visited Jamaica House during the refurbishment period, because the refurbishment took place under the Community Programme Scheme. We were very pleased that our project was chosen for the visit. He spoke with several of us about our plans for Jamaica House, and unveiled a plaque to commemorate his visit." – *Travis Johnson*

> "My best experience as a member of the Society was to meet Prince Charles face-to-face and to shake his hand and talk to him. Prince Charles asked me this question that I will never forget. He wanted to know if when we had committee meetings if we had disagreements. My answer to him was that from time to time we disagreed." – *Lynford Fletcher*

> "My best memory was meeting Prince Charles in 1987 when he came to Jamaica House. It was lovely. That's one of the most memorable things because it's not everyday you get to meet royalty in a derelict house. Talking to him was good also. He asked me about all sorts. How long have I been here? What do I do here? Why did I come here? Where do I live? What's Chapeltown like? Are there rats roaming about? Then the reporters swooped down on me after he was finished talking to me to find out what we were talking about." – *Nettie White*

Before the Society commenced using the building officially, the Bishop of Jamaica, the Right Reverend Neville DeSouza visited and blessed the building on July 31, 1988.

By October 1988, the Society started using the building. The first event that was held there was a Domino Match on October 1st. The first General Meeting was held in the same month with over sixty-three people in attendance. In 1989, the Society held its Annual General Meeting in the building for the first time. The Society's mettle was tested again when it appeared as if Sight & Sound would not take up residence in the building. The members acted quickly and the disputation was resolved. In 1990, Sight & Sound opened its annexe in Chapeltown.

Chapter 4

Jamaica House

Jamaica House is the name the members selected for the building from a number of suggestions. The name, Jamaica House, has an even greater significance to Jamaicans. One may assume that the name is only associated with the people who own the building. In Jamaica, Jamaica House is the name given to the building which houses the Office of the Prime Minister. When the Jamaican Prime Minister, the Rt. Hon. P.J. Patterson ON, PC, QC, MP visited Jamaica House, this fact delighted him. In a conversation with Councillor Norma Hutchinson, he acknowledged that on his return to Jamaica he could say he has been to another Jamaica House outside of Jamaica.

The Jamaica Society (Leeds) opened Jamaica House with much fanfare on October 30, 1989, almost a year after the members started using the building. That day was a culmination of three years of hard work, endless meetings and negotiations. It was time to celebrate.

> "The Official Opening of Jamaica House is probably one of the most memorable occasions for me. We had spent so many years trying to find, purchase and refurbish the building, that it probably would be correct to say, we were all filled with emotions. We liased closely with the Jamaican High Commission to see whether it would be possible for the then Prime Minister of Jamaica or a Member of his Government, to visit Leeds to perform the ceremony. We were indeed very pleased, when we were informed that Senator David Coore, Minister of Foreign Affairs and Foreign Trade had agreed to officially open Jamaica House, on 30th October 1989. All plans and preparations were completed on time for that 'special day'. Senator David Coore was accompanied by the High Commissioner, Her Excellency Mrs. Ellen Bogle. There were several other dignitaries present for the Opening. Jamaica House was bursting at its seams with the number of persons present. It was a special and splendid occasion, and the members enjoyed every moment of it. The next memorable occasion was when we celebrated, the fact that we had completed all payments on the loan secured to purchase the building. The then High Commissioner, His Excellency Mr. Derrick Heaven was in attendance to share in our joys." – *Travis Johnson*

> "It was just a joy to be there to see what we had achieved and to see that in life, your goals can be achieved by hard work. I don't remember much of the opening ceremony, I was too excited because everything was too much. But I do know it was a good day." – *Yvonne English*

"The grand opening of Jamaica House was great. Absolutely. You could see the (Jamaican) flag from out there. It was a really lovely evening. There was the usual refreshment and many guests gave speeches. The bank manager from Yorkshire Bank, where we got the loan, was there and he was very impressed. In his speech, he implied that the money was well spent and that he had confidence in the Society when he was approached and was told what the money was needed for. He did not hesitate to give us the loan because he thought it was a good thing. He said it was good to know that he was right. He was really proud and happy that things turned out the way they did." – *Florence Williams*

"When Jamaica House was finished we continued to contribute money towards the building. Years later, when we learned from the Treasurer that we had finished paying for the house, we were just like one big happy family. We were proud then to hold our head high to say we have a little home in Chapeltown known as Jamaica House. It is ours, it is paid for, and we contributed to it." – *Roy Mitchell*

"One of the most memorable things about the opening ceremony of Jamaica House was that I was given the chance to go on top of the roof to hoist the Jamaican flag. I tell you, I was really proud of that." – *Finley Wray*

The pride the members felt was enormous and the work had paid off in many ways. In 1991, the Society had the pleasure of hosting Louise Bennett in Jamaica House - the person who inspired the formation of the Society in 1977 and the subsequent drive to acquire their own headquarters.

Celebrating a Community Effort

The Jamaican community in Leeds still celebrates the achievement of acquiring Jamaica House. Those who have joined the organisation after the fact share also in the sense of pride. For many members, it became their home away from home and the home that they refer to in this instance, is Jamaica. Paulette Simpson accurately sums up how Jamaicans as a whole feel about Jamaica House: "It is a little piece of Jamaica right up there in the North of England." She has also noted that the Jamaica Society (Leeds) became the only Jamaican Society in the country to acquire its own building, even though many have started before them. Other Societies have had to rent buildings or share buildings with other Caribbean Societies, but Leeds has been able to organise functions when they need, in the way they wish, because they own the building that they occupy. She continues to explain why this effort sets the Jamaica Society (Leeds) apart within the Caribbean community: "The Jamaica Society (Leeds) is also looked upon as a model Society. Which in fact it is. One of the things is that the Jamaica Society is not only known among the Jamaican community in the UK, but in Jamaica as well. Because as you say Leeds they say Jamaica House. Anybody who has passed through Leeds with any seriousness from the Prime Minister to the Governor General, they know about Jamaica House. So, that is a remarkable achievement. It started with a small group committed enough to pay the loan themselves. It shows the power of unity within our community." The members of the Society are all too aware of the difference their efforts have made to their immediate community and the impact it has had further afield.

"I felt very satisfied. I felt what a great achievement it was because we were the only ones within the Jamaican community who had our own home and we could say, 'Yes, this is Jamaica House'. There are other groups within the community but we had achieved something on a very big and grand scale. I felt very, very proud. I was proud of the people who were very heavily involved from the beginning, like Nettie White, Travis Johnson, Liz Powell, Roy Powell, Betsy Johnson and Len Fletcher. I've worked with them. Whatever I have done, I felt very proud to be the person who was willing to take part, and proud to be a Jamaican working with other Jamaicans together in unity. It was very important for us to own our own building because of the experiences that had taken place - where they held meetings at other premises and the lights were turned out. We got together and bought our own place so that we wouldn't have to experience such an embarrassing situation again." – *Theresa Condor*

"Of all the Jamaican societies that they have in this country we are the only one that own our own house - our own place. We feel proud that we've got our own house at Chapeltown. A lot more started before us but yet we can say, 'Oh yes we have a house, our own house'." – *Nettie White*

"We felt good, because we felt at home. Everybody would always refer to Jamaica House as his or her home. I remember this chap, whenever he came up the House, he never says, 'I am at Jamaica House'. He always says, 'I am at home. I've come home'." – *Finley Wray*

"What we have at Jamaica House is that it is ours. At the first Social that we had at Jamaica House after it was refurbished, I felt good. Travis took us right to the top of the building and showed us everything right through and through. I was surprised because I did not know that it was something like that. I remember Len telling me that they got this building and how they were going to pay for it. I have only one regret that I was not more involved in the beginning in working towards renovating the building. When it was finished, I was embarrassed that I was not one of those involved. There were some Jamaicans around in my area (Hyde Park) trying to do something like Jamaica Society and I was involved in that but it failed. Jamaica House is something you can be proud of. It is an achievement. Because for a start we have somewhere we can call our own and it is very convenient." – *Samuel Barrett*

"I felt quite proud. No other Caribbean nationality in Leeds had got their own building. There is the West Indian Centre but that is for everybody, but to have your own as Jamaicans makes you quite proud. I think whatever we need to do, whether it is learning about our culture it is there and we don't need to ask anyone permission to put on an event. When people are booking the building, people feel Jamaica House is a place of safety. The first activity that I attended at the Jamaica House was a Social Evening and I was impressed to see everyone mixing with each other. People were friendly to each other and it was really good: the interaction, the food, the laughter. They have really stayed with me." – *Irene Henry*

"As Jamaicans abroad, we have achieved something. We have achieved Jamaica House where other Jamaicans can come and be at home. As for the wider community, we have also achieved it as black people who have worked hard for it." – *Yvonne English*

"There was a feeling of pride in the Jamaican community when we got that place. It has helped the reputation of Chapeltown, in my opinion. When we have functions at Jamaica House people volunteering in the kitchen are so united. Those who attend the functions do so with an open mind and free heart. I just like to know that I am here helping the community, the membership and the old folks. Jamaica House is about unity, friendship, trustworthiness, honesty, brotherly and sisterly love." – *Lynford Fletcher*

"As far as I know, we're the only Jamaica Society in the North or in the country that owns our own building. In the early days when we finished our meetings, we didn't have a place like here where we could have a meal or a cup of tea. But now, since we have a house of our own, and we have our meetings, we have a get together after the meeting and we have a meal. This was only possible because everybody seems to muck in and do what is best for the Society." – *Roy Mitchell*

"It's wonderful to have our own building. This is what you would call the headquarters of the

Jamaica Societies in England. It's really great. I just think that Jamaicans wanted their own space to share with others, and we did it!" – *Florence Williams*

"Going back to the Windrush era and a lot of people came up on *Windrush* said that even worshipping they found it difficult when they first came, because they'd go into a church where they felt it was the right place to worship and they were told that 'your people don't worship here.' The Society when they used to meet in other places as well and it came a certain time they had to leave and it was demeaning and embarrassing. In order for the Society and its members to have pride within themselves, they have to set themselves certain goals and one of the goals was to own a building. I'm very proud that they have succeeded in owning their own building. As I say, it's giving pride back to the community, not just to Jamaicans but to friends of Jamaicans." – *Councillor Norma Hutchinson*

"We are Jamaicans we should have somewhere for us, but at the same time we are saying that no one should be excluded from joining. But it's nice to know it belongs to Jamaicans; that makes it part of Jamaican soil - literally. Especially when we fly the Jamaica flag, at least that's how it feels. My husband has been in the Forces and we have served overseas, and wherever you go overseas and you go to a hospital that belongs to the Force, it's classed as British soil. So, in my estimation, Jamaica House represents Jamaica." – *Bev Lattibeaudiere*

"In so many ways, the achievement of Jamaica House was truly a dream realised. Being at Jamaica House gives a feeling of being at home. Often one hears members express the view that when they come through the gates at Jamaica House, it gives the feeling of being in Jamaica. Equally, it is often so difficult to pull ourselves away from Jamaica House, even after we have concluded the business of that particular visit. There are times when we sit around for hours, just talking or reminiscing. The good thing about it is that members or friends have said, that they feel free to drop in at Jamaica House as long as someone is in the House." – *Travis Johnson*

As the members celebrated owning their building, they were faced with the added task of its maintenance, and deciding the types of events it would be used for and the best ways to make the building accessible to the Chapeltown and Harehills community. The Society experienced the immediate benefits. Existing groups within the organisations had a permanent space for operation: the Domino Group, the Drama Group and the Choir. The decision was taken that individuals and community groups could have access to the building.

> "Jamaica House is fairly well used. It is used for most activities of the Society, for example, meetings, seminars and social events Members and friends use it for birthdays, anniversaries and wedding celebrations. It is often used for funeral repasts. Other community organisations, statutory bodies and the Local Authority also use Jamaica House for meetings, seminars and training courses. Annually, we host a number of meetings and seminars for financial institutions from Jamaica on promotional tours. It is likely that Jamaica House will be made available for most events that can be accommodated, as long is it meets with the Objects of the Society." – *Travis Johnson*

> "When it comes to funerals, a Jamaican, whether he is a member or not, can use Jamaica House for the repast. There are also lots of other ways in which Jamaica House is helping its members and the wider community." – *Lynford Fletcher*

The Society has worked out a system of designated caretakers who volunteer to supervise the building when it is hired for functions by individuals or community groups. The Society was able to host or cater for the 80th birthday parties for its two oldest members, Edley White and Louise Reid, the present facilities making it possible for members to volunteer their time to plan and cater for such occasions. Edley White was overcome with emotions and gratitude because of the support he received from the Society on this occasion.

The Society has also offered office space for community projects and organisations. The Sight & Sound project operated from the first floor of Jamaica House until 1991, and between 1992 and 1999, the Society provided space for the Black Mental Health Forum. Since October 2000, Community Links has occupied the same floor.

After the official opening, there was still minor work to be completed around the building. Members participated in doing work to tarmac the car park, to clean the gutters, to do joinery work and small painting jobs. The Building Sub-committee was later commuted to House Management Sub-committee, co-ordinated initially by Roy Powell, who took responsibility for the caring of the hall and the gardens. After his departure, a pair of equally dedicated stalwarts, Allen Ebanks and Lincoln Cole volunteered to keep the hall and garden in tip top shape.

> "I have been doing the garden soon after it was landscaped with the help of others. The names that readily come to mind are Roy Powell, Cleveland Wood and Roy MacDonald. My present helper is my good friend Con (Lincoln Cole). It has become a challenge for us to have the lawn looking lush and green because the large trees block out the sunshine and suck up the moisture from the lawn. Another task, Con and I have taken on is the cleaning and polishing of the tim-

ber wood floor of the main hall. Every time we do the floor, my thoughts go back to Roy Powell who had done it before us for a number of years. His high standard of work is very hard to follow." – *Allen Ebanks*

"It is most heartening to receive compliments about Jamaica House and in particular, the gardens. I think the credit for the garden should be directed mainly to three of our members: Allen Ebanks who took responsibility for it shortly after Jamaica House was opened, Roy Powell who assisted Allen until 1999, and Lincoln Cole who joined with Allen since 1999. We are truly grateful to them, as well as to those other members who have ensured that the garden at Jamaica House is well kept." – *Travis Johnson*

After all the members have gone through to acquire and renovate Jamaica House, they have seriously considered going through the whole process again, by putting in a bid for 279 Chapeltown Road. Though the bid was not successful, it still remains a dream to expand the building. The Society would like to be in a position to hold larger public meetings which it is not possible at the moment.

"What I would like to see is for the Society to expand the building we've got, so that we could have lots more facilities. We would be able to hold more people inside when we have big cultural events." – *Theresa Condor*

"I would like to see the building enlarged. The size of the building that's what's holding us back. We don't have the space to do the things we want to do. My wish now is for the car park to be developed so that members can get to use it." – *Lynford Fletcher*

A Legacy

The complexity of raising funds while overseeing the building tasks was a juggling act which the members managed very well. On reflection of those frenzied days during the refurbishment, Travis Johnson concurs that "while the building was being refurbished trying to raise money was one of the problems, while the Task Force and the City Council grants were awarded to assist, additional fundraising had to be done and it became an ongoing activity throughout that period." It never dampened their spirits. They were spurred on by their spirit of volunteerism; an unquestionable dedication which was the secret of their success.

"I'm one of the hardest workers that they've got actually. I'm always willing to help to do whatev-

Jamaica House: *A symbol of black pride.*

er. Not because I am the Deputy Chairperson, Assistant Secretary or an Executive member doesn't stop me from working hard. This is our Society and if it needs help then I help. Whatever I do, I do so because I want to do it for the Society. I mean nobody could force me to come down and cook for a Social. But I feel it's a part of my duty to come and to help regardless…" – *Nettie White*

"I volunteer to do what the Society wants doing, just name it, from the kitchen right up to the top, I am willing to do anything. I'm just one that take on any role that is there to do as long as I can. Because my experience in this place is one of unity." – *Robert Chrouch*

It is this unity of mind that has sustained the Jamaica Society (Leeds) and has been its biggest asset. The members are supported at all levels by the Executive Committee and by each other. Their commitment and sacrifices do not go unnoticed. It has been illustrated in a report to the Annual General Meeting by Lizette Powell where she thanked the members for another successful year in the Society's history: "Jamaica's National Motto, Out of Many, One People is a source of unity and strength and an inspiration to all of us. We look back with pride at our progress, we look forward to greater heights of attainment in the future." The foundation that the Society has laid here will have an impact on future generations. While many enjoy the fruits of their labour they are keen to see it passed on to their children and grandchildren. Jamaica House was partly constructed with that view in mind.

"It is an inheritance for the children so that they know that this place is left here for them. We don't want them to be in the same position as us, when there was no place for us to have meetings comfortably." – *Samuel Barrett*

"The building is there for the community and for our children's children growing up. We have something to show them that we worked for and that when we put our heads together, we get things done." – *Lynford Fletcher*

"The way Jamaica House is structured it is clear it is not for one person. No one can say that it isn't yours but it is mine, because it is for us all. We know that when we've passed on, Jamaica House is for the generation behind us; we have laid the foundation for them." – *Robert Chrouch*

The building is indeed a great legacy to leave behind for the next generation. But the greatest legacy that the Society will have left behind is a lifelong lesson the next generation can take with them and apply to every aspect of their lives - that "without discipline we cannot succeed, and with disorder we will fail." This was Sir Alexander Bustamante's advice to the Jamaican workers on May 28, 1938. The Jamaicans in Leeds drew on this national heritage as a source of inspiration, and showed the community that co-operation, discipline, dedication and hard work - lots of it - can lead to success. They created their own history.

Like the history of the Jamaican people, the history of the Jamaica Society (Leeds) is encapsulated in the words of the prolific Norman Manley: "I affirm of Jamaicans that we are a great people. Out of the past fire and suffering and neglect, the human spirit has survived - patient and strong, quick to anger, quick to forgive, lusty and vigorous, but with deep reserves of loyalty and love and a deep capacity for steadiness under stress and for joy in all things that make life good and blessed."

SATURDAY NIGHT, SUNDAY MORNING

Stories stick like this bonding dough underneath my fingernails.
Standing up in the too hot humidity of my Nanna's kitchen,
I am no longer in Sholebroke View –
I am thousands of miles away running up and down in dutty red dirt and trying to avoid having to tie down the goats.

Memories spin like the long thin worms dropping into the bubbling fire pot.
Learning how to cook is not a simple ting.
Age 7 – tugging at my Nanna's apron string – this is where I want to be forever.
And then you get to hear big people talk whilst they cut up big people food like yam and sweet potato
And you get to hear labrish, excuse me gossip about Sister P from over Ridge Hill.

And I get pictures about places I've never been – about dropping out of trees and cool sea breeze.
About places where it never snows and why my granddad only has toenails on 8 of his toes.
'It wasn't the pain I was cryin' for – it was the licks ah woulda get if daddy ever find out mi did a fars' wid de machete'

And now I'm 17 – Nanna's gone – and to tell the truth – I still can't cook.
But I can tell a very good story –
New page, new chapter, same book.

Laurah Pitter, 17
© 2002

5 THE NEXT GENERATION

There is no doubt that the Jamaica Society (Leeds) has grown in tremendous leaps and bounds over the past twenty-five years. As members of the Jamaica Society (Leeds) look back at their lives and their work both as individuals and as a collective, there are many things of which they can be proud. In identifying the Society's single greatest achievement, many members point to the acquisition and renovation of Jamaica House. In many ways this achievement is a monument to the personal journey that many Jamaicans have made since their migration to this country. It started as a dream, the first steps were filled with uncertainty, obstacles and disappointments, but the dream was kept alive by hope and determination. After working ceaselessly against all the odds, the dream became a reality. While Jamaica House stands as the Society's signature achievement, the Society's accomplishments are more multifaceted. The members explored these successes. Interestingly, their retrospectives were also intrinsically tied to the future. They were looking for clues in their past achievements for ways to move forward.

The Way Forward

"At the moment the Jamaica Society (Leeds) serves a good purpose. We go around and visit the sick, we are concerned when someone dies and supports the bereaved family. Part of our culture is observed by carrying out these funeral rites. But as an organisation, the Society needs to have more things for the young people. I stuck around the Society because there was a friend there in my age group, but I also like to know what is going on here and in Jamaica. The young people do come, but they do not stick around because you've got to get them interested in something. The young people would come if the Society had more things to stimulate them. On a day like a Saturday, the children could come and learn more about the Jamaica Society and what it stands for. Young children, who have been born here and not heard about Jamaica, could come to Jamaica House. The second and third generations need to know about the culture, they need something to hold on." – *June Wood*

"I think to a large extent as an organisation we have been fairly successful. When we first met to form the Jamaica Society (Leeds) we had set ourselves three goals: one, that we aim to establish a fully constituted organisation, two, that it would be a registered charity and three, that we would acquire a building to use as headquarters. We have achieved all three goals. Over the many years we had set ourselves other goals, most of which we have achieved, of course there are a few that we have not. We recognise that the meeting room at Jamaica House is too small to accommodate large events, we are currently exploring all possible avenues of how to increase its size. I think the Society has reached the stage where it needs to employ someone as a co-ordinator to be responsible for day-to-day administration. We have worked closely with the Jamaican High Commission and look forward to continue years of close liaison. We are fortunate to have been honoured with visits from the Governor General of Jamaica, Sir Howard Cooke, and the Prime Minister of Jamaica, Rt. Hon. P.J. Patterson. We will continue to welcome and receive dignitaries and friends from Jamaica. It is an undeniable fact that a number of our members are more senior in age and some are feeling burnt out. Therefore, there is an urgent need for younger people to come forward, probably initially to share in the management responsibilities, as a lead-in to taking over full management. There is no doubt that we have failed to attract a reasonable amount of young people into membership of the Society. I believe that although the level of participation of younger people is negligible at present, somehow I feel that in the not too distant future a lot more will gravitate towards the Society." – *Travis Johnson*

"The Jamaica Society has been successful in the goals that it has set for itself. The goal was to establish this building, which they have achieved. Also their charitable activities are there to help people from Jamaica and within the community, that is to help people who are ill, disabled and lonely are looked after; to help children with education and to organise cultural events for the children so they can learn about Jamaica. We also bring people together so that they can share their experiences and enjoy social evenings. In the future, I hope the Jamaica Society will mean as much to the next generation as it did to us." – *Theresa Condor*

"I'd like to see the Society become stronger, and for the younger people to be more active in it because we are passing on one by one. So, I would like to see young people counted in. I have encouraged my two sons in Leeds to come to the Society. One time, when they had a meeting here and we invited as many young people to come. My two sons came they enjoyed it very much and liked what was going on, but they don't feel that it's something they want to take part in as a member on a regular basis." – *Robert Chrouch*

"For one, we've achieved the building and I'm sure that if there was another, they would be able to. At the moment, I am not as active as I should be in the Society but I would really like to see us with a bigger house where there is a nursing home for older people, a crèche for children, and nursery for the kids. I would also like to see younger people involved. We've got quite a few young members and I think that the ones that are in now should spread the word around. They are aware that the Society is here and it's not here only for the older ones, but for the younger ones as well. Yes, they do visit us from time to time, but I hope that they will walk in our footsteps and carry on where we left off." – *Yvonne English*

"In the future, I would like to see more of the younger people taking an interest in the Society to carry on the work we have started. I wouldn't like the Society to finish just here. We will not live to see what is going to happen ultimately, but we know the mainstay is our younger generation." – *Roy Mitchell*

"My concerns are that not enough young people are coming along to give us the support, and to underwrite the future of the Society. In other words, the second and third generations of West Indians don't seem to be coming in to help and work like we did, because they have a different focus. We were like strangers in a strange country. They are already here; this is their country. So they may not feel the same urge to be together and to share a common unity like we did when we first started." – *Glen English*

"From the women's point of view, I would like to see more health issues taken on board. I think we need to be more aware of the younger Jamaicans in the community. Because I think the young people of today are not necessarily first generation Jamaicans, they are second and third generation Jamaicans. Although they are British born, they are of Jamaican parentage. I think we should be inviting the younger generation into the Society and help them to develop a sense of being Jamaicans: realising where their parents came from and to develop their sense of being people from the Caribbean. I feel in a sense our young people are lost. They have lost their sense of belonging and I think have lost a feeling of knowing who they really are." – *Bev Lattibeaudiere*

"The thing about it with the Society is that we just have to see if we can get as much young people in so it can keep going. But it might not keep going the way we started it. The older members must give them the responsibility of the running of the Society so that one day, they can take over. But we can't expect the younger people just to walk in and do it the way the Jamaican people do it, like to collect money that everyone has thrown together, and come together and volunteer to do the same amount of work that we did. Young people now have so many different clubs, plus the opportunities that they have, they can ignore the Society if they want." – *Samuel Barrett*

"We'd like to see the Society be more forceful in the things that are happening in Chapeltown. In this day and age it is getting hard for the young people. We should help to tackle the drug situation in the area, help the old people to parent and guide the young people by giving them counsel. The Society needs to help to make Chapeltown better." – *Lynford and Norma Fletcher*

"I would like to see more young people involved in the Society. I would like to see the Society taking on more issues that affect Jamaicans in the community. Because when you live in a community where you have good and bad, I would like to see organisations saying enough is enough. We cannot let a few bad apples spoil it for us Jamaicans. It makes it bad for the rest of us who are trying to lift our heads up and do something in the community. Not all Jamaicans are the same". – *Councillor Norma Hutchinson*

"I would like to see the Society go further in looking after our elderly people like getting our own nursing home. But I really would like to see younger people coming into the Society and participating in what we have to offer, and so that they can learn about their background. I see them losing it if we don't get more young people here. I don't know why it seems so hard. I think that the Society needs to put on projects where young people can come in and perhaps learn like the Jamaican dialect and culture." – *Yvonne Hylton*

"I think for the future I would like to see an expanded Care Group. I would also like to see support groups for single mothers who have young ones growing up without the support of grandparents, aunts and uncles. The strength of the Society has always been in the high value in which we hold our culture. We need to instil in the next generation the value of holding on to their culture, and encouraging the younger ones to take over as we grow older." – *Irene Henry*

The members' ideas on the future path of the Society are diverse. They range from expanding the services to persons of pension age, to taking on the issues affecting the younger generation primarily drugs, violence and education. Education through knowledge of their cultural background is identified by most. Though the views on the future are varied, it is indeed clear where the survival of the Society lies - the next generation.

What lies behind this process of documenting in their own words, the experiences of Jamaicans in Leeds and their contribution to the city, is the expectation that these stories may serve as a beacon that will light the path for the next generation of members. Over the years, there have been only a handful of members who are second generation Jamaicans and their participation has been sporadic. The challenge that faces the

Jamaica Society (Leeds) is how it can conspicuously re-invent itself so that it attracts membership from successive generations.

Paulette Simpson, a representative from the Jamaican business community who is very aware that bodies like the one she represents have a vested interest in seeing organisations like the Jamaica Society (Leeds) continue to grow once the first generation has passed on. She has expressed her concerns about the Society's survival: "One of my only fears for the Society (at the moment and I can see them addressing it), is one of succession. When this set goes, who will step in and maintain the momentum that has been carrying on for so many years? I see them bringing in young persons. They are of a different ilk, these young people, and you have to think about your strategies of including them in a positive way, not only to organise events. A lot of organisations have died because there is no one to take it on. However, I have seen them inviting young people to take an active role in the management of the Society."

Clinton Cameron thinks that the challenge for the Jamaica Society (Leeds) is to command the respect and loyalty of the young people. He cautions that if the next generation becomes "absorbed into the society at the bottom, having accepted their position at the bottom, some may not be prepared to do what is necessary to make the changes and move upwards. They may become comfortable knowing their place." He also believes that the problem is further compounded by the fact that "people who have been born here and been through the education system here, only know about the Caribbean islands from what they have been told, or from visiting it as tourists. They do not have deep attachments to their island communities. In many ways, I think that as a community, we have lost that."

Father Taylor also sees education as one of the pressing needs at the moment. He acknowledges that the Jamaica Society (Leeds) has begun to do that at the moment 'through art in the widest sense.' In terms of a possible solution to getting more young people into the Society, Father Taylor's advice is that this generation needs to "let go, to let grow."

> "I think that the most senior members of the Society are ready in principle to hand over to the next generation. The hardest thing is letting go and that would take an enormous amount of courage. But they have *to let go* in order *to let grow*. If they don't do that, they will carry on, and carry on, and carry on doing - I'll put it in inverted commas - 'the same old things'. So that's something I think they've got to watch. I'm saying that because I know that we as a church have got to watch that, and I say that to a lot of our church people, 'you've got to let go, to let grow - all those wonderful seeds that are waiting to come up to flower'." – *Father Taylor*

The Second Generation: Holding on to Their Identity

The issue of the younger generation's interest in the Jamaica Society (Leeds) is in fact a question of identity. It is rooted in how they see themselves. Are they British, Jamaican British, black British or all of the above? Negotiating a Caribbean identity was hard enough for the first generation. Lizette Powell pointed this out in her 1985 address at the Service of Thanksgiving for Jamaica's Independence: 'We are Africans who have never lived in Africa, speaking European languages and educated in European cultural traditions. We are also an amalgam of African, European and Asian and have built a new identity as West Indians.' This hybrid identity has brought about a culture which expresses in the deepest sense, a proud and admirable history. Some of the Society's members say they have made an effort to share with their offsprings stories about their lives in Jamaica - how to cook Jamaican food and how to speak Jamaican.

"I told my son about life in Jamaica. When he was eight years old, I took him back home to Jamaica to meet his relations. I told him we came from Lucky Valley. Lucky Valley is where citrus fruits, tobacco, grapefruits, limes and all sorts grew. My father worked as a foreman in that area. Every Saturday, we would go down there and we would spend all day Saturday there and come back Sunday night, and then we would get ready for school on Monday morning. We went to Marley Hill School. I have also told him how we had to carry water and firewood on our heads before we went to school. Then, we would go straight to school after that. After we came back from school, we had our duties to do: to go and fetch water again, to look some firewood, and to feed the pigs, the donkeys and the cows. Also early mornings, we had to get up and milk the cows with our father who would then go and sell the milk. The first milk from the cow we used to drink it, hot from the cows breasts. It was sweet!!!" – *Francis Williams*

"I have shared with my children who are born in the UK about growing up in the parish of St. James. I grew up in a section of the island which in those days was rich in bananas, tropical fruits, sugar canes, coffee, ginger, pimentos, cocoa beans, ackees, lovely coconuts and vegetables. Lots of these products were exported to other countries. Living in the countryside there was plenty of fresh fruits, our family had a lot of land. Our house had seven apartments with a huge garden where I used to play outside with my friends. My father was a postman and my mother was a seamstress." – *Phyllis Hines*

"It's a lot of work to get young people to know that they have a very valuable cultural background, especially since they were born here and have gone to school here. I think about what

I have done for my own children here. My children know everything they need to know about where I have come from because I made sure of that. I think that as children are growing up in the home, that's where the cultural education has got to start. At the end of the day, one's parents' background is important too." – *Yvonne Hylton*

The second generation Jamaicans who have had contact with the Jamaica Society (Leeds), either as members or having assisted in some way with their activities, have strong connections to their parents' heritage. They recall their parents telling them stories about Jamaica, which have had a very strong impact on their own sense of identity as young people growing up in the UK.

"I am Jamaican, my parents are Jamaican, so I see myself as being of Jamaican heritage. My Mom told me a lot about Jamaica, particularly stories about when she was growing up in St. Ann. The stories she told us were quite fascinating actually, it was better than watching TV. She used to tell us about her grandfather and his farm and the different animals that he had on the farm. I think what fascinated me the most, actually, was trying to imagine my mother riding a horse. Her grandfather had horses and there were certain horses she was allowed to ride and some she was not. One of the stories that she told me was about her stealing a ride on one of the forbidden horses. I think the horse was called something like Mayflower. She was riding this horse with no saddle and she got to this piece of land called Top Mountain and she just let the horse go. I can just imagine Mom with the winds going as she was riding along.

"Someone in the area saw her, so by the time she got back home, her granddad knew she was riding this horse. Of course, she got into trouble for that. It was those stories that fascinated me. She also told me a lot about what my great grandfather was like; she used to give me quite good descriptions of him. Apparently, when he used to go to town, he always rode his horse and he would wear his riding gear: the hat, jodhpurs, the boots and whip. When he came back from town, my mother would meet him at a tree. She would run out into the yard to this tree and wait for him at this tree. He would come and always have a little parcel wrapped up in brown paper with something in there for her: a dress or a piece of material or something else. These stories that my parents used to tell me was about us having a connection to her place of birth. It is also about identity, having a grounding as to where you are coming from, where your roots are. Also I think to an extent the society that we live in, don't actually accept us as being British. They refer to us as West Indian, black or Jamaican, but obviously, we are legally British because we are born here." – *Marcia Hylton*

Chapter 5

"My heritage is a combined one. Firstly, I am aware of my African ancestry and secondly my parents are from the Caribbean, so I am African Caribbean. But equal to that I am also British because I was born in the UK. My grandmother told me a lot about Jamaica but the most memorable stories came from my grandfather. He used to sit and talk about his childhood in Jamaica and teach me some of the Jamaican songs. When you are young you don't appreciate the value of listening to the stories your grandparents are sharing with you. But a lot of those stories they remain with me. I used to go to school singing, *Brown Gal in the Ring* and *Carry me Ackee Go a Linstead Market*. The stories that I heard from my grandfather and grandmother have helped me to accept my Jamaican heritage, because my heritage supports me as a human being."
– *Khadijah Ibrahiim*

"My auntie told me Anancy and *duppy* (ghost) stories. She talked about life on the family land, how they used to have to get up early in the morning to go and help in the field before they get to school. She would always make us laugh. People like my mom and my aunt's favourite saying was: 'When we were growing up…' As parents they were always cautious with whom their children mixed with, so another memorable saying was: 'Show me your friend and I'll tell you what type of person you are' and 'if you do wrong in this world it's going to come right back on you'. But the Jamaican saying went like this: 'if you spit in the sky, it's gonna come right back in your face.' These stories and sayings had quite a positive effect on me. I feel very proud of my Jamaican roots. If anybody asks me, 'where are you from?' - my first response is I am of Jamaican descent".– *Sandra Simpson*

"Growing up we were told a lot of Anancy stories, I'm sure we had a book. I also remember the folk songs from when I was little. Songs like *Carry Me Ackee Go a Linstead Market*. I remember, we had to learn them whether we liked it or not. I think my parents shaped my identity and have made me who I am - a conscious black woman." – *Angelique Johnson*

"I am British of Jamaican parentage both sides I accept. From ever since I can remember, I've always heard about Jamaica. I've heard stories about the characters in my family and Jamaican folklore like Anancy stories and also about the history of Jamaica. I suppose these stories must have informed my identity otherwise, I don't think I would have made so many trips to Jamaica." – *Susan Pitter*

Visiting Jamaica is the necessary rites of passage for these second generation Jamaicans. For some, their parents took them to give them first hand knowledge of life in Jamaica. It is also a tradition that the second generation has kept up with their children - the third generation of Jamaicans born in the UK. The journey to Jamaica is significant on so many levels for these British born Jamaicans. Returning to their ancestral home provides them with a greater understanding of their heritage and just how the stories that they have heard are very relevant to forming their identity within a predominately white society.

"When I was a child, I remember my aunt specifically saying when she used to plait my hair that 'it was tough like a coconut brush.' So when I went to Jamaica, one of the first things I had to see was a coconut brush. I said to my grandma, 'Auntie Rose said that my head is tough like a coconut brush' and I asked her what was it and she showed me, and I thought 'No!' Fond memories of my dearest auntie! However, when my sister and I first went to Jamaica in the '70s, I had this negative image of it even though we had a lot of positive input from our family. There was this negative image still in our heads, because in school you got the impression that in Jamaica there was only extensive poverty. So when we arrived in Jamaica, what I found quite surprising was seeing black Jamaican people in high-powered jobs. That was a bit of a culture shock for us. When I saw black people in professional jobs, it just made me think. I asked myself why are black people always perceived as the ones who should be in low manual working jobs? Going to Jamaica was a good eye opener actually.

"When I came back to school, I decided to work my socks off. At high school in particular, we weren't encouraged at all. I remember the careers teacher saying to me that it's a pity I wanted to pursue a career in nursing, it would be better if I looked at a job in a factory. That kind of comment definitely affected my confidence. Because teachers are highly regarded in Jamaica, I think that our parents' generation left our education up to the schools and also our parents had to work hard on shifts. So when we went to school, we were expected to accept what they said. Today, I am a public health practitioner and also a midwife. I also have two degrees: a degree in Social Policy and a degree in Public Health. So there, Mr. Careers Teacher at Roundhay High School! I've got a son age eleven. Though, we've got books on Jamaica, I thought it would be really important this year for my son to actually see where his Nan came from. So we visited Jamaica in August 2002". – *Sandra Simpson*

"I have been to Jamaica once. Most of what my mother had talked about had changed a lot. I think what made the most impact was going back to the house where my mother was actually born and where she grew up. It was fascinating. Because in my head I had a picture of what it looked like but it was different, yet it was an absolutely awesome experience. I remember that we were walking down to the house and our uncle was waiting to receive us, but my sister and

I walked passed the house because there was this bit of land where you could look over the hill. We could see for miles and we could see the sea in the distance. I remember the beauty of the landscape and it was just awesome how beautiful the land was. I felt proud. I felt a connection to it. I felt like I had come home. I didn't want to leave and I felt upset knowing we had to come back to England. My two older sons have been to Jamaica except Josh. Josh is sort of upset that he hasn't been yet. But he knows a lot about Jamaica and about its National Heroes like Paul Bogle and Sir Alexander Bustamante." – *Marcia Hylton*

Knowledge and understanding of Jamaica's history are integral to shaping the next generation's sense of cultural identity. For many second generation Jamaicans, this knowledge came to them through stories told by their parents and other close relatives. It is a tradition that the second generation Jamaicans have preserved - the oral tradition of storytelling. When Jamaican relatives and friends visit the UK, they encourage their children to listen to the stories that are relayed about childhood exploits in Jamaica, Jamaican legends and folklore, and significantly, lessons from Jamaica's history and from the lives of Jamaican icons and National Heroes. Storytelling at family gatherings is integral to Jamaican family culture.

"I feel honoured and blessed because in terms of trying to define who I am as a person at a young age came from my aunt, one of my dad's sisters. She was born in Jamaica and came to the UK at a very young age. My aunt always taught me the value of my blackness, if you will. I was hearing those names of Marcus Garvey and Nanny of the Maroons from the age of seven. Like many Black Britons, I was also introduced to the work of Linton Kwesi Johnson after the riots. I have three children: the eldest Jadey is eighteen, my daughter Rheima who is ten and Ali who is seven. I am hoping as a mother I have achieved something in terms of passing on information about their culture. I have made it my duty to pass on the knowledge that my parents and grandparents have passed on to me. I have come to realise how stories have developed for generations. An aspect of our culture is our oral tradition. So even if our stories are not documented, they should be spoken. Storytelling that is my background, so it is important to speak to my children about their grandparents and to put them into contact with their grandparents. I don't have to tell my mother to tell my children stories, because my mother is a great storyteller, you just have to mention back home in Jamaica and her face lights up. I firmly believe that it is important for our children to hear what their parents or grandparents have to say." – *Khadijah Ibrahiim*

"My aunt had a party in 2002 and we had our family coming from all over the world. There was a particular uncle, it was amazing just to listen to him as a older head. Some nights, we would not even sleep because he was telling us Anancy stories. Josh, my son, knows Anancy stories and loves it to bits. He heard about Anancy and the Magic Spoon; how Anancy tricked people into getting food into his pot when he didn't have any. Stories and family times like these I think are so important. As old as I am, I was listening to the stories that my uncle was telling the children. I was so sorry that he had to leave. One thing that I was sorry about really was not being able to find out more about my background. I wanted to know more about his parents because I think my uncle's great grandparents were slaves, so it was kinda close, not so far removed - I wanted to find out more about that.

"My uncle also made the Jamaican connection with my sons' names, for instance my son, Marcus is named after Marcus Garvey, Jamaica's first National Hero. He told my little son, Joshua that they called Michael Manley, Joshua, and he explained why Michael Manley was given that nickname. He encouraged them that they should go on and do good things with their lives. My sons have strong connections to their heritage; they very much see themselves as being of Jamaican origin. They have problems seeing themselves as British. If you are to ask them what are their origins, they would tell you Jamaican as opposed to being British. I remember when Josh's school had an International Day, Josh wore a shirt with the Jamaican flag on the back and a teacher commented that she didn't know that that was the Jamaican flag. Josh was able to talk to her about Jamaica, explaining that was where his grandparents came from and he even knew that his granny came from St. Ann in Jamaica." – *Marcia Hylton*

"I have passed my knowledge about Jamaica to my daughter. Although I have to say that my father is still very much a part of that and my mother when she was alive as well. So in that sense, I think the stories have shaped my identity very much and my daughter's. The Jamaican stories have fostered a sense of pride in my background and my origin; something that I think is quite passionate amongst Jamaicans, and that passion has been passed down to me." – *Susan Pitter*

If there are substantial numbers of second generation Jamaicans who see the value in retaining their cultural heritage, then the Society may have a greater chance of survival than previously feared. However, it does not answer the question: why aren't they attending in larger numbers?

"The only reason why I probably haven't joined is because my parents are at Jamaica House all the time, so I don't have a babysitter. That has limited my ability to commit myself to going to all the meetings and to sit on committees. I understand the need for the younger generation to get involved, but I believe, we have different views. We are from a different generation and we grew up here, so the way we view things are not the same as our parents. There are some similarities, but we're different. Having said that, a group of second generation Jamaicans and I have actually organised the Children's Christmas Party for 2002. We met once and we put forward our proposal and the Executive welcomed it warmly. I've also volunteered and served at the Senior Citizens' Dinner. Nevertheless, I think the Society serves some of my needs. If I want to have a function, I can book Jamaica House. My extended family has used Jamaica House. I also think that they do serve the needs of my children probably more. They have put on excellent events for children. I'd love to see my children have the knowledge that I have about the history of Jamaica and its people. I would like to see the Society continue with the educational activities such as a Saturday club, or events in the holiday period - maybe music, maybe some drama or maybe some computers." – *Angelique Johnson*

"I am not a member of the Jamaica Society (Leeds). However, I have been invited to become a member. I have the application form but I have not completed it yet. Even though the Society has been around for twenty-five years, I was not really aware of their existence. I just thought it was a few people who walked under the banner of this name doing things for their own self-gain. I have realised now after being welcomed into the Society by Travis Johnson and by other members who have said 'you should come back and do this', that my impressions were wrong. If the Jamaica Society (Leeds) is for change and it is a Society for education and growth, I definitely have to be a part of it. As someone of Jamaican parentage, it is important that I feel that there is an establishment that I can go to get information about Jamaica. The Jamaica Society from my understanding provides that information. Plus, my children have been part of the History project that the Jamaica Society has been running. I have seen the results of the work that they have done and the joy that it has brought them. They have come home and shared with me some of the information that they gained from the classes. That information can only be beneficial to their growth. What the Society can provide and is trying to provide for the third generation coming up is a place where they can come and gain knowledge about Jamaica, because some people may never get to go to Jamaica. They may never get to visit where their grandparents or great grandparents have come from, but we can paint the picture for them."
– *Khadijah Ibrahiim*

"No, I am not a member. Why have I never joined? There's no real reason why. My mother is a member, and Mrs. Johnson keeps on encouraging me to join. I have helped to organise a Christmas party along with others in my age group, but we want to do it with a difference. It's good having different generations at the Jamaica Society because we have different perspectives. I can see the Society serving the needs of my child, because he is not always going to get information of our historical background in school, but not just provide that information for our children but for the community. I participated in the creative writing session with my son and it made me reflect and realise how truly important my Jamaican background is to me, and also the importance of Jamaican patois in forming our identity. When I was younger, patois was considered by some people to be speaking incorrect grammar, because it is the informal language of the Jamaican people. When I went to Jamaica I bought my sister a book on how to speak patois, that was one of the best presents she ever had in her life. She was just so thrilled with it that she felt the need to share it with this English guy she is dating. He equally enjoys patois and tries to speak it." – *Sandra Simpson (Since this interview, Sandra has become a member of the Society)*

"I am ashamed to say I am not officially a member. I have not actually got around to completing the application form. However, I have been to various meetings and I have participated in some of its activities. Over the past months, I have become involved in this community health initiative, the Community Health Awareness Project that happens here at Jamaica House. Because of my background in nursing, I felt that I had some skills that I could contribute to this project. Also, my son has participated in the History project and it has given him that extra knowledge of knowing that his grandparents came from Jamaica. He spoke to me about it. He was telling me of the stories that Paul Aiken had discussed with them and he has put down these things in his computer work. He told me the story about the man who brought his wife and children from Jamaica for £28 each, and he said it was so cheap. So, I think the Society has relevance to my children in that they see it as an organisation to pass on the knowledge of our culture. In a way you can see it being easily lost. If we don't have something to pass on to our children then their whole identity can be gone. I think the Jamaica Society plays a big part in giving that to me and other people of Jamaican heritage." – *Marcia Hylton*

Some of the second generation Jamaicans do not seem to be in a hurry to become members. However, they have found ways in which they can serve the Society on the sidelines, by contributing their skills and talents in relevant areas. Others have identified child care as a deterrent to fuller participation, and the difference in perspectives being identified due to the gap between the generations. Regardless, there is an apparent interest in the Jamaica Society, but the next generation is patiently and respectfully waiting its turn. They understand just how much the Jamaica Society means to their parents' generation. One thing that they have all agreed on is that in order to get successive generations interested in the Society, it has to provide activities that stimulate an interest in Jamaican culture and history. Only young people who have a strong sense of their cultural heritage and the desire to contribute meaningfully to their community, will carry on this legacy left by the first set of Jamaicans to migrate to Leeds. The few second generation Jamaicans who are members have also pointed to the fact that it is their strong awareness of their Jamaican cultural heritage that has influenced their decision to participate in the Society. Ian Lawrence grew up with parents who had instilled in him a strong sense of his Jamaican roots. Additionally, his encounter with the Society as an apprentice architect influenced his decision to become a member. For Ann Elliot, it was holding her daughter's christening party at Jamaica House that was the catalyst. She has not regretted her time with the Society as she has deepened her knowledge of her roots and she values the time she gets to spend with Jamaicans. The second generation members are keen to point out that the Society already has the key to its longevity.

> "I chose very carefully to join the Jamaica Society and have served on the Executive. I know that I would not have had an interest in the Jamaica Society, if my parents hadn't told me about growing up in Jamaica. It's all about getting that experience across. I think the Society needs to be looking at encouraging younger people to take an interest in their heritage. My daughter is seventeen, and I know that she has that strong knowledge of Jamaica, because it's been passed down from my parents to me and from me to her." – *Susan Pitter*

As generations become further removed from relatives who were born and raised in Jamaica, the responsibility of passing on the knowledge of Jamaican history and culture to successive generations needs to be a community responsibility. Passing on the heritage is not the only consideration. The way in which the history is taught - the content and perspective - is equally important. The Governor General of Jamaica has made suggestions on how to approach the transference of our Jamaican heritage.

> "I get the impression that the first generation of Jamaicans have passed on some of the culture, the values and the attitudes. But I also get the impression that the real history - the romantic history of our people - does not seem to be part of the programme. It is an imperative in my mind that the ordinary Jamaican should know their total history; the suffering, but also the achievements and the successes. We seem to emphasise that our parents used to work in the cane fields. True, they used to work in the cane fields and made the European nations great because of the wealth of sugar. But we had the ordinary Jamaican who post slavery built bridges and great houses and violins and they also built free villages. We are not telling the circumstances from which the people came, the massive evolution: the growth in education, the growth in science and technology, the growth in health - and they need to. I think it is an imperative for the Jamaican

people to be told their total history. I am not ashamed to tell people that I come from the cane fields, because, my grandparents worked in the cane fields. In spite of this, we have produced a great people. Intellectually, we are as good as any." – *Sir Howard Cooke, Governor General of Jamaica*

The Third Generation: Honouring their Ancestral Past

The first and second generations have pointed the way forward for the Jamaica Society (Leeds). In order to ensure that successive generations participate in the Society, it has to take up the challenge to be both guardian and disseminator of their historical legacy. History has long since been a tool of empowerment. The complete history of the Jamaican people can be used as a source of unity and self worth. It offers a deep sense of self and belonging. As generations of Jamaicans chart a path for themselves to personal success and achievements, they are tapping into the spirit of independence and self-determination that drove their ancestors to overcome the problems of race, cultural denigration, enslavement and exploitation. It is therefore imperative that the younger generation recognise and affirm these aspects of their heritage.

Holding on to, and drawing on their cultural heritage played a crucial role in the survival of Caribbean people in their early years in the UK. It has been so throughout history. The tradition in many African societies has been to pass on the knowledge of their lineage to their children. The practice continued in the Caribbean and can be heard in traditional folklore, folksongs, proverbs and rhymes. Today, Jamaican poets, storytellers and artists have captured and portrayed historical experiences. The mediums that Caribbean artists have used to process these stories have taken them on a journey of self-discovery and have unmasked the inner spirit of their ancestors.

The Society continued in this noble tradition, and brought the first, second and third generations together to listen to a re-telling of their history and to explore new and dynamic ways of documenting their understanding of their Caribbean heritage. The project, *Our Journey! Our History!* was conceived as an interactive, cross generational and multimedia approach to documenting the stories of the first generation of Jamaican people to settle in Leeds post World War Two, and to highlight their social and cultural contributions to their community. The young people were able to document this history by using both traditional methods and multimedia technologies. They participated in one or more of the five types of workshops that were on offer: art, desktop publishing, creative writing, video documentation and storytelling. The first generation of Jamaicans also participated in the workshops which were, for the most part, facilitated by second generation Jamaicans.

Following in the footsteps of renown Jamaican poets, artists and writers such as Claude McKay, Una Marson, Roger Mais, Andrew Salkey, Albert Huie, Kapo, Gloria Escoffery and many more, the young people fulfilled Marcus Garvey's wishes of affirming their ancestry and claiming their history. An awareness and understanding of themselves and their place in history became clearer. This is evident in the poem, *Like a Glove* which was written by 17-year-old Laurah Pitter in the first creative writing workshop:

> I like this.
> I like sitting here smelling the morning in anticipation of what I can do today.
> What can I do today?
> For you, for me, for us?
>
> I like this.
> I like the idea that for 30 minutes this whole page is mine
> – and you know that.
>
> I like the idea that I'm sitting here – the last in the chain that stretches way back.
> I like that.
> I like old school, new school and I like the fact that I like it like that…

The participants started working from their present knowledge of themselves and their culture shaped primarily by what they have learnt through the media and popular culture. In the painting by Marcus Hylton, he has positively placed the knowledge of himself and his identity within the context of modern Jamaican music.

Reggae Roots Culture
by Marcus Hylton, 12

While Laurah Pitter laments the distortion of her heritage by the media in her poem, *Today's Lesson is ...Labelling Theory*. This is a poem that echoes the militancy of Linton Kwesi Johnson and the passion of Jean Binta Breeze. Khadijah Ibrahiim, the creative writing facilitator introduced the participants to the works of these two Jamaican poets, the former being Britain's most celebrated dub poet and the latter, a well known performance poet on both sides of the Atlantic. Laurah's poem makes the connection to Roy Mitchell and Glen English's comments in the storytelling workshop. Both men, served as ground crew in the RAF during World War Two and talked about the lack of consistent acknowledgement of Jamaican people's contribution to Britain, instead there have been a lot more emphasis on the "bad deeds". Laurah feels that the negative media portrayal impose a severe limitation on how her people are perceived

> I am constrained by the name I am given.
> I am constrained by a category I am put in.
> I am constrained by a misinterpretation of a nation.
>
> I am black. But what does that mean?
> Is it belonging to a group rich in culture, history and music?
> Or is it wrong?
> Is it being stopped from walking the street due to my rich coffee colour?
> Because I am offensive to the eye?

Laurah feels the negative media portrayal impose a severe limitation on how her people are perceived.

> ...But what does that mean?
> Is it coming from an island paradise of white sand, blue sea and an intrinsic beat?
> Or is it wrong?
> Is it blood thirsty, money hungry, gang-banging violence?
> A violation of immigration?
>
> I'm your blud.
> A youth.
> But what does that mean?
> Your friend, amigo, partner or family?
> A young person growing up with dreams?
> Or is it wrong?

> Is it an intimidating rabble of rebels in a gang?
> See it's all in your interpretation of a nation.
> Depending on how you see my self-fulfilling prophecy.
> Oppressed by the name you call me...

The young people were also aware of the impact that a negative sense of self can have on an individual or community of people. In a dark, angst-ridden and untitled poem, Laurah battles with the cultural, social and racial ghettoisation of her people. She however, ends the poem on a hopeful note that it is a battle worth fighting for, and it is one she is sure she will win.

> From the soil of my soul,
> I create this ghetto within.
> Where dark and deadly shadows
> Infiltrate my mind
> With illegal chemical substance.
> Where fear is transformed
> Into a saline solution
> Which rains down from my eyes –
> Torrential.
> From the concrete of my feet,
> I create this ghetto within.
> Where street life vandalises my conscious –
> Leaving a montage of names and expletives
> Just to let you know
> 'I woz 'ere'.
>
> From the soil of my soul,
> I create this ghetto within.
> Where barbed wire and corrugated zinc
> Protect my grieving heart
> From pain and deceit –
> Just in case.
>
> From the concrete of my feet,

> I create this ghetto within.
> Where violence inhaled
> Pollutes my lungs and
> Seeps through my veins
> To be excreted like
> Some over concentrated brew
> Through my over worked hands –
> Disillusioned.
>
> From the soil of my soul
> And the concrete of my feet,
> I create this ghetto within –
> Until I can pack up my insecurities
> And move to the suburbs.

The thrust of the workshops was to ensure that the young people were not impeded or discouraged by the plethora of negative information about their racial, cultural and ancestral origins. Because the primary lesson that they can learn from their history, is one of overcoming against all odds. This message is present in the stories of the first generations of Caribbean people to come to the UK which the third generation uncovered in their video interviews and through their participation in the workshops. In order for the young people to gain a historical perspective on the first generations journey to, and experience in Britain, they explored the most significant journey in the history of Caribbean people of African descent: the forced journey from Africa to the Caribbean as slaves. In spite of the unspeakable horrors of slavery, their ancestors survived, and never abandoned their desire for freedom and equality. Rheima Ibrahiim, 11 and Ben McIntosh, 12 made the link between their Caribbean and African ancestry in their paintings of the same name, *My Ancestors' Journey*. While the poem, *Writing Oral History* by Lee Chrouch, 14 reverberates with his own sense of disbelief about his people's history as well as the profound sense of loss that the African slaves experienced as they grappled with being forcibly uprooted.

> My Mom and Dad told me
> That once there were slaves my age
> From Africa, who were always in a cage.
> When the slaves were shipped over on a boat
> My Mom and Dad told me that they never wore even a coat.

  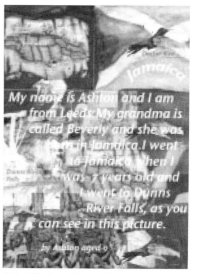

My Ancestor's Journey
by Rheima Ibrahim, 11

My Ancestor's Journey
by Ben McIntosh, 12

My Visit to Jamaica
by Ashton Lattibeaudiere, 9

> My Mom and Dad told me
> The slaves were treated like dirt,
> All the white man did was hurt, hurt, hurt.
>
> My Mom and Dad told me
> That this happened in Jamaica
> These slaves were my ancestors from Africa.

For 8-year-old, Joshua Hylton, the sessions made him understand and come to terms with the label of African Caribbean. In his Time Line, he wrote:

> My name is Josh. I was born in Leeds in 1994. My family is African Caribbean because my Nana came from Jamaica but I know that some of my ancestors came from Africa…I am also going to a history project at Jamaica House learning about my past by using computers.

However, the third generation do not live in strict isolation of their cultural heritage, even though their parents are the first generation of Caribbean descendants to have been born in Britain. Some have had the privilege of visiting the Caribbean. Working closely with the art facilitator, Marcia Brown, a young participant, Ashton Lattibeaudiere, 9 reproduced a computer-generated artwork of his memory of his first trip to Jamaica when he was only seven years old. Others only have the sweet memories of their grandparents' tales about their lives in Jamaica to fuel their imagination. Many of these stories passed on at family gatherings. *Story Time* by Troy Lawrence, 18 evokes the true essence of a cross generation Caribbean family gathering; where food, music, dominoes and the mellowing influence of Caribbean rum create the perfect atmosphere for a journey down memory lane.

> "When I was in Jamaica," said Granddad. As soon as he said that I knew that I was about to be taken on a journey.
> This was no ordinary journey but one that filled with music and a vast amount of culture.
> The dominoes viciously struck the table, each one following the other like earthquake.
> The room was filled with the sweet smell of rum which was often tampered by the harsh taste of tobacco smoke.
> Each man using his little codes to signal his partner from across the domino table.
> The jokes float around the room like the sweet smell of perfume…"

In *Saturday Night, Sunday Morning*, Laurah Pitter wrote that her first connection to her grandparents' homeland were made through these stories. They stimulated and fed her curiosity and imagination as early as seven years old, before she made one of her many journeys to Jamaica.

> Memories spin like the long thin worms dropping into the bubbling fire pot.
> Learning how to cook is not a simple ting.
> Age 7 – tugging at my Nana's apron string – this is where I want to be forever.
> And then you get to hear big people talk whilst they cut up big people food
> like yam and sweet potato and you get to hear labrish, excuse me, gossip about
> Sister P from over Ridge Hill.
> And I get pictures about places I've never been – about dropping out of trees
> and cool sea breeze. About places where it never snows and why my granddad
> only has toenails on 8 of his toes.
> 'It wasn't the pain I was cryin' for – it was the licks ah woulda get if daddy
> ever find out mi did a fars' wid de machete'…

A Day At the Beach
by Ali Ibrahim, 7

Jamaican Fishermen *by Moses Joseph, 9*

Birds of Jamaica
by Ashton Lattibeaudiere, 9

Jamaican and British School Children *by Cory Fletcher, 12*

The inspiration for the young people's creative works also came from books about Jamaica. They used their fertile imaginations and walked the seven-mile stretch of Negril's white sand beaches and surveyed the splendour of their Motherland through the coffee scented mist of the Blue Mountain Peak, and brought to life their impressions of life in Jamaica.

Jamaican Foods
by Ital Joseph, 10

The younger generation have not always placed the same emphasis on their cultural heritage as their predecessors. In the storytelling workshop, the facilitator, Ansell Broderick remarked that in his work with young people in schools, he would usually pose the question: 'where are your parents or grandparents from?' The weak response has often been: 'somewhere in the West Indies.' It was in these workshops that 10-year-old James Robinson discovered that his grandmother came from Jamaica, a fact that altered his outlook on the future which he articulated in his Time Line:

> When I grow up I want to go to university to be a doctor. I want to make a difference as a black doctor because I don't see many black doctors. Some day I want to go to Jamaica to see where my Nana was born.

Though the participants had a sense of their history and could place some of their daily practices within the wider context of their cultural heritage, the majority did not have comprehensive knowledge of their grandparents' experiences when they first arrived in the UK: their participation in World War Two and their arrival on the *SS Empire Windrush* which led to a large inflow of people from the Caribbean in search of economic opportunities. Ansell Broderick in the storytelling workshop painted a picture for the young people with his rhythmic poems, *The Less I See* and *Island in the Sun*. When these poems were performed, the participants were taken on what Ansell called 'a journey of the mind'. It was a journey that has opened their eyes for the first time to their history - the history of Caribbean people in Britain. Laurah Pitter describes her awakening in the poem, *Further Education*.

> I sat down on the cold plastic chair. History on a Saturday? Really, who cares?
>
> *First 15 minutes*
> Nah man, this isn't how it's supposed to be – I prefer hectic bass lines not heavy drum beats. But

I'm feeling this. I'm feeling the vibrations run through my veins – like old ones and young ones are one and the same. And I know what they mean – oppression and prejudice. Ya get mi? Seen!

First 30 minutes
Old folks talking – story of my life. An hour of this – please send me the knife. But wait – I've never heard about this before, grandparents in botany and uncles in war. So why was this hidden from me? I'm gonna bus' this in lesson. Ya get mi? Seen!

First 45 minutes
Nah man, this ain't too bad. You might think I'm jokin', trust me I'm glad. Windrush ain't just a name anymore. Really, I can feel a cool breeze rush through the door. And it grabs me and I can feel this kinda swelling in my head. It's pride. You never taught me that Mr. Deputy Head.

Last 15 minutes
Really I never want this to end. I never thought I would make a 70-year-old friend. Imagine I could have wasted a day on MTV Base - only thing my head would be full of was bling bling and space.

The participants celebrated their new knowledge in their Time Lines and paintings:

My name is Ali Shabazz Ibrahiim-Broderick… I am seven years old… My dad and my mother's parents are from Jamaica. My Nana tells my mom, Khadijah a lot about Jamaica and she tells me too… I am doing a computer and history class at the Jamaica Society (Leeds). I joined the class late but I came just in time to learn about the *Windrush* and how Caribbean people came to the UK. I like the Windrush story and pictures. The Windrush story lets me know why Black people like myself live in Britain.

I am going to a history project at Jamaica House learning my past by using computers… The class is about my history and my ancestors' history. I learnt about the *Empire Windrush* and that Caribbean people came to England on this ship. I also learnt that the people weren't treated right when they first came to the UK and they did not like it. – *Joshua Hylton, 8.*

This summer, I attended a programme at Jamaica House. We learnt about history using the computer. I also did a test about Caribbean people who came to Leeds. Caribbean people came here over 50 years ago. The people who came from the Caribbean are linked to me because my Nana

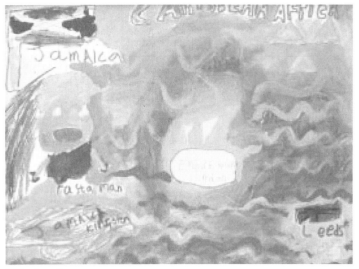

Windrush
by Joshua Hylton, 8

The Empire Windrush
by Aniah Coleman, 11

Journey from the Caribbean
by Joshua Hylton, 8

is from Jamaica. I attend a school called Bracken Edge Primary School. But I don't learn about my history there. – *James Robinson, 10.*

Joshua's painting *Journey from the Caribbean* pays tribute to the peoples of Jamaica and St. Kitts and Nevis who also came from the Caribbean and settled in Leeds. Today, Kittians and Nevians represent the largest group of Caribbean people living in the city.

In comparison to their lives today, the young participants were shocked by the conditions under which the Caribbean migrants worked and lived, and were inspired by their determination to succeed, nonetheless. These issues were also underscored in the video documentation sessions which culminated in a discussion between the first and third generations. In both the storytelling and video workshops, Roy Mitchell talked about living in shared accommodations in a back-to-back house in the 1950s with outside toilets which were at the end of a long row of houses, the lack of central heating and having to use a brick to warm himself at nights having heated it on coal fires. He also talked about working in the coalmines where his job was to maintain the machines for cutting coals. This story impelled Laurah Pitter to write a poem of appreciation to her grandfather entitled *Black Diamonds*.

> For the plantain and pumpkin and red peas based elation.
> For the paraffin heated nights of shared accommodation so that I could go to private school and get a better education.
>
> So thanks, for everything.
>
> For walking in the paradox of sullen grey streets
> Where black and white could never meet.
>
> So thanks, for everything.
>
> For the ackee and saltfish and sorrel based nights.
> For when words like 'nigger' really caused a fight.
>
> - just so I could fit in and be alike.
> Just so I could walk down the streets in baby blue Nikes.
>
> So thanks, for everything...

She is aware that the journey is not over, because Britain is counting on the contribution that her generation can make to its development as the country relied on her grandfather's contribution fifty years ago.

> For the extra £5 from down in the pit –
> Black dark outside toilets only by stars lit.
> Just so I can be determined so I never will quit –
> Be you train conductor, botanist, unhealthy or fit.
>
> So thanks, Granddad for putting shoes on my feet.
> Then, Britain needed you and now it needs me.

This appreciation is also reaffirmed in a painting by Rachel Morris, 15 which captures the sharp contrast between the hope in the eyes of the Caribbean people and the cold reception they encountered on arriving in Britain: "I chose to do this painting because it means a lot to me. It makes me think of what we have come through. There has been a lot of change… when black people first came to Britain they weren't wanted by the white people and we faced a lot of racism."

Levi Fowler, 14 could only make sense of his grandparents' experiences by outlining how he would feel if the same conditions were present in 21st century Britain, in his poem, *Oppression*.

> Me not being able to walk streets
> Just because of the colour of my skin is a terrible thing.
>
> Not being able to see blacks and white communicating together
> And not being allowed to go anywhere by myself would make me sick.
>
> It would be like I am a prisoner in my own home.
> Just day after day inside not seeing my friends at all.
> Not being able to get an education at school it would hurt me
> Just because black people and white people are enemies.
>
> Seeing blacks fighting for a right to stay in this country.
>
> If this was really happening today, then I would definitely feel
>   OPPRESSED.

Troy Lawrence, on the other hand, in his poem of the same name, looks at the long-term effect of racist and inhumane treatment on his ancestors and successive generations.

> Oppression leads to depression,
> It stops you from doing what you want to do.
>
> It comes when it wants and takes what it needs,
> And if you're lucky some day it leaves.
> You won't understand or have a clue,
> Why the oppressor takes a hold of you.
>
> The oppressor could be near or far away,
> But its grip grows stronger everyday.
>
> I change my mind for you see oppression will never leave,
>
> It whistles in the wind and through the trees,
> Over hills like a cool damp breeze.
>
> Like a cold draft it gives you chills,
> Like a child having giddy little thrills.
>
> Oppression and Oppressors are one in the same,
> For one day you're oppressed,
> Then you oppress another's name.

The young participants were encouraged that like their predecessors, they too can achieve success despite discriminating practices and racial stereotyping. Sometimes, the early Caribbean people only had the nostalgic recollections of their homeland to sustain them. Gavin Williams, 14 depicts that generation's emotional dichotomy in his painting, *From Jamaica to England* which shows how the beautiful memories of Caribbean people's tropical 'paradise' are always present in their consciousness.

In the final analysis, the young participants have learned to fully appreciate the role that history has played and can play in their lives. Paul Aiken, facilitator of the desktop publishing workshops made the link between a people's knowledge of their history and their future. Sir Philip Sherlock and Dr. Hazel Bennett concluded

Coloured Folks Get A Cold Welcome
by Rachel Morris, 15

From Jamaica to England
by Gavin Williams, 14

Jamaica House: Our Legacy
by Dean Hyde, 13

Don't forget Your Roots
by Akilah Cohen, 12

Dual Heritage
by Gavin Williams, 14

in their Afrocentric study, *The Story of the Jamaican People*, that it is Jamaican people's "passion for freedom and justice that gives continuity and a sense of moral purpose to Jamaican history." As future generations respond to the issues within their community, they can do so with a clear understanding of their place in history.

In the absence of any emphasis on Caribbean history in mainstream education, the young people have identified this as the role for community organisations such as the Jamaica Society (Leeds) in their Time Lines and paintings.

> I think that the Jamaica Society can help people of my age group by teaching them about their history and heritage, by helping us to develop a sense of identity. I hope to go to university next year to study Sociology and Media communications with the intention of pursuing a career in advertising. I want to do this kind of job because I see people like me being disempowered and portrayed in stereotypical ways in the media and I would like to present a different, positive perspective of stereotyped groups. – *Laurah Pitter, 17*

> I think the Society can help us to find out more about Black History since I don't do it in High School. [The Society] can help by doing things like these more often. – *Levi Fowler, 14.*

> The Jamaica Society (Leeds) has done a lot already for the black community, but to help me and many other children like myself they could organise more events like this history project. Jamaica House is where Black history and culture come alive through a burst of colourful stories, music sound and sights. Growing up in a black community and having a lot of black friends, I have seen a lot of misled and miseducated youths. This is not the life for me. I hope to change the stereotype of young black people in this society because it takes only one person to make a difference. – *Troy Lawrence, 18*

June Wood attended the storytelling and video workshops with her daughters and has summed up what the workshops have achieved for the third generation: "The sessions were trying to give young people positive role models, by teaching them about our people's past experiences. Which is good, because my young children didn't have much knowledge about their culture in the first place." Evidently, the perspectives of the third generation are in many ways similar to that of the second generation. They both agree on the importance of their historical and cultural heritage to Caribbean descendants living in Britain. The paintings *Don't Forget Your Roots* by Akilah Cohen, 12 and *Dual Heritage* by Gavin Williams, 14 implore young people not to forget their roots. The message in their work underscores Marcus Garvey's most famous epitaph: "A people without a knowledge of their history; is like a tree without roots."

RIDDIMS TALKING

Riddims talking
Talking from de inside and come out
Talking with a lingo dat
CYAN Stop

Mi say de Riddims is talking
It just lift itself up
And come out of mi mouth top with de yard man beat
It just a…just a…just a
A Skeng na…a skeng na…a skeng na
And den sit down EASY…pan
Mi
Voice
Box

Riddims talking
Mi just a say wat me 'ave fe say
Tough top mouth front and jaw dem nah lock

Mi nearly tun over
Spin over
Fall over
And drop

You see a true mi a wait
Siddown pan Massa man gate
Thinking I couldn't hear nothing
See anything
Or be anything

Cos Mumma say…Cuh yah

POEM

Miss Tiny say...Watchcha nuh
So mi tek a stop
And mi draw back dat deh same Riddims track
And go inside which part mi consciousness did siddown
And I check out de I an' I
Oh yes people
I am feeling IRIE
Right there pon top

Cos like a lightning
A thunder clap
A warning
Wid no deceiving
Is de same Riddims
De Riddims just rocking and bubbling
De same Riddims what mi long time mumma and pappa was talking
De same Riddims what mi ancestors was drumming
Oh yes people 'ave de same Riddim wat I an' I is talking.

Khadijah Ibrahiim ©2001

6 THE JOURNEY CONTINUES

The history of the Jamaican community in Leeds is intrinsically linked to the history of the Caribbean people living in and around the city. It is difficult to isolate the two. However, it was after the formation of the Jamaica Society (Leeds) that one was able to take a concentrated look at the social and economic contributions that Jamaicans have made to the City of Leeds and to Jamaica. Individual Jamaicans have made their mark in Leeds as church and community workers, lay magistrates, local councillor and Lady Mayoresses, but it was their function as a collective force that gave their historical experiences greater meaning.

The Jamaican people's history was a painful journey towards achieving a sense of belonging in the wider British society. Their greatest weapon against feelings of alienation and displacement was unity. If history is the landmark by which we are directed into the true course of life, the Jamaican community in Leeds has been on the right path - that of collective endeavour. The emergence of the Jamaica Society (Leeds) was underscored by a sense of community. As a unified body, Jamaicans were bolstered by their commonality – their national origin, cultural heritage, spiritual values and ancestral memories. The same ancestral energies that were influencing social changes in their homeland at that time in history, were directing their energies in a similar manner in the UK.

Jamaicans' involvement in British society began before World War Two, but their presence as settlers in the UK in significant numbers began in 1948. Their participation in World War Two showed that they could function effectively in any sphere as part of a workforce or a unit. They showed unswerving dedication to the British Empire, even though back in colonial Jamaica their people were still striving to free themselves from British domination. It was a testament to their generosity of spirit.

As one of the first set of Caribbean people to settle in Leeds, the Jamaicans assumed many pioneering roles as a visible Caribbean community began to emerge. They have left behind the legacy of the Leeds Caribbean Cricket Club which is still around today - the oldest Caribbean organisation in the city. The Jamaicans moved beyond the realm of the Cricket Club to assist with the formation of the Aggrey House which addressed the most immediate problem of finding accommodation that Caribbean people faced in the 1950s. They could not stand idly by while their compatriots were denied housing because of their colour, and suffered the indignity of squeezing themselves and their families into overcrowded and filthy living spaces. In the post war economy where jobs were plentiful, Caribbean people bolstered the Leeds economy by filling the labour shortfall in engineering, chemical and clothing factories, and in the hospitals and the transport sector. Jamaicans made themselves available to new arrivals by passing on advice on securing employment. They had come out of a culture where *one hand wash' the other* and they found a place for it at a time when Britain was cold, alien and unwelcoming. Their community spirit was also signified by a knowing nod as they passed each other on the streets, even if they were complete strangers.

As the Caribbean community in Leeds expanded, Jamaicans joined other Caribbean nationals to lobby for social change. They worked to improve the quality of life within the community in order to ensure that their experiences were unencumbered by inequality and injustices. They also wanted their children who were born in the UK to have the full benefits of being British citizens. Together they established service delivery, educational and social welfare organisations, agencies and institutions within the Chapeltown and Harehills community - some of which are still around today.

Evidently from the accounts in this book, the Jamaicans' struggles became their successes. There were times when they worried that they would not have achieved their goals. But in spite of the rocky start, a number of Jamaicans have carved out a comfortable existence for themselves and their families in Britain. Allen Ebanks has repeatedly emphasised that fact: "Life has turned out well for me. This country has been good to me. I mean the lifestyle - the bills are getting paid, and I don't owe anybody anything. On the whole, it's been good for us." Audrey Henry has acknowledged that her achievements are reflected in the lives of her children. She has proudly stated that she has 'raised six children in Leeds and the police has never been to her house'. Her children work in professions that range from engineering, dentistry, nursing to being a director of a computer firm in the US, and she is "right proud of them."

Unfortunately, for most, an important goal that they will not have achieved is returning to Jamaica to live out their retirement. A significant number have resettled in Jamaica, happy with their decision. Some Jamaicans have lived here for over fifty years and have never set foot on Jamaican soil since they have left. Family circumstances and ill health have been the preventative factors. Others have cited the fact that their family members and friends who they had left behind in Jamaica have died or migrated. Consequently, returning home became a daunting prospect.

The Jamaicans in Leeds have never been better organised and resourceful than when they got together under the ambit of the Jamaica Society (Leeds). Jamaica House stands majestic as a verification of this conviction. It represents almost seventeen years of free work days, the continuous search for financing and thousands of hours of volunteer time. The touchstone by which the commitment of the Jamaican community can be measured, is found in Edley White's account that four heart attacks would not stop him from missing a work day. The members of the Jamaica Society (Leeds) are an inspiration to each other. Robert Chrouch believes that saying thanks is simply not enough considering the sheer volume of the members' contributions over the twenty-five years. If their contributions were quantified, they would run in the region of hundreds of thousands of pound sterling. But he wants to express his gratitude nonetheless to the members of the Jamaica Society (Leeds): "They know that everybody working there are volunteers. Nobody is getting paid to do it. I would also like to see them all appreciated for the work that they're doing. I thank them ever so much. I don't know if I can thank them enough for the hard work that they have put into Jamaica House. I keep thinking, even the women in the kitchen, these women working so faithfully time after time, I just want to say thank you."

The Society has spread its brand of community service to the wide cross section of the local population. Its membership includes indigenous British people and non-Jamaicans like Calvin Ford, a Barbadian who joined the Society because he was visited by the Care Group when he took ill in 1990. Thereafter, he also joined the Care Group. They too can claim the Society and Jamaica House as their own. Members of the Jamaican business community have done just that. As associates of the Society, they speak about the organisation with a profound sense of belonging, but more so, they rely on some of its distinctive characteristics in the implementation of their work. Experience has taught Paulette Simpson of the Jamaica National Building Society a useful strategy: "It is well known throughout the UK that if you want to get a feel for the Jamaican community, you want to create a bond with the Jamaican community - not only in Leeds but across the northern region - you would work alongside the Jamaica Society (Leeds)." According to Delores Cooper of the Jamaican diplomatic corps: "The Jamaica Society Leeds is one of the leading organisations in this country, and I am certain of this as Community Relations Officer at the Jamaican High Commission… they are like a tower of strength to me in the execution of my work."

Its reputation is well deserved because the Society has taken care of its people that even members who now reside in other countries still provide financial support. They cannot forget the difference that the Society has made in their lives. It was the bridge between their new lives in the UK and their old lives in Jamaica. It filled many gaping holes: by acting as a surrogate family, offering bereavement support, finding lost relatives, providing advice on matters of social importance, and catering to a section of the population that can still remember when places for recreation were closed to them or limited in number - a memory that resonates deeply with the first generations of Jamaicans. The Society has flung its doors wide open to an impressive list of Jamaican dignitaries and visitors, extending their warm hospitality for which they are renowned.

The Society is eager to pass on the legacy of Jamaica House and the Society's passion for community service to the next generation of Jamaicans when the time comes. By collecting over seventy-five hours of interviews and conducting over one hundred hours of workshops, the Society's cross generational approach to oral history has achieved much more than being a retrospective. It has tried to influence the future participation of successive generations in the work of the Jamaica Society (Leeds). Their history revealed the far-reaching impact of community volunteerism and organisation. Therefore, the members hope that by leaving behind this book, their past efforts and achievements will reverberate for sometime with future generations, inspiring them to continue in their footsteps. Jamaicans built an organisation with their eyes firmly fixed on the future. If they have succeeded in implanting their national pride, national character and national heritage deep into the consciousness of future generations of Leeds born Jamaicans, then all that the members of the Jamaica Society (Leeds) and the wider Jamaican community have achieved, will not have been in vain. Marcus Garvey promised that "what you do today that is worthwhile, inspires others to act at some future time." If successive generations continue to build on the firm foundations of their predecessors' past accomplishments, whatever they strive for in the future will yield even greater rewards - and the work of the pioneering generation will last forever.

CHAPTER 6

Our Legacy for the Next Generations

Epilogue

Writing *A Journey Through Our History* was equally revealing to me as it was for the young people who participated in the workshops. Born in Jamaica, this part of my people's history was unknown to me. On my less historic journey to the UK, I arrived just in time to witness the Caribbean community celebrating the fiftieth anniversary of the arrival of the *SS Empire Windrush*. I attended a public event in November 1998 organised by the Jamaica Society (Leeds) where its exhibition, *Had We Not Come* was on display. I was quick to embrace this new knowledge. Their journey became my journey, because their history is an extension of the history of all Jamaicans even though it took place in the Caribbean Diaspora. This experience will remain an invaluable one and it has been a privilege to have been given such a wonderful opportunity. Through the stories, I could recognise not just the indefatigable Jamaican spirit but our ability to laugh in spite of adversity. The stories also made me realise how tremendously grateful and indebted future generations of Jamaicans born in Britain should be to this generation. The Jamaican people who came in the 1940s to the early 1960s are in my eyes, heroes and heroines: whether it was their presence on the larger public stage of local and national activism or the personal sacrifices they made for their families and communities. Post war Britain had much to offer Jamaicans in terms of economic opportunities (with unexpected social drawbacks), but they and their Caribbean brother and sisters were to bestow on the wider British society a greater legacy - a chance to expand its civilisation to recognise all people as worthy of dignity, equality and respect.

Melody Walker
January 2003

Biographical Notes

The following are short biographies of the members of the Jamaica Society (Leeds), their associates and friends, Jamaican community leaders and workers, Jamaican dignitaries and the second generation descendants who were interviewed for this publication.

Founding Members

Yvonne ENGLISH arrived in the UK to join her parents in 1965. She went straight into nursing and also studied Social Work. She worked in these two areas until retirement. She was involved in family placement of children of minority ethnic groups. She volunteers in one of HM Prisons and with the Genesis Project for young mothers. She is also involved in the church. She is one of the founding members of the Jamaica Society (Leeds) and has served as co-ordinator of the Fundraising and Social Sub-committee.

Elizabeth JOHNSON arrived in the UK in October 1961 to study as a State Registered Nurse. She then completed her studies as a State Certified Midwife, a post in which she worked for thirty years. She is the proprietor and manager of Angels Home Care Services. She is one of the founding members of the Jamaica Society (Leeds) and is the current Secretary.

Travis JOHNSON OBE, BH(M), JP came to the UK from Jamaica in 1962. He worked for over twenty years in the field of race relations. He was appointed a Justice of the Peace in 1981 and still serves on the bench as a Lay Magistrate. He has been involved in a number of community initiatives such as the Community Action & Support Against Crime (CASAC) of which he was a founding member and chairperson for eight years. In 1999, he received an OBE for his work with this organisation. He was also awarded the Badge of Honour, BH(M) by the Government of Jamaica for his work with the Jamaican community in Leeds. He has served on the Board of Visitors for one of HM Prisons for ten years and as a Governor of a college for Further Education and a Comprehensive school. He is a member of the Independent Review Panel – NHS Complaint Procedure and a member of the West Yorkshire Probation Board. He has also served as a member of the General Synod of the Church of England and is Lay Canon of Ripon Cathedral and Church Warden at St. Aidan Church. He is one of the six founding members of the Jamaica Society (Leeds) and is currently the Chairperson of the Society.

Ratrica 'Nettie' WHITE came to the UK in 1958 and studied nursing. She worked in general nursing until she retired. She has sat on the board of the Leeds Racial Equality Council for a number of years and has served on the Board of Visitors for HM Prison Services. She is also actively involved in the church. She is a founding member of the Society and has held the positions of Vice Chairperson and Co-ordinator of the Women's Group in the Society over the years. She is currently the Assistant Secretary.

Members Jamaica Society (Leeds)

Samuel BARRETT was encouraged to come to the UK in 1956 by his friend. He settled in London for three months until he came to Leeds. He worked in a number of factories around the city and in 1978 he went to work as a machine operator with GKN in Kirkstall until his retirement. He joined the Jamaica Society (Leeds) in the 1980s and is a member of the Executive Committee.

Robert CHROUCH came to the UK in 1955 because many of his friends in Jamaica were coming in search of jobs. He did a wide range of jobs. His last employment was in the chemical industry for thirty-five years. He is a member of the Jamaica Society (Leeds) since the early 1980s.

Theresa CONDOR came to the UK in 1965 to join her parents at the age of fourteen. She worked in the area of Customer Services for private sector firms. She joined the Society in 1987 and held the following posts: Vice Chairperson, Assistant Secretary and Co-ordinator of the Care Group. She is currently a member of the Executive Committee.

Lincoln COLE came to the UK from Jamaica in April 28, 1958 with his cousin. He worked in London and Nottingham until he settled in Leeds some months later. He joined the Jamaica Society (Leeds) in the late 1980s. He is currently a member of the Executive Committee.

Mavis COLE settled in Leeds in 1961 with her brother and sister. She worked in the clothing sector for several years before retiring. She is a member of the Jamaica Society (Leeds).

Elma DAVIS settled in Gloucester when she came in 1959 until she came to Leeds in 1968. She worked in an engineering firm for a number of years. She is a member of the Care Group of the Jamaica Society (Leeds).

Allen EBANKS arrived in 1957 as a young man of nineteen years and settled in Birmingham before he came to Leeds. He worked in the engineering and transport sectors for a many years and then subsequently as a postman before he retired. He is a member the Executive Committee of the Jamaica Society (Leeds) and the House Management Committee.

Glen ENGLISH, MBE arrived in the UK in April 1944 as RAF ground crew personnel in World War Two. He settled in Leeds after the war where he worked as a draughtsman in an engineering firm. After working for several years in design engineering, he taught engineering until he retired. He is one of the founding members of the Leeds Caribbean Cricket Club which was formed in the late 1940s and also a founding member of Aggrey House formed in the 1950s. He is one of first Caribbean community workers in Leeds and spearheaded a number of projects. He was one of the early members of the Jamaica Society (Leeds) and held the position of Treasurer in the early 1980s. He is currently the Vice Chairperson of the Society.

Lynford FLETCHER came to the UK in June 1961 following in the footstep of his father. He spent five years in Huddersfield before settling in Leeds in 1966. He joined the Society in 1984 and is currently the Treasurer.

Norma FLETCHER settled in the UK in October 1961. She joined the Jamaica Society (Leeds) in 1984 and has been a long standing member of the Care Group. She is often seen volunteering in the kitchen catering for functions.

Adnence Audrey HENRY came to Leeds with her elder sister in October 1961. Like many Caribbean women, she worked at Burton's Tailoring. She joined the Jamaica Society (Leeds) in the 1980s and became a member of the Care Group. She is one of the women who frequently cater for functions at Jamaica House.

Irene HENRY came to the UK at the age of sixteen as a student in 1962 and studied at Bradford University. She works for the Local Authority as a Locality Home Care Manager. She joined the Jamaica Society (Leeds) in 1990 and became a member of the Care Group.

Phyllis HINES settled in Leeds in 1960 with her husband. She was invited to the UK by her brother and sister. She worked in nursing until retirement.

Yvonne HYLTON came to the UK to join her parents in 1961. She first settled in Preston until she moved to Leeds where she worked in the field of caring until retirement. She has been active in the community and the church. She was a deaconess in the church and member of the Churches Race Advisory Group. Her community work involved lobbying against poor housing and working for the Leeds Black Elders' organisation as a Community Development Worker for a number of years. She has been a member of the Jamaica

BIOGRAPHICAL NOTES

Society (Leeds) for many years and has co-ordinated the Society's Choir and Women's Group. She is currently a member of the Executive Committee.

Bev LATTIBEAUDIERE joined her parents in the UK in June 1958 at the age of twelve and grew up in Bristol. When she left school, she went into nursing and now works in the field of oncology. She eventually settled in Leeds with her husband. She has been the co-ordinator of the Jamaica Society (Leeds) Women's Group for the past three years, and more recently, the Community Health Awareness Project.

Roy MITCHELL arrived in the UK in late November 1944 as an RAF ground crew in World War Two. After the war, he was one of the first Jamaicans to settle in Leeds and subsequently joined the Leeds Rifles for the next fourteen years. He married a German nurse and worked in the field of engineering until he became a freelance painter/decorator. He is an active member of the Jamaica Society (Leeds) and has been a member of the Executive Committee.

Icyline PARKER came to Leeds in 1963 to join her father the late Joseph Parker, retired Public Health Inspector from Jamaica and Lay Preacher in the Anglican Church. She started working as an auxiliary nurse on April 14, 1963 and retired thirty-four years later. She is a member of the Jamaica Society (Leeds) and its Care Group. She works tirelessly as part of the Society's catering team.

Maizie PINNOCK settled in Leeds in April 1962. She worked as an auxiliary nurse for thirty-five years. She is a member of the Jamaica Society (Leeds), she volunteers for the Care Group and can be seen catering for the functions held at Jamaica House.

Louise REID came to join her brother in 1955 who lived in Preston. Her first job was at Preston Steam Laundry until she moved to Leeds and worked at Burton's Tailoring. She raises money for charities both locally and overseas by designing clothes and showcasing them at fashion shows. She is the oldest female member of the Jamaica Society (Leeds).

Edley WHITE came to the UK in 1954 and worked in the engineering sector. He was the playwright and co-ordinator of the Jamaica Society (Leeds) Drama Club and is the oldest member of the Society.

Florence WILLIAMS arrived in the UK in April 1962 and came to Leeds to join her brother. She is an Executive member of the Jamaica Society (Leeds) and for a total of nine years she chaired the Social and Fundraising Sub-committee.

Marylyn Francis WILLIAMS settled in Leeds in 1961. She worked for over thirty years in catering. She was active in the trade union and was a shop steward for her co-workers in the Social Services department where she worked for twenty-four years. She now owns and runs a café on Chapeltown Road called Dunn's River Café. She joined the Jamaica Society (Leeds) in 1980.

June WOOD arrived in the UK on August 21, 1971 at the age of eleven to join her mother. She currently works as a Care Worker in a Day Centre for the elderly. She joined the Jamaica Society (Leeds) in the 1980s and was elected to the Executive Committeein 2000. She co-ordinated the Society's first printed Annual Report.

Finley WRAY came in 1957 and spent thirty-five years in the UK then migrated to the USA to join his family. He worked as a carpenter for most of his years in the UK. He was a member of the Executive Committee of the Jamaica Society (Leeds) in the early 1990s and chaired the Care Group during that period.

Jamaican Dignitaries and members of the Jamaican Business Community

His Excellency the Most Honourable Sir Howard COOKE ON, GCMG, GCVO, CD, Governor General of Jamaica holds the highest office in Jamaica as the representative of the Queen. He was installed as Governor General of Jamaica on August 1, 1991. For twenty-three years, he worked in the teaching profession and later in the insurance industry in Jamaica. He entered politics in 1938 as a founding member of the People's National Party and subsequently became Chairman of the Party. He entered the Jamaican Parliament in 1962, served as a Senator until 1967 and as a member of the House of Representatives between 1967 and 1980. He has demonstrated an interest and involvement in sports, community organisation, the church and Jamaican culture. Among his many awards, he was awarded a special plaque for distinguished service from the Commonwealth Parliamentary Association. He has visited the Jamaica Society (Leeds) in 1994 and 2002, since his instalment.

Ambassador the Honourable David MUIRHEAD OJ, OC was High Commissioner to the UK between 1999 and 2002. He had worked closely with the Jamaica Society (Leeds) during his tenure.

Delores COOPER OD is the Community Relations Officer at the Jamaican High Commission in London.

Paulette SIMPSON is the chief representative of the Jamaica National Building Society. She first worked with the Jamaica Society (Leeds) when she was previously employed as the UK representative of Jamaica National Commercial Bank.

Biographical Notes

Local Public Figures and Community Workers

Clinton CAMERON, MBE settled in Leeds in May 7, 1960. He has been involved in several community-based organisations. He currently chairs Unity Housing Association.

Veryl HARRIOTT came to the UK in 1961 and settled in Leeds. She became very active in the community in a number of areas. She was founding member of the Leeds Afro West Indian Brotherhood and established the Chapeltown Citizens' Advice Bureau and later worked with the national body for Citizens' Advice Bureaux. She also worked in the field of race relations as a regional officer for National Association for Race Equality Council. She is an assessor to the Courts on the Race Relations Act. She is a Governor for the Colleges of Building and Technology.

Councillor Norma HUTCHINSON came to the UK in September 1965 and worked in the field of nursing. During that time she became an active trade unionist for NUPE. She was a shop steward at the Meanwood Park Hospital in Bradford, she then moved to Leeds and worked at the St. James's Hospital. As a trade unionist, she chaired the Regional Race Equality Committee and the National Race Equality Committee. She was an active member of the Labour Party and she was the first Jamaican to be elected as a city councillor in 1991.

Celine NORTH came to the UK in 1956 at age sixteen. Having served the community in various capacities, she became the first Lady Mayoress in the City of Leeds to be born in Jamaica in 2002 to 2003.

Father Alan TAYLOR is the Vicar of the Parish and Canon of Ripon Cathedral, St. Aidan Anglican Church, Roundhay. He is also a city councillor and has worked extensively with the various migrant groups in and around the city.

Windrush Passenger

Alford GARDNER joined the RAF in Jamaica as a ground crew personnel and came to the UK in June 1944 as part of the war effort. He returned to Jamaica after the war and returned on the *SS Empire Windrush* in 1948 and settled immediately in Leeds with his brother. He was an early member of the Leeds Caribbean Cricket Club.

Second Generation Jamaicans

Marva BUCHANAN was born in Jamaica and came to the UK in 1965 at the age of ten to join her parents who left Jamaica in the 1950s. She has lived for the past thirty-eight years in England – the last eight in Leeds. She has worked in schools, community theatre, film, video and radio as a performer and arts educator specialising in Drama and English. She has written education resource packs to support theatre plays for Nottingham and West Yorkshire Playhouses. She has acted as an adviser to young writers and developed scripts for short films and videos. She also has co-edited, with Merle Collins, an anthology of short stories for young people entitled "Inside Ant's Belly" for The National Association for the Teaching of English. Her poems appear in this publication under the nom de plume - MarvaB.

Marcia HYLTON is of Jamaican heritage. Born in Leeds, her parents came to the UK in the late 50s to early 60s. Her mother is a member of the Jamaica Society (Leeds). Marcia has volunteered with one of the Society's most recent project, Community Health Awareness Project. She currently works as a Clinical Skills Tutor at the University of Leeds

Khadijah IBRAHIIM was born in Leeds to Jamaican parents. Her paternal grandparents came over in the late 1950s. Her mother arrived in the 1960s. Her grandparents were active in the community. Her grandfather, Trevor Wynters was a member of the Leeds West Indian Afro Brotherhood and her grandmother Lucinda Wynters organised educational and health programmes within the community. Khadijah is a performance artist, poet and playwright. She has experience devising and leading creative writing workshops and has worked in, or travelled to the Middle East, West Africa, South Korea and Jamaica. Her poems have been recently published in a curriculum package for English Literature along with poems by Linton Kwesi Johnson for the Oakpark River Forest High School, Chicago. She is currently doing research into the Caribbean community in Leeds and is involved in arts education through her organisation, SEMA Grassroots.

Angelique JOHNSON is a second generation Jamaican. Both of her parents settled in the UK in the early 1960s. She has volunteered for a number of years at the Jamaica Society (Leeds) Senior Citizens' Christmas Dinner and Children's Christmas Party. Her parents are foundation members of the Society. She works full time as a Housing Support Worker, securing tenancies of 16-25 year olds. She is also a part time Individual Support Worker.

Ian LAWRENCE was born in the UK to Jamaican parents who came in the 1950s. He works as a Quantity Surveyor for the Leeds City Council. He joined the Jamaica Society (Leeds) in 1998 and became involved in the co-ordination of the Windrush exhibition, *Had We Not Come*. He was a member of the Executive for two years and coordinated the Children's Activities Day.

BIOGRAPHICAL NOTES

Susan PITTER was born and raised in Leeds to Jamaican parents who came in the early 1960s. She has been active within the community. She has been involved with Leeds Carnival, the BBC Leeds Caribbean programme, *Calypso* and has organised various community events. She was appointed a Lady Mayoress of Leeds, 2000-2001 by the then Lord Mayor of Leeds, Councillor Bernard Atha. She became the first black woman to be appointed to the post and the first of Jamaican descent. She is a member of the Jamaica Society (Leeds) and was a member of the Executive Committee.

Sandra Simpson was born in Leeds to Maizie Pinnock who came to the UK in 1962. She has served in a voluntary capacity at the Jamaica Society (Leeds) Children's Christmas Party and the launch activity of the Community Health Awareness Project. She is a public health practitioner, having been a midwife for eleven years.

List of Young Participants

Lee CHROUCH, 14
Akilah COHEN, 14
Anaih COLEMAN, 11
Rhea FLEMING, 14
Cory FLETCHER, 12
Levi FOWLER, 14
Jellisia FRAZIER, 13
Laura GATSWOOD, 13
Robyn GILBERT, 15
Ayesha HUGGINS, 14
Cory HUGGINS, 7
Natalie HUGHES, 13
Dean HYDE, 13
Marcus HYLTON, 12
Joshua HYLTON, 7

Ali IBRAHIIM, 7
Rheima IBRAHIIM, 11
Samantha JAMES, 13
Ital JOSEPH, 10
Jasmine JOSEPH, 7
Moses JOSEPH, 9
Shasha JOSEPH, 8
Ashton LATTIBEAUDIERE, 9
Malachi LAWRENCE, 7
Troy LAWRENCE, 18
Sonech MAYNARD, 15
Ben MCINTOSH, 12
Chamelle MCKAIN, 14
Rachel MORRIS, 15
Tasha PARKINSON, 18

Laurah PITTER, 17
Sholah RICHARDS, 14
James ROBINSON, 10
Alex ROBINSON, 11
Tancia ROBINSON, 12
Dominic SIMPSON, 12
Ryan SMALL, 12
Gavin WILLIAMS, 14
Iona WILLIAMS, 14
Blair WITTER, 10
Shazmin WITTER, 10
Jordan WITTER, 8
Ebony WOOD, 6
Holly WOOD, 10

Workshop Facilitators

Paul AIKEN, Desktop Publishing Facilitator

Ansell BRODERICK, Storytelling Facilitator

Marcia BROWN, Art Facilitator

Garnet DORE, Art Facilitator

Jenny EUGENE - JEEP Partnerships, Video Documentation Facilitator

Khadijah IBRAHIIM - SEMA Grassroots, Creative Writing Facilitator

Musufing NJIE, Creative Writing Facilitator

Linton ROBINSON, Desktop Publishing Facilitator

Glossary

Bauxite is a claylike mineral found in soil usually rust–coloured, with a high proportion of alumina. Bauxite is mined in Jamaica and other countries to produce aluminium. The processing of bauxite to produce of aluminium begins with the removal of the topsoil and the ore is taken and stored in a dry place. Then, the bauxite is processed into alumina which looks like a chalky white powder. In the end, the alumina is melted and the final product aluminium is extracted The discovery of bauxite was made in Jamaica by Sir Alfred DaCosta in the 1940s, who could not understand why his crop yield was so poor. Soil analysis revealed that it contained fifty percent alumina. (Source: Philip Sherlock, *Keeping Company With Jamaica*, pp. 24-26)

Day Work is a communal practice which involves persons in the community coming together to help each other, an individual or a family to carry out certain tasks: clearing a field, digging, planting, harvesting, house building and house moving. When one grants this favour to a member of a community, the expectation is that the favour will be returned. It is widely believed that Day Work was inherited from Africa, more specifically of Dahomean origin. Consequently, this practice can be found throughout the Caribbean. It is however known as coumbite in Haiti, gayap in Trinidad and jollification in Nevis. (Source: Olive Senior, *A-Z of Jamaican Heritage*. p. 49)

Dinki Mini has an atmosphere of celebration even though it occurs after a death. It involves spirited and festive music. The intention is to lift the spirits of the family and friends of the deceased. Throughout the celebrations, instruments such as shakas, katta sticks, condensed milk tins, grater, tambo and benta are used. It is widely acknowledged that Dinki Mini comes from the Congolese word 'ndingi' which means lamentation or funeral song and was practised openly throughout slavery. Today, the Dinki Mini dance is still done in the parishes of St. Mary, St. Ann, St. Andrew and Portland. (Source: Jamaica Information Service website.)

Free Villages were established throughout Jamaica in their hundreds by the ex-slaves and supported by the missionaries following emancipation in 1938. The enterprise demonstrated by the ex-slaves to construct these free villages is a testament to their fierce determination to be totally free. The planters were vehemently opposed to their freedom and tried to find ways to bound them to the plantation under similar conditions that existed during slavery. As emancipation left the freedmen and women homeless, free villages became one of the most important ways of ensuring their total independence of the planters and plantation life. Many of the villages in Jamaica were established under this system, the first free village that was built in the

Caribbean was Sligoville in St. Catherine, Jamaica in 1834. Porus, Sturge Town, Bethel Town, Mt. Carey and Islington are the other known free villages in Jamaica. (Source: Olive Senior, *A-Z of Jamaican Heritage*. pp. 64-65.)

Kumina is an ancestor worship religion. It was brought to Jamaica by the Bantu people who migrated freely to island as indentured workers in the 1840s to 1860s, many of whom settled in St. Thomas. However, Kumina groups were also found in Portland, St. Catherine, Kingston and other areas. The Bantu people are from Democratic Republic of Congo, and the language identified with Kumina is the Ki-Kongo. Kumina is a practice that ensures that the dead gets a proper burial, complete with the appropriate ceremony. The belief is that if this is not done, the spirit of the deceased will wander the world haunting the living. Kumina ceremonies involve singing, dancing and drumming, which are key elements in its observation. Kumina dancers have been known to be possessed by ancestral spirits during the ceremonies. Over the years, dance companies of Jamaica have included kumina in its repertoire, the most notable being the National Dance Theatre Company of Jamaica. (Source: Olive Senior, *A-Z of Jamaican Heritage*. pp. 91-92)

Maundy gifts are distributed to persons who have been selected for their Christian service in the Church and the community at a special service held on Maundy Thursdays. The recipients receive a red purse which contains an allowance for clothing and provisions, and a white purse contains Maundy coins – two pences, three pences, and four pences - as many coins are the Sovereign's age. The Royal Maundy goes far back as the 12th century and from the 15th century, the number of recipients selected reflected the Sovereign's age. (Source: The History of the Royal Maundy.)

Mento is a folk and dance music that preceded ska, rocksteady and reggae, and was as popular as those forms of music. Mento is more than just the music; mento is dance, mento is song lyrics. Mento music, dance and lyrics possess certain characteristics that are specific to this genre. Also, certain instruments are specific to a traditional mento band such as the Rumba box, banjo, guitar, shakers and graters. (Source: Olive Senior, *A-Z of Jamaican Heritage*. p. 104)

National Heroes of Jamaica: Jamaica has seven National Heroes. The Order of National Heroes is the highest honour the country bestows on an individual, and the honour is restricted to Jamaican nationals and they are styled 'The Right Excellent…'

The Right Excellent Nanny of the Maroons is a National Heroine of Jamaica, she is known as a exceptional military tactician and chieftainess. She ably led the Maroon people during the First Maroon War from

1720-1739 against the British. Her brilliance at planning and executing guerrilla warfare is legendary and used the element of surprise and entrapment against the British with superb effectiveness. Nanny who is of Ashante origin was believed to have supernatural powers, she was the spiritual leader of her people. She encouraged the continuation of African customs, legends, music and songs as a source of pride in their cultural identity.

The Right Excellent Samuel Sharpe (1801-1832), National Hero of Jamaica, 19th century slave leader and martyr was the mastermind behind the 1831 Slave Rebellion. The insurgence began on the Kensington Estate in St. James and was instrumental in bringing about the abolition of slavery. Sam Sharpe became a "daddy" or leader of the Baptist church in Montego Bay and was known for his intelligence and his merits as a strong leader. Because of his role in the 1831 Rebellion, Samuel Sharpe was hanged on May 23, 1832. Two years later, the Abolition Bill was passed by the British Parliament and in 1838, slavery was abolished. His most famous words were: "I would rather die upon yonder gallows than live in slavery".

The Right Excellent Marcus Mosiah Garvey is Jamaica's first National Hero. He was born in St. Ann's Bay on August 17, 1887. Garvey is known for the formation of the Universal Negro Improvement Association (UNIA) in Jamaica, which came out of his observation of the poor living conditions of black people. The UNIA became an international organisation; it was built on the precepts that black people from the Caribbean and Africa should be self-governed. It also fostered self-help economic projects, protested against racial discrimination and held cultural activities. In 1916, Garvey took his message of freedom to the black people in the USA. His activities were considered subversive by US officials and he was imprisoned, then deported. He returned to Jamaica in 1927, and continued his political activism by forming the People's Political Party in 1929. He was unsuccessful in national elections but won a seat on the local council. Many believed that Garvey's ideas were far too progressive for the world in the 1920s and 30s. He left Jamaica again for England where he died in 1940. His body was brought back to Jamaica in 1964 and buried in the National Heroes Park in Kingston. Garvey's legacy was the philosophy of racial pride, African unity, self-reliance and self-government for black people.

The Right Excellent George William Gordon was the self-educated son of a slave mother and a planter father, a lawyer to several sugar estates in Jamaica. George William subsequently became a landowner in St. Thomas. Gordon entered politics because he was sickened by the repressive system under which black people in Jamaica lived in the post slavery economy. He was stonewalled because it was difficult to represent the interest of a people who did not qualify to vote. Gordon concentrated nonetheless on subdividing his own lands and selling farm lots to the people for next to nothing. He was also known for organising a system whereby small farmers could sell their produce for market value. Gordon's activities were considered illegal because he encouraged the Jamaican people to rise up and resist their oppressive living conditions. When the 1865 Morant Bay Rebellion occurred Gordon was arrested and charged for collusion. He was tried by court martial which was illegal even then. He was convicted and sentenced to death. He was executed on October 23,1865.

The Right Excellent Paul Bogle, was a Baptist deacon in Stony Gut, a few miles north of Morant Bay. He was allowed to vote at a time when only 104 people in the parish of St. Thomas were allowed the privilege, primarily because he was born free. No one is sure of Bogle's exact date of birth but it is believed he was born about 1822. He was a supporter of his contemporary George William Gordon. On October 11 1865, Bogle led a march to the Morant Bay court house to protest against poverty and social injustice and the repressive actions of the central government authority. Following the march, violence erupted between the protesters and the official forces. Close to 500 people were killed. Bogle was sentenced to be hanged on October 24, 1865, while others were flogged and punished. Bogle's protest was successful, it led to changes in the courts and changes which made it possible to improve the lives of the Jamaican people.

The Right Excellent Norman Washington Manley was born on July 4, 1883 in Manchester. A brilliant scholar, athlete, and lawyer, he was one of the central figures in the troubles of 1938 and donated time and advocacy to the cause of improving the working conditions of the working class. Manley founded the People's National Party (PNP) in September of the same year and was its President until his retirement thirty-one years later. Manley's PNP was a leading supporter of the trade union movement, and led the struggle for universal adult suffrage. He was a strong advocate of the Federation of the West Indies which was established in 1958. When Jamaica withdrew from the Federation, Norman Manley set up a joint committee to decide on a constitution for separate independence for Jamaica. He chaired the committee with great distinction and then led the team that negotiated Jamaica's independence from Britain. Norman Manley died on September 2, 1969.

The Right Excellent Alexander Bustamante rose to prominence in Jamaica when he mobilized the masses against the social and economic injustices that were endemic to the system of government during the time when Jamaica was still a crown colony. Bustamante was known for his flurry of letters to the Gleaner which brought to the public's attention the social and economic problems of the poor and underprivileged in Jamaica. Bustamante became the champion of the working classes, particularly during the period of social unrest in 1937 and 1938. He took on the Colonial Governor, and he famously declared "Long live the King! But Denham must go." By 1943, he founded the Jamaica Labour Party and won the first general election

under universal adult suffrage in 1944. In 1962, Sir Alexander became Jamaica's first Prime Minister. He retired from active politics in 1967 and ten years later, he died on August 6.
(Source: Jamaica Information Service leaflets)

National Honours: Jamaica bestows many honours and awards. Among them are the Order of Jamaica, OJ, the fourth highest honour one can receive. The recipient is entitles to the prefix, 'the Honourable'. OD is the Officer of the Order of Distinction, the fifth highest honour; the Order of Distinction also has the Commander rank, CD. The Commander rank is the higher of the two. The second highest honour, the Order of Nation, ON is usually conferred to the Governor General of Jamaica. The current Governor General, His Excellency the Most Honourable Sir Howard Cooke also holds the following awards and honours: GCMG - Knight and Cross of St. Michael and St. George; GCV - Knight and Cross of the Victorian Order.

Nine-Night is similar in its purpose and observation as Kumina that of giving the dead a proper burial to prevent wandering spirits. However, this old folk custom is a ceremony that is held on the ninth night after someone dies, and at the home of the deceased or the family. In some places in Jamaica, only the ninth night is observed. But most hold a 'set up' every night after the death, and the ceremony culminates on the ninth night. In St. Mary, Jamaica, this 'set up' is called 'dinkie mini' or 'gere' in other areas. At a set up, there is singing, dancing and stories. On the ninth night there is the singing of hymns and rituals for the dead.
(Source: Olive Senior, *A-Z of Jamaican Heritage*. p. 118)

Pardner is an informal way of saving whereby a group of people 'throw a hand' each week with one member of the group and each member takes turn to 'draw' the total sum. (Source: Olive Senior, *A-Z of Jamaican Heritage*. p. 123)

Bibliography

Annual Report of the Housing Committee year ended 31st March 1935-year ended 31st March 1964, Leeds City Council Housing Committee.

Annual Reports and Minutes of the Jamaica Society (Leeds) 1980-2002

Black, Clinton: *History of Jamaica*, (Longman Caribbean Ltd., 1983)

Blood and Fire, BBC2 documentary, 2002

Building Sub-committee Reports 1987-1988, Jamaica Society (Leeds).

Chapeltown News, 1972-1976 editions, Chapeltown News Collective, Leeds

Claypole, William et al: *Caribbean Story, Book One: Foundations*, (Longman Caribbean Ltd., 1980)

"Confidence of immigrants shaken by Commonwealth Immigration Act 1968", *Yorkshire Evening Post*, April 10, 1968

"Courses for Young Immigrants Urged", *Yorkshire Evening Post*, April 10, 1968

Duke, Christopher: *Colour and Rehousing: A Study of Re-development in Leeds*, (Institute of Race Relations/Special Series, 1970)

Farrar, Max: *The Struggle for "Community" in a British Multi Ethnic Inner City Area – Paradise in the Making*, (The Edwin Mellen Press, 2002)

"40, 000 Leeds Homes without Bathrooms", *Yorkshire Evening Post*, February 26, 1957

Francis, Vivienne: *With Hope In Their Eyes: The Compelling Stories of the Windrush Generation*, (Nia, 1998)

Garvey, Amy Jacques: *Garvey & Garveyism*, (Colliers Books, 1974)

BIBLIOGRAPHY

Garvey, Amy Jacques: *The Philosophy & Opinions of Marcus Garvey*, (The Majority Press, 1986)

"Help for Unexpected Jamaican: Welfare men board ship", *Yorkshire Post*, June 22, 1948

"Immigrant & the Police", *Yorkshire Evening Post*, August 9, 1972

Lazenby, Peter: "Staged-managed: Role of people from outside in Leeds disturbances", *Yorkshire Evening Post*, July 13, 1981

Lean, Geoffrey: "When East Meets West: New Britain: *Yorkshire Post*, January 23, 1973, January 26, 1973, January 27, 1973

Mays, Jeb: *Jamaica: Caribbean Challenge*, (The Epica Task Force, 1979)

Murray, Robert: *Lest We Forget: The Experience of World War II Westindian Ex-Service Personnel*, (Nottingham Westindian Combined Ex-Services Association in association with Hansib Publishing Caribbean Ltd. 1996)

Naylor, Derek: "In Bonfire's Ashes – The Days of Hope of a Suburb," *Yorkshire Evening Post*, November 12, 1975

Naylor, Derek: "The Colony Within", *Yorkshire Evening Post*, June 27, 1973, June 28, 1973, June 30, 1973.

Philips, Mike et al: *Windrush: The Irresistible Rise of Multi-Racial Britain*, (Harper Collins, 1998)

"Police Battle with 200 in Leeds Bonfire Night Riot", *Yorkshire Evening Post*, November 6, 1974

Ranston, Jackie: *From We Were Boys: The Stories of the Magnificent Cousins Manley and Bustamante*, (The Bustamante Institute of Public and International Affairs, 1989)

"Re-writing England's History - in Black", *Guardian* 1962 edition

Rowley, Allan: "Mistah…This Is My Home Now", *Yorkshire Evening Post*, August 29, 1958

Senior, Olive: *A-Z of Jamaican Heritage*, (Heinemann Educational Books Caribbean Ltd., 1987)

Sherlock, Philip et al: *The Story of the Jamaican People*, (Ian Randle Publishers, Kingston and Markus Wiener Publishers, Princeton, 1998)

Sigworth, Eric: "Back to Back Amid Affluence," *Yorkshire Post*, May 10, 1962

"Spotlight On Leeds: Mecca of Vice: Where prostitutes are just part of the scenery", *Yorkshire Evening Post*, January 31, 1974

Sternbery, William: Race Bill to Cut Out Ghettos, *Yorkshire Evening Post*, April 8, 1968

Tanna, Laura: *Jamaican Folktales and Oral Histories*, No. 1 Jamaica 21 Anthology Series, (Creative Production and Training Centre in collaboration with Institute of Jamaica Publications Ltd., 1987)

"That Bloody Bonfire Could Explode on us all – says Race Relations Expert", *Yorkshire Evening Post*, November 12, 1975

The Norman Manley Memorial Lectures 1984-1995, (Hansib Caribbean in association with The Norman Manley Memorial Lecture Committee, 1996)

"Three injured: alleged attacks by coloured men," *Yorkshire Post*, June 21, 1948

"Too Many People, Too Few Homes – Ghetto report", *Yorkshire Evening Post*, January 7, 1976

"Vice District Worse Than Soho", *Yorkshire Evening Post*, April 5, 1968

"Violence Flares on Leeds Streets", *Yorkshire Evening Post*, July 13, 1981

Windrush '98 – *Had We Not Come?!?* Jamaica Society (Leeds) Exhibition, 1998

"Youths baited coloured man – Magistrate", *Yorkshire Evening Post*, April 30, 1969

About the Writer

Melody Walker was born in Jamaica where she graduated from the University of the West Indies with a BA (Hons). She completed her MA in Communications Studies at the University of Leeds in 1999, and in 2003 completed her PGDip in Screenwriting. Melody has written, produced and directed programmes for television and video in Jamaica where she also worked as the co-ordinator for a women's media organisation: designing and implementing communications projects with a gender focus, conducting workshops and seminars in Jamaica, the Caribbean and internationally, producing video documentaries, writing articles for Caribbean and international feminist publications, and developing training resources on gender, media issues and popular culture. She has also co-edited a reggae music festival magazine and worked as production and publicity co-ordinator on several music concerts and festivals.